ON THE WATER, MICHIGAN

Your Comprehensive Guide to Water
Recreation in the Great Lake State

By **ERIC FREEDMAN**

Huron-Superior-Michigan Press

On the Water, Michigan

Copyright 1992 by Eric Freedman

Huron-Superior-Michigan Press
Box 776
East Lansing MI 48826

No part of this book may be reproduced without written
permission. Printed in the United States of America

Cover design: Michele Telschow
Cover photos: Michigan Department of Natural Resources
and Michigan Travel Bureau
Layout: DG Designs, Okemos MI

Library of Congress Catalog Card Number 92-70557

ISBN 0-9631741-1-8

DEDICATION
To Mary Ann, Ian and Cara
for sharing Michigan's diverse waters with me.

ALSO BY ERIC FREEDMAN
Pioneering Michigan

TABLE OF CONTENTS

Page

Introduction Welcome to Michigan Waters   1
Chapter   1 Recreational Harbors   5
Chaper   2 Marinas on the Water   17
Chapter   3 Off-Water Marinas   47
Chapter   4 Public Boat Launches   55
Chapter   5 Canoe Liveries   117
Chapter   6 Tubing Liveries   137
Chapter   7 Wild, Scenic & Natural Rivers   143
Chapter   8 Fishing   154
Chapter   9 Scuba Diving   163
Chapter 10 Underwater Preserves   177
Chapter 11 Boat Charters   187
Chapter 12 Cruises & Tours   225
Chapter 13 Passenger Ferries   231
Chapter 14 State Parks & Recreation Areas on the Water   239
Chapter 15 National Parks & Army Corps of Engineers   255
Chapter 16 State Forest Water Access   263
Chapter 17 National Forest Water Access   273
Chapter 18 County & Regional Park Watercraft Rentals   281
Chapter 19 Wildlife Refuges on the Water   285
Chapter 20 Boating, Canoeing, Scuba & Fishing Courses   289
Chapter 21 Whitewater Rafting   299
Chapter 22 Kayaking & Rowing   303
Chapter 23 Waterskiing & Surfing   307
Chapter 24 Maritime Museums   311
Chapter 25 Historical Markers   321
Chapter 26 Lighthouses   339
Chapter 27 Special Delights on the Water   349
Chapter 28 Manufacturers & Boat Shows   359
Chapter 29 U.S. Coast Guard Stations   369
Chapter 30 Sheriff's Marine Divisions   375
Appendix A Travel & Recreation Information Sources   384
Appendix B Books & Resources   403

KEWEENAW

ONTONAGON

HOUGHTON

GOGEBIC

BARAGA

IRON

MARQUETTE

DICKINSON

ALGER

LUCE

SCHOOLCRAFT

DELTA

MACKINAC

CHIPPEWA

MENOMINEE

EMMET

CHEBOYGAN

PRESQUE ISLE

LEELANAU

CHARLEVOIX

OTSEGO

MONTMORENCY

ALPENA

ANTRIM

BENZIE

GRAND TRAVERSE

KALKASKA

CRAWFORD

OSCODA

ALCONA

MANISTEE

WEXFORD

MISSAUKEE

ROSCOMMON

OGEMAW

IOSCO

MASON

LAKE

OSCEOLA

CLARE

GLADWIN

ARENAC

HURON

BAY

OCEANA

NEWAYGO

MECOSTA

ISABELLA

MIDLAND

TUSCOLA

SANILAC

SAGINAW

MUSKEGON

MONTCALM

GRATIOT

LAPEER

KENT

GENESEE

ST CLAIR

OTTAWA

IONIA

CLINTON

SHIAWASSEE

OAKLAND

MACOMB

ALLEGAN

BARRY

EATON

INGHAM

LIVINGSTON

VAN BUREN

KALAMAZOO

CALHOUN

JACKSON

WASHTENAW

WAYNE

BERRIEN

CASS

ST JOSEPH

BRANCH

HILLSDALE

LENAWEE

MONROE

MICHIGAN TRAVEL BUREAU

WELCOME TO
MICHIGAN WATERS

When it comes to water recreation, Michigan is the Great Lake State -- and a lot more. It's also the Great Inland Lakes State, the Great Rivers State and the Great Underwater Preserves State.

Michigan has over 800,000 registered boats.

It borders on four of the five Great Lakes -- Michigan, Superior, Huron and Erie -- more than any other state or Canadian province, and no spot in the state is more than 90 miles from at least one of the Great Lakes. They are the subject of legends, songs and true tales of bravery and foolhardiness. French explorer Samuel de Champlain dubbed Lake Huron "La Mer Douce," or the Sweetwater Sea, when his canoe first reached it in July of 1614. As our inland seas, the Great Lakes carry mythical and maritime heritage as well, but can pose a fatal challenge to recreational and commercial watercraft. Hundreds of wrecks -- some still undiscovered -- prove it.

The state's Great Lakes shoreline is 3,288 miles in length, longer than California's Pacific coast or Florida's combined Atlantic and Gulf coasts. In fact, Alaska is the only state with more coastline.

There are 240 public beaches along the state's Great Lakes coasts. As the Michigan Sea Grant Program observes, "There are wide beaches where the grasses struggle to anchor the sands. There are narrow beaches that just barely separate the trees from the water. There are cozy beaches hemmed in by rocky ledges. And there are vast beaches where the sand erupts into towering dunes."

Michigan's 11,000-plus lakes range from mega-sized to mini. Superior, the giant, covers the largest surface area of any body of fresh water on the globe and contains the second-largest total volume of water of any lake. In fact, Superior's 31,700-square-mile area is larger than 11 states and could cover Rhode Island 25 times.

Houghton is the largest of the inland lakes, spreading out over 20,004 square acres or 31 square miles. At the opposite end of the size spectrum are such tiny lakes as Priest Lake in Kalkaska County, Devils Washbasin in Ogemaw County, No Name Lake in Washtenaw County, Twin Lake in Lapeer County and the appropriately named Two Bit Lake in Oscoda County, each covering about an acre.

1

There are lakes with such unusual names as Peck & Rye, Billy Good, Little John Brown, Shavehead, Prison and Little Wolf, as well as more than 20 that are Crooked or Round, over 30 that are Long or Mud, and at least a dozen that are Lost, with a plethora of No Name Lakes and a few literally named Un-Named.

As for rivers and streams, Michigan's stretch about 36,350 miles through busy downtown business districts, suburbs, farmland and wilderness. Some are environmentally pristine, others tragically polluted but undergoing private, community and government-sponsored cleanups. Government programs safeguard some; drives are underway to put hundreds more miles under federal, state or local protection against development, overuse and environmental degradation.

Michigan offers more than 1,200 public boat launches, 70 protective harbors, hundreds of marinas and charter boats, dozens of canoe liveries. Ferries connect the mainland with islands. Tour companies offer cruises. Charter captains provide access to prime fishing and scuba diving spots. There are waterfront festivals, fishing tournaments, races, rowing clubs and boat shows galore.

You can examine nautical history on shore at maritime museums or underwater among Great Lakes wrecks. You can raft through whitewater rapids, tube along calm rivers, sleep in a lighthouse, dine on a boat, visit a commercial fish breeder, even earn college credit for canoeing and sailing classes.

On the Water, Michigan is the first comprehensive guide to water-related recreation opportunities in this water-oriented state, covering activities for landlubbers as well as experienced sailors and outdoor adventurers.

Equally important, *On the Water, Michigan* is an independent guide. There are no ads, and no business or organization paid to be listed. The goal is to serve you, the reader, with more useful information than you'll find in any other single source.

Listings are as complete as possible at time of publication, although circumstances do change. New businesses open and others close. While the state finances the development of more public boat launches and the acquisition of additional park and forest land, some government agencies are forced by budget problems or liability concerns to cut back on recreational programs.

To ensure comprehensiveness, you'll find some facilities listed more than once. For example, a boat launch in a state park would appear in both the chapter on launches and the chapter on state parks.

We welcome reader suggestions, comments and updates for future editions. You can write to Huron-Superior-Michigan Press, Box 776, Lansing MI 48826.

Chapter 1

RECREATIONAL HARBORS

Michigan's Great Lakes recreational harbor program began in 1947 with the goal of having every boater within 15 shoreline miles of safety. As the years passed, 70 protective harbors and public marinas have been developed -- some small, some large -- with financial support from the state tax on marine fuel, from municipal government contributions, from the U.S. Fish and Wildlife Service and from the U.S. Army Corps of Engineers.

The state Waterways Commission can designate at least 50 percent, and in some instances up to 100 percent, of dock space at recreational harbors for transient boaters. The few harbors of refuge without transient accommodations are marked in the listings. Slips are made available on a first-come, first-served basis. During busy seasons, the maximum stay at public docks is seven consecutive days, except for a four-day limit at Mackinac Island.

Most of the harbors are run by local governments, with fees regulated by the Waterways Commission based on the overall length of the vessel. There is a flat fee rate for boats under 24 feet in length; larger craft are charged on a per-foot basis, with the rate-per-foot higher for longer boats. In addition, there is a flat rate charged for temporary daytime mooring.

VHF-FM radio communication services are available at 49 of the harbors. Channel 16 (156.8 MHz) is set aside as the principal channel for distress, monitoring and calling. Channel 9 (156.45 MHz) is the working channel.

Some harbors, particularly the smaller ones, do not provide all basic services. Often those services or facilities can be found at nearby private marinas or on shore.

SOUTHEAST

	Harbormaster	Gas & diesel	Water	Electricity	Pump-out	Showers	VHF-FM
MACOMB COUNTY Metro Beach Metropark Lake St. Clair (313) 463-4581	✓		✓	✓	✓	✓	
MONROE COUNTY Bolles Harbor Lake Erie		G	✓	✓			
ST. CLAIR COUNTY Port Huron Lake Huron (313) 985-5676 (313) 982-0200	✓	G&D	✓	✓	✓	✓	✓
Charles Moore Boat Harbor, St. Clair Lake St. Clair (313) 329-4125	✓	G&D	✓	✓	✓	✓	✓
WAYNE COUNTY St. Aubin Park, Detroit Detroit River (800) 338-6424	✓		✓	✓	✓	✓	✓
Erma Henderson Marina Detroit Detroit River (313) 267-7143	✓		✓	✓	✓	✓	
Lake Erie Metropark Lake Erie (313) 379-5020			✓	✓	✓	✓	

* after name means no transient accomodations

6

	Harbormaster	Gas & diesel	Water	Electricity	Pump-out	Showers	VHF-FM

CENTRAL

BAY COUNTY
Liberty Harbor, Bay City
Lake Huron
(517) 894-8280

| | ✓ | | ✓ | ✓ | ✓ | ✓ | ✓ |

HURON COUNTY
Caseville
Lake Huron
(517) 856-4590

| | ✓ | G&D | ✓ | ✓ | ✓ | ✓ | ✓ |

Harbor Beach
Lake Huron
(517) 479-9707
(517) 479-3363

| | ✓ | G&D | ✓ | ✓ | ✓ | ✓ | ✓ |

Port Austin
Lake Huron
(517) 738-8712

| | ✓ | G | ✓ | ✓ | ✓ | ✓ | ✓ |

SANILAC COUNTY
Lexington
Lake Huron
(313) 359-5600

| | ✓ | G&D | ✓ | ✓ | ✓ | ✓ | ✓ |

Port Sanilac
Lake Huron
(313) 622-8818
(313) 622-9610

| | ✓ | G&D | ✓ | ✓ | ✓ | ✓ | ✓ |

NORTHEAST

ALCONA COUNTY
Harrisville
Lake Huron
(517) 724-5242

| | ✓ | G&D | ✓ | ✓ | ✓ | ✓ | ✓ |

* after name means no transient accommodations

	Harbormaster	Gas & diesel	Water	Electricity	Pump-out	Showers	VHF-FM
ALPENA COUNTY Alpena Lake Huron (517) 356-0551	✓	G&D	✓	✓	✓	✓	✓
ARENAC COUNTY Au Gres Lake Huron (517) 876-8729	✓	G	✓	✓	✓	✓	✓
CHEBOYGAN COUNTY Cheboygan (City) Lake Huron			✓	✓		✓	
Cheboygan (County) Lake Huron (616) 627-4944	✓	G&D	✓	✓	✓	✓	✓
Cheboygan Lock* Lake Huron (616) 627-9841							
Mackinaw City Lake Huron (616) 436-5269	✓	G&D	✓	✓	✓	✓	✓
IOSCO COUNTY East Tawas Lake Huron (517) 362-2731	✓	G&D	✓	✓	✓	✓	✓
PRESQUE ISLE COUNTY Hammond Bay Lake Huron (517) 938-9291	✓	G	✓	✓	✓	✓	✓

* after name means no transient accommodations

8

	Harbormaster	Gas & diesel	Water	Electricity	Pump-out	Showers	VHF-FM
Rogers City Lake Huron (517) 734-3808	✓	G&D	✓	✓	✓	✓	✓

NORTHWEST

ANTRIM COUNTY

Elk Rapids Lake Michigan (616) 264-8174	✓	G&D	✓	✓	✓	✓	✓

BENZIE COUNTY

Frankfort Lake Michigan (616) 352-9051	✓	G&D	✓	✓	✓	✓	✓

CHARLEVOIX COUNTY

Boyne City Lake Michigan (616) 582-6597 (616) 582-6611	✓		✓	✓	✓	✓	
Charlevoix Lake Michigan (616) 547-3272	✓	G&D	✓	✓	✓	✓	✓
East Jordan Lake Michigan (616) 536-2166	✓	G&D	✓	✓	✓	✓	✓
St. James Harbor, Beaver Island Lake Michigan (616) 448-2252	✓	G&D	✓	✓	✓	✓	✓

* after name means no transient accommodations

Recreational Harbors

	Harbormaster	Gas & diesel	Water	Electricity	Pump-out	Showers	VHF-FM
EMMET COUNTY Crooked River Lock* Lake Huron (616) 548-2271							
Harbor Springs Lake Michigan (616) 526-5355	✓	G&D	✓	✓	✓	✓	✓
Petoskey Lake Michigan (616) 347-6691	✓	G	✓	✓	✓	✓	✓
GRAND TRAVERSE COUNTY Traverse City Lake Michigan (616) 922-4903	✓	G	✓	✓	✓	✓	✓
LEELANAU COUNTY Greilickville Lake Michigan (616) 946-5463	✓		✓	✓	✓		
Leland Lake Michigan (616) 256-9132	✓	G&D	✓	✓	✓	✓	✓
Northport Lake Michigan (616) 386-5411	✓	G&D	✓	✓	✓	✓	✓
Suttons Bay Lake Michigan (616) 271-6703 (616) 271-3051	✓	G	✓	✓	✓	✓	✓

* after name means no transient accommodations

	Harbormaster	Gas & diesel	Water	Electricity	Pump-out	Showers	VHF-FM
MANISTEE COUNTY							
Arcadia Lake Michigan (616) 889-9653	✓	G&D	✓	✓	✓	✓	✓
Manistee Lake Michigan (616) 723-1552	✓	G&D	✓	✓	✓	✓	✓
MASON COUNTY							
Ludington Lake Michigan (616) 843-9611	✓	G&D	✓	✓	✓	✓	✓
MUSKEGON COUNTY							
Hartshorn, Muskegon Lake Michigan (616) 724-6785	✓		✓	✓	✓	✓	✓
White Lake Municipal Whitehall Lake Michigan (616) 894-9689	✓	G&D	✓	✓	✓	✓	✓
OCEANA COUNTY							
Pentwater Lake Michigan (616) 869-8301	✓		✓	✓	✓	✓	✓
SOUTHWEST							
BERRIEN COUNTY							
New Buffalo Lake Michigan (616) 469-2600							

* after name means no transient accommodations

11

	Harbormaster	Gas & diesel	Water	Electricity	Pump-out	Showers	VHF-FM
St. Joseph Lake Michigan (616) 983-5432	✓		✓	✓	✓	✓	
OTTAWA COUNTY Grand Haven Lake Michigan (616) 847-3478	✓	G	✓	✓	✓	✓	
VAN BUREN COUNTY South Haven Lake Michigan (616) 637-3171	✓		✓	✓	✓	✓	✓

UPPER PENINSULA

	Harbormaster	Gas & diesel	Water	Electricity	Pump-out	Showers	VHF-FM
ALGER COUNTY Grand Marais Lake Superior	✓	G&D	✓	✓		✓	✓
Munising Lake Superior				✓	✓		
BARAGA COUNTY Baraga Lake Superior (906) 353-6237					✓		
CHIPPEWA COUNTY De Tour Harbor Lake Huron (906) 297-5947	✓	G&D	✓	✓	✓	✓	✓

* after name means no transient accommodations

	Harbormaster	Gas & diesel	Water	Electricity	Pump-out	Showers	VHF-FM
Charles Harvey, Sault Ste. Marie Lake Superior (906) 632-6741	✓		✓	✓	✓		✓
Whitefish Point Lake Superior							
DELTA COUNTY Escanaba Lake Michigan (906) 786-9614	✓	G&D	✓	✓	✓	✓	✓
Fayette Lake Michigan							
Gladstone Lake Michigan (906) 428-4915	✓	G	✓	✓	✓	✓	✓
GOGEBIC COUNTY Black River Lake Superior (906) 667-0261		G	✓	✓	✓		
HOUGHTON COUNTY Grand Traverse Bay Lake Superior							
Houghton* Lake Superior							
Houghton-Hancock Lake Superior (906) 482-6010	✓	G&D	✓	✓	✓	✓	✓

* after name means no transient accommodations

	Harbormaster	Gas & diesel	Water	Electricity	Pump-out	Showers	VHF-FM
KEWEENAW COUNTY							
Copper Harbor Lake Superior (906) 289-4410	✓	G	✓	✓	✓	✓	✓
Eagle Harbor Lake Superior (906) 289-4416	✓	G	✓	✓	✓	✓	
Lac La Belle Lake Superior		G					
LUCE COUNTY							
Little Lake Lake Superior	✓	G	✓	✓			
MACKINAC COUNTY							
Bois Blanc Lake Huron				✓			
Hessel Lake Huron (906) 484-3046	✓	G	✓	✓	✓	✓	✓
Mackinac Island Lake Huron (906) 847-3561	✓	G&D	✓	✓	✓		✓
Naubinway Lake Michigan	✓		✓	✓		✓	
St. Ignace Lake Huron (906) 643-8131	✓	G	✓	✓	✓	✓	✓

* after name means no transient accommodations

	Harbormaster	Gas & diesel	Water	Electricity	Pump-out	Showers	VHF-FM
MARQUETTE COUNTY Big Bay Lake Superior (906) 345-9353	✓	G	✓	✓	✓		✓
Presque Isle Harbor Marquette Lake Superior (906) 228-0464	✓	G&D	✓	✓	✓	✓	✓
MENOMINEE COUNTY Menominee Lake Michigan (906) 863-8498	✓	G&D	✓	✓	✓	✓	✓
ONTONAGON COUNTY Ontonagon Lake Superior	✓	G	✓	✓	✓	✓	✓
SCHOOLCRAFT COUNTY Manistique Lake Michigan (906) 341-6841		G	✓	✓	✓	✓	✓

* after name means no transient accommodations

Chapter 2
MARINAS ON THE WATER

For many boaters, marinas make the sport feasible with docking space, fuel, repair facilities and knowledgeable staff able to provide information about lake and river conditions, technical problems, local attractions and navigation.

This chapter lists marinas that operate under Michigan Department of Natural Resources permits and that responded to a detailed survey about their facilities and services. The information is compiled from survey replies and DNR records. It does not include marinas which limit their services to members and, therefore, are not available to the general boating public. You'll also find marina services covered by the chapter on recreational harbors, Chapter 1.

In addition to the services covered in this list, boaters may also want to inquire about restrooms, showers, fuel, shuttle service, food, campgrounds, motels, restaurants and winter storage. Check into reservation, deposit and minimum stay policies. Also, if you don't have your own boat, some marinas offer rentals as either a sideline or their major activity.

Services not found at a marina are often available nearby, including restaurants, convenience stores, public boat launches and lodging.

The waterway listed below each marina's telephone number is the one on which it is located. Often, that waterway connects with others; for example, Saugatuck marinas are located on Kalamazoo Lake, which has access to Lake Michigan, and Oscoda marinas are on the AuSable River, which connects with Lake Huron.

	Total slips	Transients	Sales	Repairs	Parts	Launche ramp	Pump out	Hoist	Electric	Water	VHF-FM radio

SOUTHEAST

JACKSON COUNTY

	Total slips	Transients	Sales	Repairs	Parts	Launche ramp	Pump out	Hoist	Electric	Water	VHF-FM radio
Wolf Lake Marina Inc. 9145 Wolf Lake Jackson MI 49201 (517) 536-8666 Big Wolf Lake	44		✓	✓	✓	✓					

LAPEER COUNTY

	Total slips	Transients	Sales	Repairs	Parts	Launche ramp	Pump out	Hoist	Electric	Water	VHF-FM radio
Columbiaville Village Marina 449 McCormick Drive Lapeer MI 48446 (313) 667-0080 Holloway Reservoir	10					✓					

MACOMB COUNTY

	Total slips	Transients	Sales	Repairs	Parts	Launche ramp	Pump out	Hoist	Electric	Water	VHF-FM radio
Aggressive Marine 32393 S. River Road Mt. Clemens MI 48045 (313) 463-1234 Clinton River	131	✓	✓	✓	✓			✓	✓	✓	
Blue Water Marine 30201 S. River Road Mt. Clemens MI 48045 (313) 468-6960 Clinton River	15			✓	✓			✓	✓	✓	
North Bay Marine Ltd. 48930 Jefferson Ave. New Baltimore MI 48047 (313) 725-2628 Salt River	6		✓	✓	✓	✓		✓	✓	✓	✓

	Total slips	Transients	Sales	Repairs	Parts	Launch ramp	Pump out	Hoist	Electric	Water	VHF-FM radio
Propeller Basin & Sales 48740 Jefferson Ave. New Baltimore MI 48047 (313) 725-0041 Lake St. Clair	52			✓	✓		✓	✓	✓	✓	
Residential 48800 Jamaica New Baltimore MI 48047 (313) 725-0810 Salt River	8								✓	✓	
Ship Chandler Marina 32489 S. River Road Mt. Clemens MI 48045 (313) 465-1231 Clinton River	22						✓	✓	✓	✓	
Sun & Sail Marine Inc. 31040 N. River Road Mt. Clemens MI 48045 (313) 463-4800 Clinton River	27	✓		✓				✓			
Sun Up Marina 48770 Jamaica New Baltimore MI 48047 (313) 725-1411 Salt River	85			✓	✓	✓	✓	✓	✓	✓	
MONROE COUNTY Lake Pointe Marina 11234 U.S. Turnpike S. Rockwood MI 48179 (313) 379-2904 Huron River	145	✓				✓	✓	✓	✓	✓	

	Total slips	Transients	Sales	Repairs	Parts	Launch ramp	Pump out	Hoist	Electric	Water	VHF-FM radio
Luna Pier Harbour Club Box 424 10420 S. Harold Drive Luna Pier MI 48157 (313) 848-8777 Lake Erie	393	✓		✓	✓	✓	✓		✓	✓	✓
Shelter Cove Marina 2929 E. Sterns Road Erie MI 48133 (313) 723-7458 Lake Erie	80	✓	✓	✓	✓	✓	✓		✓	✓	✓
Trout's Yacht Basin 7970 Harbor Road Monroe MI 48161 (313) 242-5545 Bolles Harbor	100	✓		✓	✓	✓	✓	✓	✓	✓	
OAKLAND COUNTY Oxbow Landing Beach & Marina Club 9552 Elizabeth Lake Road White Lake MI 48387 (313) 698-2622 (313) 339-3998 Oxbow Lake	32	✓		✓		✓					
ST. CLAIR COUNTY Algonac Harbour Club Box 438 1999 Pte. Tremble Road Algonac MI 48001 (313) 794-4448 St. Clair River	383	✓		✓	✓		✓	✓	✓	✓	✓

	Total slips	Transients	Sales	Repairs	Parts	Launch ramp	Pump out	Hoist	Electric	Water	VHF-FM radio
Bay Port Marine 8815 Dixie Highway Fair Haven MI 48023 (313) 725-6769 Swan Creek	16	✓	✓	✓	✓	✓		✓	✓	✓	
Belle River Marina 1226 S. Belle River Marine City MI 48039 (313) 765-5556 St. Clair River	10	✓		✓	✓		✓	✓	✓	✓	
Black River Marine 207 Water St. Port Huron MI 48060 (313) 982-3990 Black River	12	✓	✓	✓	✓		✓	✓	✓	✓	✓
Cuthbertson Boat Works 6231 M-29 Pearl Beach MI 48052 (313) 794-4552 St. Clair River	6	✓		✓	✓			✓		✓	
Harmony Marina Motel 7745 Harmony Court Fair Haven MI 48023 (313) 725-1331 Swan Creek	19	✓							✓	✓	
Sassy Marina 9000 Merrill Drive Algonac MI 48001 (313) 794-9333 St. Clair River	330	✓		✓			✓	✓	✓	✓	

	Total slips	Transients	Sales	Repairs	Parts	Launch ramp	Pump out	Hoist	Electric	Water	VHF-FM radio
St. Clair Marina Inc. 700 Marine Drive St. Clair MI 48079 (313) 329-9047 St. Clair River	70			✓	✓	✓		✓	✓		
Sunset Harbor Marina 1784 N. Channel Harsens Island MI 48028 (313) 748-3082 St. Clair River	105	✓		✓	✓		✓	✓	✓	✓	
Tashmoo Marina South Box 28006 7650 South Channel Harsens Island MI 48028 (313) 748-3330 St. Clair River	80	✓		✓	✓		✓	✓	✓	✓	
Terry's Marina & Yacht Harbour Brokerage 8839 Dixie Highway Fair Haven MI 48023 (313) 725-8964 Swan Creek	153	✓					✓	✓	✓	✓	
WASHTENAW COUNTY Midwest Aquatics Group 8930 Dexter-Pinckney Road Pinckney MI 48169 (313) 426-4155 Portage Lake	197		✓	✓	✓						✓

	Total slips	Transients	Sales	Repairs	Parts	Launch ramp	Pump out	Hoist	Electric	Water	VHF-FM radio
WAYNE COUNTY C-Porte Marina 11 Cherry St. Trenton MI 48183 (313) 671-1600 Detroit River	24	✓	✓					✓	✓	✓	
Damark Marine Specialties 29021 Wilson Ave. Gibralter MI 48173-9731 (313) 676-2880 Detroit River	0		✓	✓			✓			✓	
Gregory Boat Co. & Detroit Boat Basin 9666 E. Jefferson Detroit MI 48214 (313) 823-1900 Detroit River	86	✓	✓	✓	✓		✓	✓	✓	✓	
Page's Marine Service Box 14517 467 Harding Detroit MI 48214 (313) 331-5897 Detroit River	12	✓		✓	✓			✓	✓	✓	
River's Edge Marina 4685 W. Jefferson Ave. Ecorse MI 48229 (313) 386-3353 Detroit River	125	✓		✓	✓	✓	✓	✓	✓	✓	

	Total Slips	Transients	Sales	Repairs	Parts	Launch ramp	Pump out	Hosit	Electric	Water	VHF-FM radio
Sinbad's Restaurant & Marina 100 St. Clair Detroit MI 48214 (313) 822-7817 Detroit River	86	✓		✓	✓		✓	✓	✓	✓	
Stowaway Ltd. 29001 Wilson Ave. Gibralter MI 48173-9731 (313) 675-7869 Detroit River	0						✓				✓

SOUTHWEST

ALLEGAN COUNTY

	Total Slips	Transients	Sales	Repairs	Parts	Launch ramp	Pump out	Hosit	Electric	Water	VHF-FM radio
Deep Harbor Marina 3301 Woodhams Drive Portage MI 49002 (616) 327-3647 (616) 857-4833 (616) 792-6652 Kalamazoo River	90	✓				✓	✓		✓	✓	✓
Point Pleasant Marina 201 Washington Ave. Douglas MI 49406 (616) 857-4759 Kalamazoo River	15	✓							✓	✓	
Sergeant Marine Box 316 31 Butler St. Saugatuck MI 49453 (616) 857-2873 Kalamazoo Lake	52	✓					✓		✓	✓	✓

	Total slips	Transients	Sales	Repairs	Parts	Launch ramp	Pump out	Hoist	Electric	Water	VHF-FM radio
Skipper's Cove 419 Lake St. Saugatuck MI 49453 (616) 857-5091 Kalamazoo Lake	12								✓	✓	
Walker's Landing Box 1015 Holland 49422 (616) 857-2013 (616) 335-5533 Kalamazoo River	20	✓					✓		✓	✓	
BERRIEN COUNTY Brian's Marina & Service 285 Anchors Way St. Joseph MI 49085 (616) 983-0760 St. Joseph River	225	✓	✓	✓	✓		✓	✓	✓	✓	✓
Pier 33 Marina 250 Anchors Way St. Joseph MI 49085 (616) 983-0677 Lake Michigan	220	✓	✓	✓	✓	✓	✓	✓	✓	✓	✓
Wolf's Marine Inc. 250 W. Main St. Benton Harbor MI 49022 (616) 926-1068 St. Joseph River	32		✓	✓	✓						
BRANCH COUNTY Brannan's Place 4375 Wayne Beach Coldwater MI 48036 (517) 238-2303 Coldwater Lake	15	✓				✓					

	Total slips	Transients	Sales	Repairs	Parts	Launch ramp	Pump out	Hoist	Electric	Water	VHF-FM radio
Lake Drive Marine 26212 Lake Drive Coldwater MI 49036 (517) 238-4651 Coldwater Lake	10		✓	✓	✓	✓					
CASS COUNTY Camp Wildwood 23040 Phillips St. Edwardsburg MI 49112 (616) 699-5331 Juno Lake	50	✓			✓	✓					
KALAMAZOO COUNTY Gull Harbor Marine 12173 East D Ave. Richland MI 49083 (616) 629-4507 Gull Lake	42	✓	✓	✓	✓				✓	✓	
KENT COUNTY Murray Lake Marina 11319 Lally N.E. Lowell MI 49331 (616) 897-4116 Murray Lake	21	✓	✓	✓	✓	✓					
OTTAWA COUNTY Anchorage Marina 1800 Ottawa Beach Road Holland MI 49424 (616) 399-1802 Lake Macatawa	189	✓	✓	✓	✓		✓	✓	✓	✓	

	Total slips	Transients	Sales	Repairs	Parts	Launch ramp	pump out	Hoist	Electric	Water	VHF-FM radio
Barrett Boat Works 821 W. Savidge St. Spring Lake MI 49456 (616) 842-1202 Spring Lake	200			✓	✓		✓	✓	✓	✓	
Cutler's Landing Inc. 17540 Fruitport Road Spring Lake MI 49456 (616) 842-3713	50								✓	✓	
Eldean Shipyard & Yacht Sales 2223 S. Shore Drive Macatawa MI 49434 (616) 335-5843 Lake Macatawa	195	✓	✓	✓	✓		✓	✓	✓	✓	
Eldean Yacht Basin Ltd. 1862 Ottawa Beach Road Holland MI 49424 (616) 786-9300 Lake Macatawa	371	✓	✓	✓	✓		✓	✓	✓	✓	✓
Fricke Marine Inc. 1719 Pennoyer St. Grand Haven MI 49417 (616) 842-7889 Grand River	36							✓	✓	✓	
Grand Haven Municipal Marina 101 N. Harbor Drive Grand Haven MI 49417 (616) 847-3478 Grand River	57	✓					✓		✓	✓	✓

	Total slips	Transients	Sales	Repairs	Parts	Launch ramp	Pump out	Hoist	Electric	Water	VHF-FM radio
Grand Valley Marina II 1211 Jackson St. Grand Haven MI 49417 (616) 842-4670 Grand River	40	✓		✓	✓			✓	✓	✓	✓
North Shore Marina Inc. 18275 Berwyck Spring Lake MI 49456 (616) 842-1488 Grand River	118	✓	✓	✓	✓		✓	✓	✓	✓	✓
Wharf Marina 501 N. Third St. Grand Haven MI 49417 (616) 842-5370 Grand River	151			✓	✓		✓	✓	✓	✓	✓
ST. JOSEPH COUNTY Klinger Lake Marina Inc. 67708 Klinger Lake Road Sturgis MI 49091 (616) 651-6503 Klinger Lake	32		✓	✓	✓	✓		✓			
VAN BUREN COUNTY All Seasons Marine Inc. Box 431 234 Black River St. South Haven MI 49090 (616) 637-3655 Black River	46		✓	✓	✓		✓	✓	✓	✓	✓
Black River Park Dunkley Avenue South Haven MI 49090 (616) 637-1949 Black River	62	✓				✓			✓	✓	

	Total slips	Transients	Sales	Repairs	Parts	Launch ramp	Pump out	Hoist	Electric	Water	VHF-FM radio
Nichols Marine Box 565 815 Wells St. South Haven MI 49090 (616) 637-7026 Black River	0		✓	✓		✓	✓	✓	✓	✓	
Patterson Marine 270 Oak St. South Haven MI 49090 (616) 637-4453 Lake Michigan	18	✓	✓	✓	✓		✓	✓	✓	✓	✓
South Haven Municipal Marina 345 Water St. South Haven MI 49090 (616) 637-3171 Black River	128	✓				✓	✓		✓	✓	✓
Summerplace Moorings 12 N. Bailey Ave. South Haven MI 49090 (616) 637-2419 Black River	28	✓				✓			✓	✓	✓

CENTRAL

BARRY COUNTY

	Total slips	Transients	Sales	Repairs	Parts	Launch ramp	Pump out	Hoist	Electric	Water	VHF-FM radio
Mar-Bil Marine 12450 Sunset Point Plainwell MI 49080 (616) 664-4445 Pine Lake	0			✓	✓	✓					

	Total slips	Transients	Sales	Repairs	Parts	Launch ramp	Pump out	Hoist	Electric	Water	VHF-FM radio
K T Resort 7327 Delton Road Delton MI 49046 (616) 623-5396 Upper Crooked Lake	2	✓				✓					
Pine Lake Boat & Motor 1101 S. Doster Road Plainwell MI 49080 (616) 685-8690 Pine Lake		✓	✓	✓	✓	✓					
BAY COUNTY Bay City Municipal Marina, Liberty Harbor 215 John F. Kennedy Dr. Bay City MI 48706 (517) 894-2800 Saginaw River	98	✓				✓	✓	✓	✓	✓	✓
Bay Harbor Marina Box 57 5309 E. Wilder Road Bay City MI 48707 (517) 684-5010 Saginaw Bay	435	✓	✓	✓	✓		✓	✓	✓	✓	✓
Brennan Marine Box 490 1809 S. Water St. Bay City MI 48707 (517) 894-4181 Saginaw River	350	✓	✓	✓	✓	✓	✓	✓	✓	✓	✓

	Total slips	Transients	Sales	Repairs	Parts	Launch ramp	Pump out	Hoist	Electric	Water	VHF-FM radio
Hoyles Marina 135 S. Linwood Beach Linwood MI 48634 (517) 697-3153 Saginaw Bay	262	✓	✓	✓	✓	✓	✓	✓	✓	✓	✓
EATON COUNTY Grand Pointe Marina Inc. 7086 Creyts Road Dimondale MI 48821 (517) 646-6733 (517) 646-0777 Grand River	14	✓	✓	✓	✓	✓	✓	✓	✓	✓	
GENESEE COUNTY Cornwell's Country Store 16177 S. Seymour Road Linden MI 48451 (313) 735-5271 Lobdell Lake	8	✓									
Silver Spray Sports Inc. 4037 Silver Lake Road Fenton MI 48430 (313) 629-6370 Silver Lake	12		✓	✓	✓	✓					
Water Sports Marine Inc. 3460 Silver Lake Road Fenton MI 48430 (313) 629-1342 Silver Lake	40	✓	✓	✓	✓	✓		✓			

	Total slips	Transients	Sales	Repairs	Parts	Launch ramp	Pump out	Hoist	Electric	Water	VHF-FM radio
HURON COUNTY											
Beadle Bay Marina Box 1029 - Sand Point 4375 Lone Eagle Trail Caseville MI 48725 (800) 342-0850 (517) 856-4911 Saginaw Bay	155	✓				✓	✓		✓	✓	
Beadle Bay Marina Annex 6635 River St. Caseville MI 48725 (800) 342-0850 (517) 856-4911 Saginaw Bay	43	✓				✓			✓	✓	
Hoy's Saginaw Bay Marina Box 1157 6591 Harbor St. Caseville MI 48725 (517) 856-4475 Saginaw Bay	110	✓		✓	✓	✓	✓	✓	✓	✓	✓
Off-Shore Tackle 23 E. Spring St. Port Austin MI 48467 (517) 738-5247 Saginaw Bay	5		✓	✓	✓				✓	✓	✓
LIVINGSTON COUNTY											
Young's Marina Inc. 21660 Kaiser Road Gregory MI 48137 (313) 498-2494 Woodburn Lake	50		✓	✓	✓	✓					

	Total slips	Transients	Sales	Repairs	Parts	Launch ramp	Pump out	Hoist	Electric	Water	VHF-FM radio
MIDLAND COUNTY											
Sanford Lake Resort 4063 Water Road Sanford MI 48657 (517) 689-3441 Sanford Lake	4			✓	✓	✓					

NORTHEAST

	Total slips	Transients	Sales	Repairs	Parts	Launch ramp	Pump out	Hoist	Electric	Water	VHF-FM radio
CHEBOYGAN COUNTY											
Bridge Marina & Island Ferry Services 101 W. 2nd Cheboygan MI 49721 (616) 627-9445 Cheboygan River	8	✓					✓		✓	✓	✓
Burt Lake Marina Inc. Box 550 4879 S. Straits Highway Indian River MI 49749 (616) 238-9316 Inland Waterway	46		✓	✓	✓	✓		✓			
Hack-Ma Tack Inn 8219 Beebe Road Cheboygan MI 49721 (616) 625-2919 Inland Waterway	3								✓	✓	
Indian River Marina Box 426 3020 Apple Blossom Lane Indian River MI 49749 (616) 238-9373 Inland Waterway	100	✓	✓	✓	✓	✓	✓	✓	✓	✓	✓

	Total slips	Transients	Sales	Repairs	Parts	Launch ramp	Pump out	Hoist	Electric	Water	VHF-FM radio
Rivers Junction Marina Box 519 5892 River St. Indian River MI 49749 (616) 238-7215 Inland Waterway	32	✓		✓	✓	✓				✓	✓
Walstrom Marine Inc. 113 E. State St. Cheboygan MI 49721 (616) 627-7105 Cheboygan River	28	✓	✓	✓	✓	✓	✓	✓	✓	✓	✓
Waterways Campground Box 262 M-33 at Cheboygan River Cheboygan MI 49721 Cheboygan River	10	✓				✓			✓	✓	
GLADWIN COUNTY Castillo's Landing Inc. 5013 Middle Road Hope MI 48628 (517) 435-4201 Wixom Lake	5	✓				✓					
J & J's Landing Inc. 5106 Dundas Road Beaverton MI 48612 (517) 435-7145 Wixom Lake	25			✓	✓						
Lakeshore Village Marina 4069 Lakeshore Drive Gladwin MI 48624 (517) 345-2752 Tittabawasee River	40	✓		✓	✓	✓					

	Total slips	Transients	Sales	Repairs	Parts	Launch ramp	Pump out	Hoist	Electric	Water	VHF-FM radio
IOSCO COUNTY											
Fellows' Marina Box 453 440 S. State St. Oscoda MI 48750 (517) 739-2525 AuSable River	40	✓		✓		✓			✓	✓	✓
Fellows' Marine North 402 S. State St. Oscoda MI 48750 (517) 739-1921 AuSable River	45	🚤		✓		✓			✓	✓	✓
Main Pier Marina 4498 W. US-23 Oscoda MI 48750 (517) 739-8530 AuSable River	127	✓				✓	✓		✓	✓	✓
North East Michigan Marine 470 S. State St. Oscoda MI 48750 (517) 739-4411 AuSable River	60	✓		✓	✓		✓	✓	✓	✓	✓
Surfside Motel & Marina 716 W. Lake St. Tawas City MI 48763 (517) 362-6915 Tawas River	18	✓							✓	✓	

	Total slips	Transients	Sales	Repairs	Parts	Launch Ramp	Pump out	Hoist	Electric	Water	VHF-FM radio
PRESQUE ISLE COUNTY Belz & Sons Marina Inc. 14322 Highway 638 E. Alpena MI 49707 (517) 595-2502 Grand Lake	26	✓	✓	✓	✓	✓					
ROSCOMMON COUNTY B & B Sports Center Marina 431 Higgins Lake Blvd. Roscommon MI 48653 (517) 821-6549 Higgins Lake	36	✓		✓	✓	✓					
D & B Lakeview Marina 1901 M-76 St. Helen MI 48656 (517) 389-4961 Lake St. Helen	100	✓	✓	✓	✓	✓					
Harvey Marine Inc. 1699 E. Houghton Lake Road Houghton Lake MI 48629 (517) 366-5537 Houghton Lake	118		✓	✓	✓	✓		✓			
Higgins Lake Boat Yard 1234 Higgins Lake Drive Roscommon MI 48653 (517) 821-6509 Higgins Lake	25	✓	✓	✓	✓	✓		✓			

	Total slips	Transients	Sales	Repairs	Parts	Launch ramp	Pump out	Hoist	Electric	Water	VHF-FM radio
NORTHWEST											
ANTRIM COUNTY											
Elk Rapids Harbor Box 398 207 Ceadar Elk Rapids MI 49629 (616) 264-9274 East Grand Traverse Bay	213	✓				✓	✓		✓	✓	✓
Kewadin Village Marina 7208 Cherry Ave. Kewadin MI 49648 (616) 264-8914 Elk Lake	51	✓		✓	✓	✓	✓		✓	✓	
BENZIE COUNTY											
Betsie Bay Marina 100 Frankfort Ave. Elberta MI 49628 (616) 352-7200 Betsie Bay	100	✓		✓	✓		✓	✓	✓	✓	✓
Elberta Charter Boat Marina 212 Frankfort Ave. Alberta MI 49628 (616) 352-9980 Betsie Lake	28	✓					✓		✓	✓	
Frankfort Municipal Marina Mineral Springs Park 42 Main St. Frankfort MI 49635 (616) 352-9051 Lake Michigan	69	✓			✓	✓	✓		✓	✓	✓

	Total slips	Transients	Sales	Repairs	Parts	Launch ramp	Pump out	Hoist	Electric	Water	VHF-FM radio
Elberta Marina Box 8 151 Pearson Elberta MI 39628 (616) 352-7201 Betsie Bay	50	✓				✓			✓	✓	
Jacobson Marina Box 1755 4th Street & Waterfront Frankfort MI 49635 (616) 352-9131 Lake Michigan	49	✓					✓		✓	✓	✓
CHARLEVOIX COUNTY Bear Cove Marina 03039 St. Louis Club Road Petoskey MI 49770 (616) 347-1994 Walloon Lake	26		✓	✓	✓	✓		✓			
Bellinger Marine Service Box 93 125 Belvedere Ave. Charlevoix MI 49720 (616) 547-2851 Round Lake	7	✓		✓	✓			✓	✓	✓	✓
East Jordan Municipal Marina 201 Main St. East Jordan MI 49727 (616) 536-2166 Lake Charlevoix	60	✓				✓	✓	✓	✓	✓	✓

	Total slips	Transients	Sales	Repairs	Parts	Launch ramp	Pump out	Hoist	Electric	Water	VHF-FM radio
Irish Boat Shop 13000 Stover Road Charlevoix MI 49720 (616) 547-9967 Lake Charlevoix	162	✓	✓	✓	✓		✓	✓	✓	✓	✓
Susan Valley Marina 03530 M-66 South East Jordan MI 49727 (616) 536-2672 Lake Charlevoix	10		✓	✓	✓						
EMMET COUNTY Ryde Marine 9088 Marina Drive Alanson MI 49706 (616) 347-8273 Crooked Lake	40	✓		✓	✓	✓		✓			
Windjammer Marina US 31 North Box 367 Oden MI 49764 Crooked Lake	80	✓	✓	✓	✓	✓	✓	✓	✓	✓	✓
GRAND TRAVERSE COUNTY Duncan L. Clinch Marina Box 592 Union St. & Grand View Traverse City MI 49685 (616) 922-4903 Grand Traverse Bay	102	✓				✓	✓		✓	✓	✓

	Total slips	Transients	Sales	Repairs	Parts	Launch ramp	Pump out	Hoist	Electric	Water	VHF-FM radio
Fife Lakeside Resort 228 E. State St. Fife Lake MI 49633 (616) 879-3341 Fife Lake	24	✓			✓	✓			✓	✓	
LEELANAU COUNTY Glen Craft Marina & Resort 6391 Lake St. Glen Arbor MI 49636 (616) 334-4556 Glen Lake	24	✓	✓	✓	✓						
On the Narrows Marina 8137 M-22 West Glen Arbor MI 49636 (616) 334-4891 Glen Lake	10	✓		✓							
Stander Marine Inc. Box 381 111 Oak St. Leland MI 49654 (616) 256-9231 Leland River	65	✓	✓	✓	✓	✓	✓	✓	✓		
MANISTEE COUNTY Harbor Village Marina Box 120 1360 N. River Road Manistee MI 49660 (616) 938-5438 Manistee River	384	✓		✓	✓	✓	✓	✓	✓	✓	✓

	Total slips	Transients	Sales	Repairs	Parts	Launch ramp	Pump out	Hoist	Electric	Water	VHF-FM radio
Johnston's Marina Inc. 297 Sixth Ave. Manistee MI 49660 (616) 723-3934 Manistee Channel	24	✓		✓			✓		✓	✓	✓
Solberg's Boat Yard 267 Arthur St. Manistee MI 49660 (616) 723-2611 Manistee Lake	158	✓		✓	✓		✓	✓	✓	✓	
Van's Landing Box 23 Main Street Onekmana MI 49675 (616) 889-9679 Portage Lake	15	✓							✓	✓	
MASON COUNTY Thompson Marina Inc. Box 607 510 1/2 E. Lake St. Ludington MI 49431 (616) 843-3387 Lake Michigan	34	✓		✓	✓	✓	✓		✓	✓	
MUSKEGON COUNTY Balcom Marine Centre 2964 Lakeshore Drive Muskegon MI 49441 (616) 755-1332 Muskegon Lake	79	✓					✓	✓	✓	✓	

	Total slips	Transients	Sales	Repairs	Parts	Launch ramp	Pump out	Hoist	Electric	Water	VHF-FM radio
Crosswinds Marine Service 302 S. Lake St. Whitehall MI 49461 (616) 894-4549 White Lake	101	✓		✓	✓		✓	✓	✓	✓	✓
Hartshorn Municipal Marina 920 W. Western Ave. Muskegon MI 49440 (616) 724-6785 Muskegon Lake	143	✓				✓	✓		✓	✓	✓
Lakeshore Yacht Harbour 1200 Lakeshore Drive Muskegon MI 49441 (616) 726-5770 Muskegon Lake	67						✓		✓	✓	✓
Matt's Boat Livery 3500 Channel Drive Muskegon MI 49441 (616) 755-4488 Muskegon Channel	10	✓				✓					
Muskegon Conservation Club Marina Box 5319 1921 Lake Ave. N. Muskegon MI 49445 (616) 744-8326 Muskegon Lake	117					✓			✓	✓	

	Total slips	Transients	Sales	Repairs	Parts	Launch ramp	Pump out	Hoist	Electric	Water	VHF-FM radio
Pointe Marine Assn. 350 Cihak N. Muskegon MI 49445 (616) 744-3236 Lake Michigan	125	✓		✓	✓		✓	✓	✓	✓	
Ruth's Marina 1633 S. Lake St. Whitehall MI 49461 (616) 893-7675 White Lake	10	✓							✓	✓	
South Shore Marina Inc. 6806 S. Shore Drive Whitehall MI 49461 (616) 893-3935 White Lake	20	✓	✓	✓	✓	✓		✓	✓	✓	✓
Terrace Point Marina 722 Terrace Point Blvd. Muskegon MI 49440 (616) 722-4448 Muskegon Lake	114	✓					✓		✓	✓	✓
Torresen Marine Inc. 3126 Lakeshore Drive Muskegon MI 49441 (616) 759-8596 Muskegon Lake	155	✓	✓	✓	✓	✓	✓	✓	✓	✓	✓
White Bay Marina & Charters 216 S. Lake St. Whitehall MI 49461 (616) 894-4082 White Lake	83	✓							✓	✓	✓

	Total slips	Transients	Sales	Repairs	Parts	Launch ramp	Pump out	Hoist	Electric	Water	VHF-FM radio
White Lake Municipal Marina 100 Lake St. Whitehall MI 49461 (616) 894-9689	50	✓					✓		✓	✓	✓
Whitehall Landing Inc. 410 Lake St. Whitehall MI 49461 (616) 894-5622 White Lake	180	✓		✓	✓		✓	✓	✓	✓	✓

UPPER PENINSULA

CHIPPEWA COUNTY

	Total slips	Transients	Sales	Repairs	Parts	Launch ramp	Pump out	Hoist	Electric	Water	VHF-FM radio
Little Neebish HC-51, Box 432 Rains Island Barbeau MI 49710 (906) 635-0983 St. Marys River	12	✓				✓	✓		✓	✓	✓
Riverview Taxidermy & Marine HC-51, Box 84 Scenic Drive Barbeau MI 49710 (906) 647-7211 St. Marys River	7	✓		✓	✓	✓					

HOUGHTON COUNTY

	Total slips	Transients	Sales	Repairs	Parts	Launch ramp	Pump out	Hoist	Electric	Water	VHF-FM radio
H & Y Marina & Storage 1037 Crestwood Drive Houghton MI 49930 (906) 482-1349 Portage Canal	25	✓		✓		✓					

	Total slips	Transients	Sales	Repairs	Parts	Launch ramp	Pump out	Hoist	Electric	Water	VHF-FM radio
Lake Linden Village Recreation Area 401 Calumet St. Lake Linden MI 49945 (906) 296-9911 Torch Lake Has 3 finger piers	0										

Chapter 3

OFFWATER MARINAS

Off-water marinas provide many of the same services as their counterparts on the water, including boat sales and rentals,service, parts and accessories, winter storage and good advice. All the off-water marinas listed in this chapter are open year round unless noted after their telephone number.

	Power boat sales	Sailboat sales	Repairs	Parts & accessories	Rentals
SOUTHEAST					
MACOMB COUNTY					
Joe's Trailer Sales Inc. 24953 Harper St. Clair Shores MI 48080 (313) 771-9499 Seasonal				✓	
Marine Sales & Repair 30134 S. River Road Mt. Clemens MI 48045 (313) 468-0937			✓	✓	
Modern Boats & Motors 21217 Van Dyke Warren MI 48089 (313) 757-3337			✓	✓	
Tom's Marine Hardware Inc. 30060 S. River Road Mt. Clemens MI 48045 (313) 465-5401	✓			✓	

	Power boat sales	Sailboat sales	Repairs	Parts & accessories	Rentals
MONROE COUNTY					
Anderson Marina 13431 Telegraph Box 127 Flat Rock MI 48134 (313) 782-1488	✓		✓	✓	
OAKLAND COUNTY					
Cruise Out Marine 580 E. Walton Blvd. Pontiac MI 48340 (313) 377-4290	✓	✓	✓	✓	
Inflatable Boat Specialist 8130 W. Nine Mile Road Oak Park MI 48237 (313) 545-5122	✓		✓	✓	
King Marine Inc. 4440 Haggerty Road Walled Lake MI 48390 (313) 363-8387	✓		✓	✓	
Norm's Marine Service Inc. 4914 Leafdale Royal Oak MI 48073 (313) 435-0737			✓	✓	
Waterford Marine 1050 Crescent Lake Road Waterford MI 48327 (313) 673-1015	✓		✓	✓	
ST. CLAIR COUNTY					
Marysville Propeller Inc. 1465 Michigan Ave. Marysville MI 48040 (800) 832-3222, (313) 364-4360	✓		✓	✓	

	Power boat sales	Sailboat sales	Repairs	Parts & accessories	Rentals
WAYNE COUNTY					
Bernie's Marine Service 232 S. Newburgh Westland MI 48185 (313) 326-7333	✓		✓	✓	
Boats Inc. 6465 N. Telegraph Road Dearborn Heights MI 48127 (313) 274-1600 February - December	✓		✓	✓	
Hood Sails - Great Lakes Inc. 15000 Kercheval Grosse Pointe Park MI 48230 (313) 822-1400			✓	✓	
I-94 Marine 43466 N. Service Drive Belleville MI 48111 (313) 697-6800	✓		✓	✓	
K & M Marine Inc. 14990 Telegraph Road Redford Township MI 48239 (313) 533-9800			✓	✓	
King Marine Downriver 811 Biddle Wyandotte MI 48192 (313) 246-9909	✓		✓	✓	
Quality Controlled Electronics 38424 Webb Drive Westland MI 48185 (313) 721-5666			✓	✓	

	Power boat sales	Sailboat sales	Repairs	Parts & accessories	Rentals
SOUTHWEST					
KENT COUNTY					
Northview Sport & Marine 5200 Plainfield Ave. NE Grand Rapids MI 49505 (616) 363-0481	✓		✓	✓	
Pier 33 Marina 3010 28th St. SW Grandville MI 49418 (616) 532-7676	✓		✓	✓	
Pier 33 Marina 3002 28th St. SW Grandville MI 49418 (616) 538-6500	✓		✓	✓	
Pier 33 Marina 3000 28th St. SW Grandville MI 49418 (616) 538-3314	✓		✓	✓	
OTTAWA COUNTY					
Pier 33 Marina 1885 Ottawa Beach Road Holland MI 49424 (616) 399-2628	✓		✓	✓	
Thunder Marine 1890 112th Ave. Holland MI 49424 (616) 396-8900	✓		✓	✓	

	Power boat sales	Sailboat sales	Repairs	Parts & accessories	Rentals
VAN BUREN COUNTY High's Marine 409 E. Delaware Decatur MI 49045 (616) 423-7065	✓		✓	✓	
CENTRAL					
CLINTON COUNTY Beck's Propane & Marine N. US 27 Rte. 3 St. Johns MI 48879 (517) 224-6825	✓		✓	✓	✓
GENESEE COUNTY Advanced Fiberglass Services Inc. G-6138 N. Saginaw St. Mt. Morris MI 48458 (313) 785-7541			✓	✓	
Aqua Sports Marine 3235 W. Thompson Road Fenton MI 48430 (313) 629-2800	✓		✓	✓	✓
Water Wonderland Sport Center G-10092 N. Dort Highway Clio MI 28420 (313) 686-9621	✓		✓	✓	
INGHAM COUNTY Alleva's Sport & Marine 2421 N. Larch, US 27 North Lansing MI 48906 (517) 482-2471	✓		✓	✓	

	Power boat sales	Sailboat sales	Repairs	Parts & accessories	Rentals
LIVINGSTON COUNTY Wilson Marine Corp. 6095 W. Grand River Brighton MI 48116 (517) 546-3774	✓		✓	✓	
Wonderland Marine West 5796 E. Grand River Howell MI 48843 (517) 548-5122	✓		✓	✓	

NORTHEAST

	Power boat sales	Sailboat sales	Repairs	Parts & accessories	Rentals
ALPENA COUNTY LaCross Marine 1257 US 23 North Alpena MI 49707 (517) 356-3822 (517) 354-8135	✓	✓	✓	✓	
ROSCOMMON COUNTY Spicer's Boat City 4165 W. Houghton Lake Drive Houghton Lake MI 48629 (517) 366-8400	✓		✓	✓	

NORTHWEST

	Power boat sales	Sailboat sales	Repairs	Parts & accessories	Rentals
CLARE COUNTY Harrison Sports Center 117 First St. Box 247 Harrison MI 48625 (517) 539-7026	✓		✓	✓	

	Power boat sales	Sailboat sales	Repairs	Parts & accessories	Rentals
NEWAYGO COUNTY Derks Marine Inc. 8696 S. Mason Box 357 Newaygo MI 49337 (616) 652-6789	✓		✓	✓	✓
Newaygo Marine Inc. 8336 Mason Drive Box 485 Newaygo MI 49337 (616) 652-6207	✓		✓	✓	

Chapter 4

PUBLIC BOAT LAUNCHES

With more than 1,200 boat launch sites, Michigan's public access program run by state, local and regional government agencies is extensive, serving small bodies of water and streams as well as the Great Lakes and major rivers. The program is financed with marine fuel tax revenue and part of the state's water craft registration fees. Most of the sites are operated by the Department of Natural Resources through its Recreation, Parks, Forest Management and Wildlife divisions. The others are administered by the U.S. Forest Service, Huron-Clinton Metropolitan Authority, National Guard and Joint Ypsilanti Recreation Organization; by county, city, township and village governments; or by public utility companies.

DNR classifies launch ramps in these four categories:

(1) Hard-surfaced, with enough depth to accommodate most trailerable boats.

(2) Hard-surfaced, with limited water depth.

(3) Gravel-surfaced.

(4) Carry-down areas, without an improved ramp and considered suitable only for car-top boats and canoes.

There's a lot of variety available. For example, there are 10 public launch sites in the Yankee Springs State Recreation Area near Middleville, Barry County. They're located on nine bodies of water, ranging from 17-acre McDonald Lake to 2,611-acre Gun Lake, and they fit into the second, third and fourth DNR ramp categories.

Some launch sites are on one body of water but provide access to another, larger body of water. For example, the municipal ramp in Sebewaing is on the Sebewaing River, which leads to Saginaw Bay, while the municipal ramp in Frankfort is on Betsie Lake, which connects with Lake Michigan. Maps for many inland lakes are available from Michigan United Conservation Club, Bureau of Maps, Box 30235, Lansing MI 48909; the phone number of (517) 371-1041.

In most cases, there is no fee to use state-constructed or state-funded launch facilities. However, an annual or daily motor vehicle permit is required to use facilities within state parks and state recreation areas.

The listings in this chapter cover availability of courtesy piers and toilets, parking spaces and the size -- in water acres -- of inland lakes and ponds. No size is listed for the Great Lakes and their major bays, or for rivers and streams. In most cases, the number of parking spaces is given; at a few launches, parking at the access site is restricted to registered campers. Sites which are designated as handicapper-accessible are marked with an H. Under DNR policy, "access to a representative sample of water bodies, suitable for a variety of boating experiences, will be provided to offer the handicapped boater a reasonable level of equivalent experience."

	Body of water	Acres	Ramp class	Courtesy pier	Toilet	Parking spaces	Handicapper accessible
SOUTHEAST							
HILLSDALE COUNTY							
Hemlock Lake 6 mi. NW of Reading	Hemlock Lake	140	2	✓	✓	15	
Cub Lake 2 mi. SE of Cambria	Cub Lake	128	2		✓	10	
Bear Lake 3 mi. N of Cambria	Bear Lake	117	2	✓	✓	8	
Bird Lake 4 mi. S of Osseo	Bird Lake	113	2		✓	10	
Long Lake 4 mi. NW of Reading	Long Lake	213	2	✓	✓	15	
Round Lake 4 mi. N of Reading	Round Lake	74	2	✓	✓	10	
Water Works Park 2 mi. SE of Hillsdale	Baw Besse Lake	329	2	✓	✓	9	H
Lake Diane 6 mi. E of Camden	Lake Diane	500	2	✓	✓	20	
JACKSON COUNTY							
Center Lake 1 mi. SE of Michigan Center	Center Lake	730	2		✓	30	
Crispell Lake 2 mi. W of Liberty	Crispell Lake	83	3		✓	10	
Portage Lake 5 mi. W of Waterloo	Portage Lake	360	1	✓	✓	60	
Maple Grove Bridge 6 mi. N of Jackson	Grand River		2		✓	12	
Gilletts Lake 4 mi. E of Jackson	Gilletts Lake	340	2	✓	✓	28	H
Trestle Bridge 2 mi. NW of Rives Junction	Grand River		4		✓	10	

	Body of water	Acres	Ramp class	Courtesy pier	Toilet	Parking spaces	Handicapper accessible
Tompkins Bridge 1 mi. N of Tompkins Center	Grand River	2		✓	✓	15	
LAPEER COUNTY							
Nepessing Lake 4 mi. SW of Lapeer	Nepessing Lake	354	2		✓	19	
Minnewanna Lake 3 mi. E of Hadley	Minnewanna Lake	45	3		✓	10	
Big Fish Lake 4 mi. S of Hadley	Big Fish Lake	105	1		✓	30	
Davidson Lake 5 mi. S of Hadley	Davidson Lake	56	3		✓	10	
S. Br. Flint River 7 mi. N of Lapeer	Flint River		4			5	
Sawdel Lake 6 mi. N of Lapeer	Sawdel Lake	46	4			10	
Long Lake 6 mi. NE of Lapeer	Long Lake	202	2		✓	40	
Watts Lake 7 mi. NE of Lapeer	Watts Lake	73	4			20	
LENAWEE COUNTY							
Sand Lake 2 mi. NE of Springville	Sand Lake	440	2	✓	✓	24	
Allens Lake 2 mi. N of Springville	Allens Lake	63	2	✓	✓	15	
Devils Lake 1 mi. N of Manitou Beach	Devils Lake	1330	1	✓	✓	23	H
Wamplers Lake 3 mi. NE of Springville	Wamplers Lake	780	1	✓	✓	150	
Round Lake 3 mi. NE of Springville	Round Lake	5	2	✓	✓	3	
Deep Lake 2 mi. SW of Cambridge Junction	Deep Lake	65	3		✓	10	
One Mile Lake 2 mi. SW of Cambridge Junction	One Mile Lake	29	4			10	
Lake Hudson 2 mi. S of Clayton	Lake Hudson	500	2	✓	✓	30	
MACOMB COUNTY							
Harley Ensign Mem. 5 mi. E of Mt. Clemens	Clinton River		1	✓	✓	225	H
Brandenburd Mem. Park 1 mi. SW of New Baltimore	Lake St. Clair		1	✓	✓	369	
Selfridge 4 mi. NE of Mt. Clemens	Lake St. Clair		1	✓	✓	155	

	Body of water	Acres	Ramp class	Courtesy pier	Toilet	Parking spaces	Hanciapper accessible
Metro Beach 5 mi. E of Mt. Clemens	Black Creek		1	✓	✓	160	
Stoney Creek Metro Park 3 mi. W of Washington	Stoney Creek Lake	149	1	✓	✓	149	
MONROE COUNTY							
Mouilee Creek Mouth Branch 2 mi. NE of Estral	Mouilee Creek		3		✓	10	
Otter Creek Mouth 3 mi. SE of LaSalle	Otter Creek		4			6	
Halfway Creek 4 mi. S of Erie	Lake Erie		2	✓	✓	45	
Dixie Highway 1 mi. SE of Newport	Swan Creek		2	✓	✓	15	H
Sterling St. Park 3 mi. E of Monroe	Lake Erie		1	✓	✓	319	H
Bolles Harbor 3 mi. SE of Monroe	LaPlaisance Creek		1	✓	✓	290	H
Hellenberg Field Monroe	Raisin River		1	✓	✓	50	
OAKLAND							
Orchard Lake Orchard Lake	Orchard Lake	788	1	✓	✓	64	
Union Lake Union Lake	Union Lake	465	1	✓	✓	32	H
Oakland Lake 1 mi. N of Drayton Plains	Oakland Lake	235	1	✓	✓	37	
Tackles Drive 3 mi. N of Union Lake	Pontiac Lake	640	4		✓	20	
Wolverine Lake 2 mi. N of Walled Lake	Wolverine Lake	241	1			15	
White Lake 3 mi. NE of Highland	White Lake	540	1	✓	✓	14	H
Lake Orion Lake Orion	Lake Orion	506	1	✓	✓	34	
Big Lake 2 mi. SE of Davisburg	Big Lake	200	3			15	
Long Lake 1 mi. W of Union Lake	Long Lake	146	1		✓	15	
Crescent Lake 2 mi. S of Drayton Plains	Crescent Lake	90	3			8	
Loon Lake Drayton Plains	Loon Lake	234	1	✓	✓	15	H
Squaw Lake 2 mi. W of Oxford	Squaw Lake	133	1	✓	✓	45	

Public Boat Launches

	Body of water	Acres	Ramp class	Courtesy pier	Toilet	Parking spaces	Handicapper accessible
Lakeville Lake Lakeville	Lakeville Lake	460	1	✓	✓	29	
Maceday Lake 3 mi. W of Drayton Plains	Maceday Lake	419	1	✓	✓	18	H
Cedar Island Lake 7 mi. E of Highland	Cedar Island Lake	134	1			6	
Tipsico Lake 4 mi. W of Rose Center	Tipsico Lake	301	1	✓	✓	15	
Dodge Bros. No. 4 State Park 4 mi. E of Union Lake	Cass Lake	1280	1		✓	50	
Pontiac Lake 4 mi. N of Union Lake	Pontiac Lake	640	1	✓	✓	80	
Alderman Lake 2 mi. NE of Highland	Alderman Lake	40	4		✓	15	
Moore Lake 1 mi. S of Highland	Moore Lake	92	4			10	
Lower Pettibone Lake 1 mi. S of Highland	Lower Pettibone Lake	89	3			15	
Teeple Lake 3 mi. E of Highland	Teeple Lake	49	3			30	
Middle Straights Lake 3 mi. W of Orchard Lake	Middle Straights Lake	171	3		✓	10	
Proud Lake 4 mi. SE of Milford	Proud Lake	104	1		✓	25	
Heron Lake 5 mi. E of Holly	Heron Lake	132	1		✓	48	
Crotche Lake 2 mi. NE of Holly	Crotche Lake	14	3		✓	10	
Crystal Lake 2 mi. E of Holly	Crystal Lake	12	3		✓	10	
Holdredge Lake 3 mi. NE of Holly	Holdredge Lake	16	4			10	
Wildwood-Valley Lakes 6 mi. E of Holly	Wildwood, Valley Lks.	84	2		✓	20	
Graham Lakes S. 2 mi. E of Lake Orion	Graham Lake	18	4			25	
Trout Lake 3 mi. S of Lake Orion	Trout Lake	3	1			16	
Big Seven Lake 3 mi. NW of Holly	Big Seven Lake	170	1		✓	12	
Dickinson Lake 2 mi. NW of Holly	Dickinson Lake	44	1			20	
ST. CLAIR COUNTY Fair Haven 1 mi. E of Fair Haven	Lake St. Clair		1	✓	✓	42	H

	Body of water	Acres	Ramp class	Courtesy pier	Toilet	Parking spaces	Handicapper accessible
Deckers Landing N. 3 mi. S of Fair Haven	St. Clair River		1	✓	✓	35	
Algonac St. Park Roberts Landing	St. Clair River		3		✓	12	
Walker Flats Impoundment 4 mi. S of Blaine	Black River		4			10	
Ames Middle Channel 3 mi. SW of Pearl Beach	St. Clair River		2		✓	35	
Snooks Middle Channel 2 mi. S of Pearl Beach	St. Clair River		2		✓	35	
St. Clair Mun. Ramp St. Clair	Pine River		1	✓	✓	80	
Algonac Mun. Ramp Algonac	St. Clair River		1	✓		40	
I-94 Bridge Mun. Ramp Port Huron	Black River		1	✓	✓	49	
12th St. Mun. Ramp Port Huron	Black River		1	✓	✓	65	
Marine City 1 mi. S of Marine City	St. Clair River		1	✓	✓	89	H
WASHTENAW COUNTY							
Bruin Lake 1 mi. SE of Unadilla	Bruin Lake	145	2		✓	8	
Half-Moon Lake 1 mi. S of Hell	Half-Moon Lake	244	2		✓	34	
Sugarloaf Lake 1 mi. SE of Waterloo	Sugarloaf Lake	205	2		✓	6	
Ford Lake 1 mi. SE of Ypsilanti	Ford Lake	1050	1	✓	✓	50	H
Joslin Lake 1 mi. SW of Unadilla	Joslin Lake	180	2			14	
North Lake 3 mi. S of Hell	North Lake	200	2			10	
South Lake 2 mi. S of Unadilla	South Lake	193	2		✓	4	
Gallup Park 3 mi. E of Ann Arbor	Gedes Pond	261	2	✓	✓	57	
Crooked Lake 2 mi. SE of Waterloo	Crooked Lake	113	2		✓	5	
Winnewanna Impoundment 2 mi. E of Waterloo	Winnewanna	500	3			15	
Pickerel Lake 2 mi. SE of Hell	Pickerel Lake	24	4			12	
Independence Lake 3 mi. SW of Whitmore Lake	Independence Lake	204	2		✓	10	

	Body of water	Acres	Ramp class	Courtesy pier	Toilet	Parking spaces	Handicapper accessible
Mill Lake 3 mi. W of Chelsea	Mill Lake	142	3		✓	12	
Cedar Lake 3 mi. W of Chelsea	Cedar Lake	76	2			8	
Green Lake 3 mi. E of Waterloo	Green Lake	95	3			10	
Doyle Lake 3 mi. W of Chelsea	Doyle Lake	18	4			6	
Four Mile Lake 2 mi. E of Chelsea	Four Mile Lake	256	3			15	
Portage Lake 4 mi. SE of Pinckney	Portage Lake	644	1	✓	✓	25	
WAYNE COUNTY							
St. Jean Street Ramp Detroit	Detroit River		1	✓	✓	75	
Huron River Mouth 4 mi. S of Gibralter	Huron River		2	✓	✓	60	
Belleville Lake 1 mi. NE of Belleville	Belleville Lake	1270	1	✓	✓	120	
Ecorse Mun. Ramp Ecorse	Detroit River		1	✓	✓	50	
Wyandotte Mun. Ramp Wyandotte	Detroit River		1	✓	✓	59	
Elizabeth Park 1 mi. S of Trenton	Detroit River		1	✓	✓	215	
Harrison Ave. Riverfront Park Trenton	Detroit River		1	✓	✓	34	H
Riverside Park Ambassador Bridge	Detroit River		1	✓	✓	128	

SOUTHWEST

	Body of water	Acres	Ramp class	Courtesy pier	Toilet	Parking spaces	Handicapper accessible
ALLEGAN COUNTY							
Big Lake 2 mi. NE of Watson	Big Lake	137	2		✓	10	
Hacklander 3 mi. E of Douglas	Kalamazoo River		2		✓	44	
Duck Lake 2 mi. SE of Cheshire	Duck Lake	113	3		✓	7	
Green Lake 4 mi. E of Moline	Green Lake	309	2		✓	18	
Selkirk 1 mi. NE of Shelbyville	Selkirk Lake	94	3		✓	6	
Pike Lake 4 mi. S of Allegan	Pike Lake	28	3		✓	15	

	Body of water	Acres	Ramp class	Courtesy pier	Toilet	Parking spaces	Handicapper accessible
Miner Lake 4 mi. NE of Allegan	Miner Lake	257	2		✓	10	
Swan Lake 1 mi. NW of Cheshire	Swan Lake	200	2		✓	15	
Lake Sixteen 2 mi. NE of Martin	Lake Sixteen	28	3		✓	20	
Sheffer Lake 4 mi. S of Allegan	Sheffer Lake	13	4			2	
New Richmond New Richmond	Kalamazoo River		2		✓	26	
Base Line Lake 7 mi. S of Allegan	Base Line Lake	187	2		✓	15	
Allegan Dam E. 6 mi. NW of Allegan	Kalamazoo River		2	✓	✓	109	H
M-89 Bridge 6 mi. S of Hamilton	Kalamazoo River		4			4	
Swan Creek Pond 5 mi. N of Chicora	Swan Creek Pond	140	4		✓	10	
Ely Lake 3 mi. E of Pearl	Ely Lake	18	4		✓	4	
Little Tom Lake 3 mi. SE of Pearl	Little Tom Lake	17	4			3	
Main Ottawa Landing 4 mi. W of Dunningville	Kalamazoo River		4			2	
Echo Point 3 mi. NW of Allegan	Lake Allegan	1587	2			10	
Howard Shultz Park 1 mi. E of Douglas	Kalamazoo Lake	160	2	✓	✓	50	
Gun Lake Co. Park 4 mi. E of Shelbyville	Gun Lake	2611	2		✓	30	
George Schutmaat Park Hamilton	Rabbit River		2		✓	15	
Pine Creek Impoundment 2 mi. W of Otsego	Pine Creek Impound.	80	2		✓	5	
Eagle Lake 2 mi. S of Cheshire	Eagle Lake	225	2		✓	10	
BERRIEN COUNTY							
Channels 1 mi. NE of Coloma	Paw Paw Lake	900	2		✓	24	
Sherwood Bay 2 mi. N of Watervliet	Paw Paw Lake	900	2	✓	✓	24	H
Galien River 2 mi. NE of New Buffalo	Galien River		4			10	
Black Lake 6 mi. E of Sodus	Black Lake	10	2		✓	8	

Public Boat Launches

	Body of water	Acres	Ramp class	Courtesy pier	Toilet	Parking spaces	Handicapper accessible
Benton Township River Park 3 mi. S of Benton Harbor	St. Joseph River		2	✓	✓	111	
Shamrock Park Berrien Springs	St. Joseph River		2		✓	52	
Carronde Park 3 mi. S of Benton Harbor	St. Joseph River		2	✓	✓	64	
Buchanan 2 mi. N of Buchanan	St. Joseph River		2			16	H
St. Joseph River Park Niles	St. Joseph River		2			25	
Riverview Park 2 mi. E. of St. Joseph	St. Joseph River		2	✓	✓	50	
New Buffalo New Buffalo	Galien River		1	✓	✓	92	
Benton Harbor Benton Harbor	St. Joseph River		1	✓	✓	113	H
BRANCH COUNTY							
Randall Lake 3 mi. NW of Coldwater	Randall Lake	220	2	✓	✓	20	
Coldwater Lake 3 mi. N of Kinderhook	Coldwater Lake	1610	2	✓	✓	56	H
Marble Lake 2 mi. SW of Quincy	Marble Lake	780	2	✓	✓	50	
Lake of the Woods 2 mi. SE of Bethel	Lake of the Woods	335	2	✓	✓	10	
Gilead Lake 4 mi. W of East Gilead	Gilead Lake	128	2		✓	10	
Loon Lake Channel 5 mi. NW of Algansee	Loon Lake	35	3		✓	5	
Cary Lake 1 mi. SW of Batavia	Cary Lake	42	2		✓	10	
Lake George 2 mi. S of Kinderhook	Lake George	507	2	✓	✓	20	
Matteson Lake 4 mi. N of Bronson	Matteson Lake	256	2	✓	✓	20	
Lake Lavine 3 mi. SW of Kinderhook	Lake Lavine	81	3		✓	15	
Middle Lake 4 mi. SW of Quincy	Middle Lake	64	2	✓	✓	10	
Union Lake 2 mi. W of Union City	Union Lake	518	2	✓	✓	10	
Silver Lake 1 mi. S of Kinderhook	Silver Lake	192	2		✓	10	
Craig Lake 2 mi. SE of Hodunk	Craig Lake	122	2	✓	✓	20	
Quincy-Marble Lake C. Park 1 mi. SW of Quincy	Marble Lake	780	2	✓	✓	51	

	Body of water	Acres	Ramp class	Courtesy pier	Toilet	Parking spaces	Handicapper accessible
CALHOUN COUNTY							
Nottawa Lake 4 mi. N of Tekonsha	Nottawa Lake	116	2		✓	10	
Goguac Lake 2 mi. SW of Battle Creek	Goguac Lake	352	2	✓	✓	31	H
Lanes Lake 6 mi. N of Marshall	Lanes Lake	24	2		✓	5	
Duck Lake 3 mi. E of Partello	Duck Lake	630	2	✓	✓	28	
Warner Lake 3 mi. NE of Burlington	Warner Lake	59	2	✓	✓	25	
Upper Brace Lake 4 mi. SE of Marshall	Upper Brace Lake	56	3	✓	✓	20	
Lee Lake 5 mi. E of East Leroy	Lee Lake	116	2	✓	✓	5	
Prairie Lake 5 mi. W of Springport	Prairie Lake	62	2	✓	✓	10	
Winnipeg Lake 6 mi. NW of Albion	Winnipeg Lake	31	3		✓	25	
Gordon Lake 3 mi. SW of Springport	Gordon Lake	19	2		✓	8	
Wabascon Lake 1 mi. NE of Bedford	Wabascon Lake	70	2		✓	20	
Homer Homer	Kalamazoo River		4			10	
Wilder Creek 4 mi. SE of Marshall	Kalamazoo River		3			5	
River Park 3 mi. SE of Battle Creek	Kalamazoo River		4		✓	6	
20th Street 1 mi. N of Springfield	Kalamazoo River		2			6	
Curry Park Homer	Homer Lake	74	2	✓	✓	20	
CASS COUNTY							
Fish Lake 2 mi. W of Marcellus	Fish Lake	340	2		✓	13	
Dowagiac Drain 2 mi. N of Pokagon	Dowagiac Drain		4		✓	8	H
Arthur Dodd Mem. Park 2 mi. W of Pokagon	Dowagiac Creek		4		✓	20	
Magician Lake 2 mi. E of Sister Lakes	Magician Lake	498	2	✓	✓	10	H
Paradise Lake 2 mi. S of Vandalia	Paradise Lake	185	2		✓	15	
Diamond Lake 2 mi. SE of Cassopolis	Diamond Lake	1020	2	✓	✓	18	H

Body of water		Acres	Ramp class	Courtesy pier	Toilet	Parking spaces	Handicapper accessible
Hemlock Lake 3 mi. N of Marcellus	Hemlock Lake	64	3		✓	10	
Donnell Lake 1 mi. SE of Vandalia	Donnell Lake	246	3		✓	15	
Forked Lake 3 mi. NW of Jones	Forked Lake	122	4			2	
Stone Lake Cassopolis	Stone Lake	148	2		✓	10	
Driskels Lake Jones	Driskels Lake	37	3			10	
Juno Lake 4 mi. E of Edwardsburg	Juno Lake	190	2	✓	✓	16	
Harwood Lake 2 mi. NE of Jones	Harwood Lake	122	3		✓	15	
Corey Lake 2 mi. NE of Jones	Corey Lake	567	2		✓	9	
Long Lake 3 mi. NE of Jones	Long Lake	211	2			3	
Belas Lake 2 mi. NE of Vandalia	Belas Lake	58	2			10	
Kirk Lake 2 mi. NE of Vandalia	Kirk Lake	42	2			5	
Bogart Lake 5 mi. N of Jones	Bogart Lake	31	2			4	
Fox Lake 1 mi. N of Jones	Fox Lake	51	4			3	
Dowagiac Mem. Park 1 mi. E of Dowagiac	Mill Pond	174	2		✓	20	
Dewey Lake 2 mi. SE of Sister Lakes	Dewey Lake	174	2		✓	10	
KALAMAZOO COUNTY							
Barton Lake 4 mi. E of Schoolcraft	Barton Lake	347	2		✓	26	
Sherman Lake 2 mi. S of Yorkville	Sherman Lake	120	2	✓	✓	30	H
Long Lake 3 mi. E of Portage	Long Lake	575	2		✓	24	
Hogset Lake 3 mi. S of Portage	Hogset Lake	81	4			4	
Morrow Pond 3 mi. W of Galesburg	Morrow Lake	1000	2	✓	✓	32	
Eagle Lake 3 mi. E of Mattawan	Eagle Lake	224	3		✓	25	
LeFever Lake 2 mi. SW of Climax	LeFever Lake	13	3		✓	10	
Paw Paw Lake 3 mi. SE of Mattawan	Paw Paw Lake	126	3		✓	9	

	Body of water	Acres	Ramp class	Courtesy pier	Toilet	Parking spaces	Handicapper accessible
Rupert Lake 2 mi. NW of Alamo	Rupert Lake	28	3			10	
Sugarloaf Lake 3 mi. SW of Portage	Sugarloaf Lake	148	2	✓	✓	38	H
River Oaks Co. Park 1 mi. W of Portage	Morrow Lake	1000	2		✓	75	
Austin Lake 2 mi. W of Galesburg	Austin Lake	1050	2	✓	✓	43	H
Cold Brook Co. Park 1 mi. NE of Climax	Blue Lake	24	2	✓	✓	20	
Whitford-Lawler 2 mi. S of Augusta	Whitford, Lawler Lks.	35	2		✓	16	
KENT COUNTY							
Murray Lake 3 mi. S of Grattan	Murray Lake	320	2		✓	15	
Campau Lake 2 mi. E of Alaska	Campau Lake	190	2		✓	35	
Bass Lake 1 mi. NW of Gowen	Bass Lake	184	2		✓	5	
Camp Lake 2 mi. E of Sparta	Camp Lake	154	3		✓	15	
Big Pine Island Lake 1 mi. N of Grattan	Big Pine Island Lk.	223	2	✓		15	
Campbell Lake 4 mi. NE of Caledonia	Campbell Lake	60	2		✓	8	
Ada Ada	Grand River		2		✓	20	
Lincoln Lake 3 mi. SW of Gowen	Lincoln Lake	411	2		✓	15	
Lime Lake 5 mi. NE of Sparta	Lime Lake	36	3		✓	20	
Spring Lake 4 mi. NE of Kent City	Spring Lake	15	4			6	
Clear Lake 5 mi. NE of Kent City	Clear Lake	8	4			8	
Rogue River Mouth 4 mi. S of Rockford	Rogue River		2	✓	✓	36	H
Pratt Lake 4 mi. S of Lowell	Pratt Lake	160	2		✓	9	
Knapp Street Bridge 7 mi. E of Grand Rapids	Grand River		2		✓	14	
Comstock Riverside Park 3 mi. N of Grand Rapids	Grand River		2	✓	✓	45	
Grandville 1 mi. N of Grandville	Grand River		2	✓		15	
Wabasis Lake Park 3 mi. N of Grattan	Wabasis Lake	448	2	✓	✓	35	

	Body of water	Acres	Ramp class	Courtesy pier	Toilet	Parking spaces	Handicapper accessible
Eagle Lake 2 mi. SE of Augusta	Eagle Lake	73	2		✓	14	
Kalamazoo River 2 mi. SE of Augusta	Kalamazoo River		2			10	
OTTAWA COUNTY							
Lake Macatawa 4 mi. W of Holland	Lake Macatawa	2218	1	✓	✓	101	
Petty's Bayou 2 mi. E of Ferrysburg	Spring Lake	1251	2	✓	✓	20	H
Lloyd's Bayou 2 mi. E of Grand Haven	Grand River		3		✓	25	
Deer Creek Park 5 mi. SE of Grand Haven	Grand River		2	✓	✓	58	H
Holland St. Park 5 mi. W of Holland	Lake Macatawa	2218	2	✓		3	
Bruce's Bayou W. 3 mi. SW of Nunica	Grand River		2		✓	30	
Bruce's Bayou E. 4 mi. SW of Nunica	Grand River		2		✓	6	
Mill Point Park Spring Lake	Grand River		1	✓	✓	64	
Indian Channel 3 mi. SW of Nunica	Grand River		2		✓	45	
Kollen Park Holland	Lake Macatawa	2218	1	✓	✓	40	
Grand Haven Mun. Ramp Grand Haven	Grand River		1	✓	✓	105	
Pigeon Lake 3 mi. SW of West Olive	Pigeon Lake	225	2	✓	✓	63	H
Georgetown 4 mi. NW of Grandville	Grand River		1			0	
ST. JOSEPH COUNTY							
Pleasant Lake 4 mi. W of Three Rivers	Pleasant Lake	262	2		✓	10	
Klinger Lake 4 mi. E of White Pigeon	Klinger Lake	830	2		✓	20	
Fisher's Lake 4 mi. NE of Three Rivers	Fisher's Lake	320	2		✓	10	
Clear Lake 5 mi. W of Three Rivers	Clear Lake	240	2		✓	10	
Stump Bay 2 mi. E of Three Rivers	St. Joseph River		2		✓	21	
Fish Lake 3 mi. SW of Nottawa	Fish Lake	275	2		✓	10	

	Body of water	Acres	Ramp class	Courtesy pier	Toilet	Parking spaces	Handicapper accessible
Thompson Lake 4 mi. NW of Sturgis	Thompson Lake	150	2		✓	10	
Palmer Lake 2 mi. SW of Colon	Palmer Lake	448	2		✓	10	
Mud Lake 5 mi. W of Three Rivers	Mud Lake	40	4			3	
Long Lake 3 mi. S of Colon	Long Lake	222	3		✓	25	
Noah Lake 2 mi. E of Three Rivers	Noah Lake	44	3		✓	5	
Lee Lake 1 mi. W of Fawn River	Lee Lake	30	3			2	
Sturgeon Lake Colon	Sturgeon Lake	250	3		✓	20	
Mendon Mendon	St. Joseph River		2		✓	12	
Omena Lake 2 mi. N of Sturgis	Omena Lake	160	3			5	
Prairie River Lake 4 mi. N of Sturgis	Prairie River Lk.	136	3			7	
Portage Lake 4 mi. NW of Mendon	Portage Lake	510	2	✓	✓	30	
Covered Bridge Park 3 mi. N of Centerville	Sturgis Dam Imp.	480	2	✓	✓	25	H
VAN BUREN COUNTY							
Clear Lake 4 mi. NW of Gobles	Clear Lake	62	3		✓	10	
Round Lake Sister Lakes	Round Lake	187	3		✓	10	
Gravel Lake 6 mi. S of Lawton	Gravel Lake	296	3		✓	12	
Saddle Lake 4 mi. W of Bloomingdale	Saddle Lake	298	3		✓	15	
Cedar Lake 6 mi. S of Lawton	Cedar Lake	269	2		✓	26	
Brandywine Lake 1 mi. SE of Gobles	Brandywine Lake	70	3		✓	8	
Van Auken Lake 3 mi. N of Hartford	Van Auken Lake	244	2		✓	18	
Three Mile Lake 4 mi. SW of Paw Paw	Three Mile Lake	176	3		✓	15	
Huzzy Lake 3 mi. SE of Lawton	Huzzy Lake	78	3		✓	10	
Lake Cora 5 mi. W of Paw Paw	Lake Cora	197	2		✓	15	
Wolf Lake 5 mi. SE of Gobles	Wolf Lake	24	2		✓	6	

Body of water		Acres	Ramp class	Courtesy pier	Toilet	parking spaces	Handicapper accessible
Lake Eleven 3 mi. E of Grand Junction	Lake Eleven	50	3		✓	11	
Fish Lake 3 mi. SE of Gobles	Fish Lake	65	3		✓	9	
Scott Lake 4 mi. E of Breedsville	Scott Lake	98	3		✓	7	
Rush Lake 3 mi. NW of Hartford	Rush Lake	118	3		✓	7	
Hall Lake 3 mi. W of Lawrence	Hall Lake	23	3		✓	7	
Lake of the Woods 2 mi. W of Decatur	Lake of the Woods	265	2		✓	15	
Shafer Lake 3 mi. SW of Lawrence	Shafer Lake	81	3		✓	7	
Eagle Lake 5 mi. SE of Lawrence	Eagle Lake	185	3		✓	15	
Reynolds Lake 3 mi. SE of Lawrence	Reynolds Lake	88	3		✓	7	
School Section Lake 1 mi. SE of Glendale	School Section Lk.	68	3		✓	15	
Lake Fourteen 3 mi. W of Bloomingdale	Lake Fourteen	62	3		✓	8	
Three-Legged Lake 3 mi. NE of Bloomingdale	Three-Legged Lake	25	3		✓	8	
Jeptha Lake 3 mi. E of Breedsville	Jeptha Lake	48	3		✓	9	
Bankson Lake 4 mi. SW of Lawton	Bankson Lake	202	3		✓	5	
Black River Park South Haven	Black River		1	✓	✓	78	H
Lawrence Lawrence	Paw Paw River		4			8	

CENTRAL

BARRY COUNTY

Body of water		Acres	Ramp class	Courtesy pier	Toilet	parking spaces	Handicapper accessible
Middle Lake 4 mi. N of Hastings	Middle Lake	131	2		✓	16	
Jordan Lake 1 mi. W of Lake Odessa	Jordan Lake	430	2		✓	20	H
Fine Lake 1 mi. SW of Banfield	Fine Lake	320	3		✓	12	
Payne Lake 6 mi. SW of Middleville	Payne Lake	118	3			5	
Irving Road 3 mi. SE of Middleville	Thornapple River		4		✓	5	
Cloverdale Cloverdale	Long Lake	185	2		✓	10	

69

	Body of water	Acres	Ramp class	Courtesy pier	Toilet	Parking spaces	Handicapper accessible
Clear Lake Dowling	Clear Lake	184	2		✓	6	
Carter Lake 2 mi. NW of Hastings	Carter Lake	49	3		✓	12	
Duncan Lake 2 mi. S of Caledonia	Duncan Lake	127	2		✓	15	
Long Lake (Dowling) 3 mi. S of Dowling	Long Lake	98	4		✓	8	
Bristol Lake 2 mi. S of Dowling	Bristol Lake	142	4		✓	15	
Leach Lake 3 mi. N of Hastings	Leach Lake	125	3		✓	12	
Thornapple Lake 4 mi. NW of Nashville	Thornapple Lake	409	2		✓	15	
Yankee Springs Recreation Area 7 mi. S of Middleville	Gun Lake	2511			✓	52	
Fish Lake 1 mi. E of Orangeville	Fish Lake	165	4			15	
Baker Lake 4 mi. S of Middleville	Baker Lake	59	4			3	
Chief Noonday Lake 5 mi. SW of Middleville	Chief Noonday Lake	51	4			6	
Deep Lake 6 mi. S of Middleville	Deep Lake	32	2		✓	9	
Hall Lake 6 mi. S of Middleville	Hall Lake	43	3			4	
Long Lake 6 mi. S of Middleville	Long Lake	146	3		✓	5	
McDonald Lake 4 mi. S of Middleville	McDonald Lake	17	4			4	
Williams Lake 6 mi. S of Middleville	Williams Lake	18	3			8	
Bassett Lake 3 mi. S of Middleville	Bassett Lake	44	4			4	
Otis Lake 7 mi. SW of Hastings	Otis Lake	130	4			4	
Ludlow Lake 8 mi. SW of Hastings	Ludlow Lake	12	4			3	
Charlton Park 3 mi. SE of Hastings	Thornapple Lake	409	2		✓	31	
Upper Crooked Lake 1 mi. W of Delton	Upper Crooked Lk.	735	2		✓	18	
Lower Crooked Lake 3 mi. E of Doster	Lower Crooked Lk.	417	2		✓	13	
Yankee Springs Campground 8 mi. S of Hastings	Gun Lake	2611	2		✓	3	
Prairieville Township Park 5 mi. S of Delton	Gull Lake	2050	2	✓	✓	92	H

	Body of water	Acres	Ramp class	Courtesy pier	Toilet	Parking spaces	Handicapper accessible
Airport Road 3 mi. W of Hastings	Thornapple River		4		✓	10	
Middleville Middleville	Thornapple River		4			5	
BAY COUNTY							
Kawkawlin River 2 mi. SW of Kawkawlin	Kawkawlin River		3		✓	5	
Pinconning 2 mi. E of Pinconning	Saginaw Bay		4		✓	54	
Coggins Road 4 mi. SE of Pinconning	Saginaw Bay		3		✓	25	
Hampton Township Ramp 4 mi. E of Essexville	Saginaw Bay		2	✓	✓	56	
Veterans Mem. Park Bay City	Saginaw River		1	✓	✓	64	
Essexville Essexville	Saginaw River		1	✓	✓	25	
Saginaw River Mouth 4 mi. E of Kawkawlin	Saginaw River		1	✓	✓	100	H
Veterans Park 5 mi. S of Bay City	Saginaw River		1	✓	✓	10	
CLINTON COUNTY							
French Road Matherton	Maple River		3		✓	20	
Looking Glass River 4 mi. N of Bath	Looking Glass River		4		✓	15	
Muskrat Lake 5 mi. N. of DeWitt	Muskrat Lake	39	2		✓	26	
Fitzpatrick Road 3 mi. E of Hubbardston	Maple River		4			10	
Sleepy Hollow St. Park 4 mi. NW of Laingsburg	Lake Ovid	412	2	✓	✓	109	
Park Lake 2 mi. SW of Bath	Park Lake	185	2			9	
EATON COUNTY							
Butler Co. Park Bellevue	Battle Creek River		2			6	
Bunker Road 3 mi. NE of Eaton Rapids	Grand River		4		✓	13	
McArthur River Park Eaton Rapids	Grand River		2			5	
GENESEE COUNTY							
Lobdell Lake Argentine	Lobdell Lake	545	1	✓	✓	25	

	Body of water	Acres	Ramp class	Courtesy pier	Toilet	Parking spaces	Handicapper accessible
Lake Fenton 2 mi. N of Fenton	Lake Fenton	845	1	✓	✓	38	
Lake Ponemah 2 mi. NW of Fenton	Lake Ponemah	424	1	✓	✓	39	H
Holloway Reservoir 7 mi. E of Genesee	Holloway Res.	954	1		✓	74	
Bluegill 2 mi. SW of Genesee	C.S. Mott Lake	1200	1		✓	150	
GRATIOT COUNTY							
Maple Road 3 mi. W of Bridgeville	Maple River		3		✓	25	
Alma Pond Alma	Pine River		2	✓	✓	10	H
Dean Road 3 mi. E of Bridgeville	Maple River		4			10	
INGHAM COUNTY							
Hewes Lake 3 mi. SW of Dansville	Hewes Lake	17	4			10	
Lake Lansing Park N. 2 mi. N of Haslett	Lake Lansing	453	1	✓	✓	58	H
McNamara Landing 6 mi. SW of Holt	Grand River		4		✓	0	
Ferguson Park Okemos	Red Cedar River		4		✓	30	
Moores Park Lansing	Grand River		4		✓	15	
Riverfront Park Lansing	Grand River		4			0	
Burchard Park Lansing	Grand River		4			0	
IONIA COUNTY							
Morrison Lake 2 mi. NE of Clarksville	Morrison Lake	330	2	✓	✓	15	H
Long Lake 4 mi. E of Belding	Long Lake	356	2	✓	✓	20	H
Muir 1 mi. E of Muir	Maple River		3		✓	25	
Humany Dam Impoundment 3 mi. E of Belding	Humany Dam Imp.	1229	4			0	
Towner Road 4 mi. SW of Portland	Grand River		4			20	
Belding Dam Impoundment Belding	Belding Dam Imp.	60	2	✓	✓	12	
Belding Dam Belding	Flat River		2	✓	✓	12	

	Body of water	Acres	Ramp class	Courtesy pier	Toilet	Parking spaces	Handicapper accessible
Ionia Fairgrounds Ionia	Grand River		2			60	
Woodard Lake 7 mi. N of Ionia	Woodard Lake	73	2		✓	10	
Lyons Lyons	Grand River		2			5	
Webber Impoundment 3 mi. S of Muir	Webber Impound.	766	2		✓	18	
Sessions Lake 3 mi. E of Saranac	Sessions Lake	110	1	✓	✓	25	
ISABELLA COUNTY							
Littlefield Lake 3 mi. E of Brinton	Littlefield Lake	183	1	✓	✓	10	H
Stevenson Lake 3 mi. W of Vernon Center	Stevenson Lake	113	1		✓	5	
LIVINGSTON COUNTY							
Lake Chemung 4 mi. NW of Brighton	Lake Chemung	321	1	✓	✓	24	
E. Crooked Lake 6 mi. N of Lakeland	Crooked Lake	252	4			18	
Woodland Lake 1 mi. N of Brighton	Woodland Lake	290	1	✓	✓	30	H
Whitmore Lake 3 mi. SE of Hamburg	Whitmore Lake	677	2	✓	✓	50	H
Duck Lake 3 mi. N of Hell	Duck Lake	12	4			20	
Bishop Lake Campground 3 mi. N of Lakeland	Bishop Lake	119	2		✓	20	
Appleton Lake 3 mi. N of Lakeland	Appleton Lake	56	2		✓	10	
Chenango Lake 4 mi. NE of Pinckney	Chenango Lake	29	3			10	
Chilson Pond 4 mi. N of Lakeland	Chilson Pond	100	3			2	
Hiland Lake Hell	Hiland Lake	123	3			8	
Gosling Lake Hell	Gosling Lake	12	3			8	
MECOSTA COUNTY							
Lake Mecosta 4 mi. N of Altona	Lake Mecosta	297	1	✓	✓	25	
Rogers Pond 3 mi. N of Stanwood	Rogers Pond	512	2	✓	✓	7	
Chippewa Lake 1 mi. NE of Chippewa Lake	Chippewa Lake	770	1	✓	✓	20	

Body of water	Acres	Ramp class	Courtesy pier	Toilet	Parking spaces	Handicapper accessible
Haymarsh Lake Flooding 3 mi. W of Chippewa Lake	Haymarsh Lake Fldg.	250	4		✓	5	
Pretty Lake 5 mi. E of Rodney	Pretty Lake	120	2	✓	✓	3	
Townline Lake 5 mi. NE of Big Rapids	Townline Lake	120	2		✓	7	
Clear Lake 3 mi. W of Rodney	Clear Lake	130	3		✓	10	
Hillsview Lake 3 mi. NW of Rodney	Hillsview Lake	123	3		✓	5	
Brockway Lake 3 mi. S of Altona	Brockway Lake	22	2		✓	4	
River Bend Bluffs 3 mi. N of Stanwood	Muskegon River		3		✓	10	
Jehnsen Lake 3 mi. NE of Rodney	Jehnsen Lake	270	2	✓	✓	10	
Rustford Pond 2 mi. SW of Altona	Rustford Pond	20	4		✓	10	
Lower Evans Lake 4 mi. NE of Rodney	Martiny Lake Fldg.	2080	1	✓	✓	25	H
Big Evans Lake 4 mi. E of Chippewa Lake	Martiny Lake Fldg.	2080	1	✓	✓	21	
Upper Evans Lake 4 mi. E of Chippewa Lake	Martiny Lake Fldg.	2080	4		✓	6	
Winchester Dam 6 mi. E of Chippewa Lake	Martiny Lake Fldg.	2080	2	✓	✓	4	
Bergess Lake 5 mi. NE of Big Rapids	Bergess Lake	60	3		✓	10	
Tubbs Island Forest Cmpgd. 5 mi. SE of Chippewa Falls	Martiny Lake Fldg.	2080	2		✓	20	
Browers Park Marina 5 mi. W of Stanwood	Hardy Dam Pond	3750	1	✓	✓	102	
Paris Park 2 mi. N of Paris	Muskegon River		4		✓	15	
Alma Lake 5 mi. NE of Big Rapids	Alma Lake	15	4			5	
131 Bridge 3 mi. NW of Stanwood	Muskegon River		1	✓	✓	20	
MONTCALM COUNTY							
Lake Montcalm 4 mi. SW of Six Lakes	Lake Montcalm	68	3		✓	12	
Crystal Lake 1 mi. SW of Crystal	Crystal Lake	724	2	✓	✓	12	H
Horseshoe Lake 2 mi. SW of Six Lakes	Horseshoe Lake	97	2		✓	10	
Nevins Lake 3 mi. W of Stanton	Nevins Lake	53	3		✓	10	

	Body of water	Acres	Ramp class	Courtesy pier	Toilet	Parking spaces	Handicapper accessible
Dickerson Lake 4 mi. E of Langston	Dickerson Lake	255	2		✓	15	
Clifford Lake 3 mi. E of Langston	Clifford Lake	200	1		✓	10	
Derby Lake 3 mi. SW of Stanton	Derby Lake	118	2		✓	15	
Swan Lake 1 mi. N of Crystal	Swan Lake	127	3		✓	10	
Little Whitefish Lake 2 mi. W of Maple Hill	Little Whitefish Lk.	181	3		✓	10	
Muskellunge Lake Trufant	Muskellunge Lake	134	3		✓	15	
Half Moon Lake 3 mi. S of Stanton	Half Moon Lake	49	3		✓	3	
Tamarack Lake 1 mi. E of Lakeview	Tamarack Lake	310	2		✓	15	
Rainbow Lake 3 mi. NE of Trufant	Rainbow Lake	166	2		✓	5	
Cowden Lake 2 mi. E of Coral	Cowden Lake	128	2		✓	10	
Loon Lake 2 mi. W of Crystal	Loon Lake	63	3		✓	15	
Flat River 2 mi. S of Greenville	Flat River		4			6	
Clear Lake 2 mi. SW of Fenwick	Clear Lake	16	4			2	
Grass Lake N. 1 mi. S of Fenwick	Grass Lake	29	4			10	
Grass Lake S. 2 mi. S of Stanton	Grass Lake	29	4			6	
Hunter Lake 2 mi. W of Langston	Hunter Lake	46	4			5	
West Lake 1 mi. NW of Langston	West Lake	44	4			6	
Colby Lake 2 mi. SW of Stanton	Colby Lake	44	4			4	
Twin Stone Lakes East 3 mi. S of Stanton	Twin Stone Lake	21	4			2	
Triangle Lake 4 mi. E of Stanton	Triangle Lake	8	4			2	
SAGINAW COUNTY							
Hulien Road 1 mi. E of St. Charles	Bad River		2			35	
DNR Field Office St. Charles	Bad River		2		✓	35	
Miller Road 5 mi. NE of St. Charles	Swan Creek		4			30	

Public Boat Launches

	Body of water	Acres	Ramp class	Courtesy pier	Toilet	Parking spaces	Handicapper accessible
Bridgeport Twp. Park Bridgeport	Cass River		2	✓	✓	10	
M-13 Bridge 4 mi. S of Saginaw	Cass River		4			20	
Rust Avenue Launch Saginaw	Saginaw River		1	✓	✓	0	H
Saginaw Township 1 mi. SW of Saginaw	Tittabawassee River		2		✓	53	
Imerman Park 6 mi. NW of Saginaw	Tittabawassee River		2	✓	✓	52	
SANILAC COUNTY							
Lexington Public Access Lexington	Lake Huron		1	✓	✓	100	
Port Sanilac Vil. Ramp Port Sanilac	Lake Huron		1		✓	22	
Port Sanilac Port Sanilac	Lake Huron		1	✓	✓	123	H
TUSCOLA COUNTY							
Chippewa Landing Caro	Cass River		1			12	
Quanicassee River 1 mi. W of Quanicassee	Quanicassee River		1	✓	✓	35	
Murphy Lake 4 mi. E of Millington	Murphy Lake	203	4		✓	7	
Clark Road 4 mi. N of Unionville	Saginaw Bay		4			25	
Belgian Drain 2 mi. NE of Bay Park	Belgian Drain		3			50	
NORTHEAST							
ALCONA COUNTY							
Hubbard Lake Twp. 1 mi. S of Hubbard Lake	Hubbard Lake	8850	2	✓	✓	20	
East Bay 4 mi SW of Spruce	Hubbard Lake	8850	1	✓	✓	26	H
Harrisville St. Park Harrisville	Lake Huron		4		✓	30	
Black River Mouth Black River	Lake Huron		2		✓	10	
Harrisville Harrisville	Lake Huron		1	✓	✓	130	H
South Bay 8 mi. NW of Lincoln	Hubbard Lake	8850	2	✓	✓	10	
4001 Bridge 4 mi. N of Curtisville	AuSable River		4		✓	0	

	Body of water	Acres	Ramp class	Courtesy pier	Toilet	Parking spaces	Handicapper accessible
Jewell Lake Barton City	Jewell Lake	193	2		✓	0	
O'Brien Lake 5 mi. N of Curtisville	O'Brien Lake	10	4		✓	0	
Horseshoe Lake 3 mi. N of Glennie	Horseshoe Lake	16	2			0	
Sprinkler Lake 5 mi. S of Barton City	Sprinkler Lake	34	4			0	
Alcona Co. Park 1 4 mi. W of Glennie	Alcona Dam Pond	1008	1		✓	10	
Alcona Co. Park 2 4 mi. W of Glennie	Alcona Dam Pond	1008	1		✓	5	
Alcona Co. Park 3 4 mi. W of Glennie	Alcona Dam Pond	1008	1		✓	5	
ALPENA COUNTY							
Fletcher Pond 6 mi. SE of Hillman	Fletcher Pond		2		✓	46	
Ossineke Forest Cmpgd. 1 mi. NE of Ossineke	Lake Huron		4		✓	5	
Thunder Bay River Forest Cpg. 7 mi. SW of Alpena	Thunder Bay R.		4		✓	5	
Rockport 10 mi. N of Alpena	Lake Huron		1	✓	✓	100	
Alpena Mun. Marina Alpena	Lake Huron		1	✓	✓	126	H
Snug Harbor 2 mi. SE of Ossineke	Lake Huron		2		✓	10	
ARENAC COUNTY							
AuGres River Mouth 1 mi. SE of Au Gres	Saginaw Bay		1	✓	✓	297	H
Omer Omer	Rifle River		4		✓	40	
Pine River Mouth 5 mi. E of Standish	Saginaw Bay		1	✓	✓	38	
Moffatt Bridge 4 mi. E of Alger	Rifle River		4		✓	20	
Singing Bridge 4 mi. E of Delano	Lake Huron		4		✓	120	
CHEBOYGAN COUNTY							
Haakwood Forest Cpgd. 2 mi. N of Wolverine	Sturgeon River		4		✓	25	
Mullett Lake Vil. 1 mi. NE of Mullett Lake	Mullett Lake	17360	2	✓	✓	10	H
Cochran Lake 3 mi. E of Indian River	Cochran Lake	28	3			5	

Public Boat Launches

	Body of water	Acres	Ramp class	Courtesy pier	Toilet	Parking spaces	Handicapper accessible
Jewell Road 2 mi. SW of Aloha	Mullett Lake	17360	2	✓	✓	50	
Munro Lake 5 mi. E of Levering	Munro Lake	694	4			10	
Silver Lake 2 mi. W of Wolverine	Silver Lake	75	3		✓	10	
Garfield Road 1 mi. S of Cheboygan	Cheboygan River		3			0	
Meadows 1 mi. N of Wolverine	Sturgeon River		4		✓	10	
Trowbridge Road 3 mi. S of Wolverine	Sturgeon River		4			5	
Maple Bay Forest Campground 4 mi. E of Brutus	Burt Lake	16700	2		✓	7	
Long Lake 2 mi. SW of Alverno	Long Lake	400	3		✓	10	
Lancaster Lake 3 mi. E of Levering	Lancaster Lake	52	3		✓	10	
Rondo 4 mi. N of Wolverine	Sturgeon River		4		✓	15	
Black Lake Forest Cpgd. 8 mi. SE of Alverno	Black Lake	10130	2		✓	20	
Aloha St. Park Aloha	Mullett Lake	17360	2		✓	50	
Burt Lake St. Park 1 mi. SW of Indian River	Burt Lake	16700	1			23	
Cheboygan Dam Cheboygan	Cheboygan River		1	✓	✓	50	
Mackinaw City Mun. Marina Mackinaw City	Lake Huron		1	✓	✓	54	
CRAWFORD COUNTY							
Sheep Pasture 6 mi. W of Red Oak	AuSable River		4		✓	20	
Burtons Landing Forest Cpgd. 3 mi. E of Grayling	AuSable River		4		✓	20	
Black Hole 3 mi. N of Lovells	AuSable River		4		✓	6	
Horseshoe Lake 1 mi. S of Waters	Horseshoe Lake	25	4			5	
Bluegill Lake 2 mi. S of Waters	Bluegill Lake	30	3		✓	15	
Meads Landing 1 mi. N of Roscommon	AuSable River		4		✓	10	
White Pine Canoe Camp 10 mi. NW of Luzerne	Au Sable River		4		✓	5	
Stephans Bridge 7 mi. E of Grayling	AuSable River		3		✓	15	

Location	Body of water	Acres	Ramp class	Courtesy pier	Toilet	Parking spaces	Handicapper accessible
Canoe Harbor Forest Cpgd. 8 mi. W of Luzerne	AuSable River		4		✓	30	
McMaster's Bridge 6 mi. NW of Luzerne	AuSable River		3		✓	10	
Connors Flats 8 mi. NW of Luzerne	AuSable River		3		✓	6	
Steckert Bridge 2 mi. N of Roscommon	AuSable River		3		✓	5	
Guthrie Lake 5 mi. E of Waters	Guthrie Lake	123	3		✓	3	
Section One Lake 4 mi. E of Waters	Section One Lake	85	3			4	
K.P. Lake 4 mi. W of Lovells	K.P. Lake	98	3		✓	5	
Keystone Landing Forest Cpgd. 4 mi. E of Grayling	AuSable River		4		✓	15	
Chase Bridge 4 mi. NE of Roscommon	AuSable River		3		✓	5	
Smith Bridge 8 mi. W of Luzerne	AuSable River		3		✓	5	
AuSable River Canoe Camp 3 mi. E of Grayling	AuSable River		4		✓	8	
Jones Lake Forest Cpgd. 5 mi. W of Lovells	Jones Lake	43	2		✓	20	
Lake Margrethe Forest Cpgd. 5 mi. W of Grayling	Lake Margrethe	1306	4		✓	20	
Shupac Lake Forest Cpgd. 2 mi. N of Lovells	Shupac Lake	99	2		✓	10	
N. Higgins Lake St. Park 4 mi. N of Higgins Lake	Higgins Lake	9600	1	✓	✓	15	H
Manistee River Bridge 7 mi. W of Grayling	Manistee River		4		✓	10	
Camp Grayling 4 mi. SW of Grayling	Lake Margrethe	1306	2	✓		50	
GLADWIN COUNTY							
Pratt Lake 5 mi. NW of Gladwin	Pratt Lake	180	1	✓	✓	10	
Wiggins Lake 3 mi. NW of Gladwin	Wiggins Lake	345	1	✓	✓	18	
Lake Four 5 mi. N of Hockaday	Lake Four	35	3		✓	5	
Lake Lancer 2 mi. NW of Hockaday	Lake Lancer	840	1	✓	✓	36	
Wixom Lake W. 6 mi. SE of Beaverton	Wixom Lake	1980	1	✓	✓	57	H
Secord Lake 5 mi. E of Hockaday	Secord Lake	2087	3			3	

Public Boat Launches

	Body of water	Acres	Ramp class	Courtesy pier	Toilet	Parking spaces	Handicapper accessible
Secord Lake 4 mi. E of Hockaday	Secord Lake	2087	3			5	
Trout Lake Forest Cpgd. 2 mi. E of Meredith	Trout Lake	5	3		✓	5	
Hoister Lake 2 mi. NE of Meredith	Hoister Lake	23	3		✓	5	
HURON COUNTY							
Fin and Feather 1 mi. SW of Bay Port	Saginaw Bay		4		✓	20	
Harbor Beach Ramp Harbor Beach	Lake Huron		1	✓	✓	166	
Filion Road 3 mi. NE of Bay Port	Saginaw Bay		2	✓	✓	39	H
Eagle Bay 2 mi. NW of Grindstone City	Lake Huron		4		✓	20	
Stafford Co. Park Port Hope	Lake Huron		1	✓	✓	78	
Bay Port Bay Port	Saginaw Bay		1	✓	✓	25	H
Sumac Island 5 mi. N of Sebewaing	Saginaw Bay		2	✓	✓	20	
Grindstone City Grindstone City	Saginaw Bay		1	✓	✓	44	
Sebewaing Mun. Ramp Sebewaing	Sebewaing River		1	✓	✓	35	
Caseville Dock Caseville	Pigeon River		1	✓	✓	15	
Port Austin Port Austin	Saginaw Bay		1	✓	✓	114	H
Whitlock Sebewaing	Saginaw Bay		4			8	
IOSCO COUNTY							
AuSable River Mouth 1 mi. S of Oscoda	Lake Huron		1	✓	✓	162	H
Long Lake 1 mi. W of Long Lake	Long Lake	493	2		✓	54	
Floyd Lake 7 mi. N of McIvor	Floyd Lake	41	3		✓	6	
Cedar Lake 6 mi. N of Oscoda	Cedar Lake	1025	2		✓	26	
Tawas Lake 1 mi. NW of East Tawas	Tawas Lake	1600	2		✓	3	
Londo Lake 4 mi. SW of Hale	Londo Lake	176	3		✓	3	

	Body of water	Acres	Ramp class	Courtesy pier	Toilet	Parking spaces	Handicapper accessible
Van Etten Lake Forest Cpgd. 4 mi. NW of Oscoda	Van Etten Lake	1320	3		✓	6	
East Tawas Ramp East Tawas	Lake Huron		1	✓		57	
Foote Dam 3 mi. NW of Oscoda	AuSable River		2		✓	50	
Whirlpool AuSable River 3 mi. NW of Oscoda	AuSable River		2		✓	56	
Round Lake 7 mi. NW of Tawas City	Round Lake	92	1		✓	10	
MONTMORENCY COUNTY							
Rush Lake Flooding 8 mi. N of Atlanta	Rush Lake	224	3		✓	5	
McCormick Lake 6 mi. E of Vienna	McCormick Lake	100	2		✓	5	
Grass Lake 8 mi. NW of Hillman	Grass Lake	230	3		✓	10	
Lake Fifteen Forest Cpgd. 2 mi. SW of Atlanta	Lake Fifteen	81	3		✓	6	
Emerick Park Hillman	Hillman Impound.	100	2		✓	11	
Crooked Creek 1 mi. N of Atlanta	Crooked Creek		4		✓	20	
East Twin Lake Lewiston	East Twin Lake	830	2		✓	15	
Avalon Lake 3 mi. NW of Hillman	Avalon Lake	372	1	✓	✓	25	H
Gaylanta Lake 3 mi. E of Vienna	Gaylanta Lake	115	4		✓	5	
Sage Lake Flooding 8 mi. S of Atlanta	Sage Lake	51	4		✓	5	
Long Lake 5 mi. NW of Hillman	Long Lake	295	3		✓	4	
DeCheau Lake 3 mi. NW of Atlanta	DeCheau Lake	25	3		✓	10	
Crooked Lake 2 mi. S of Atlanta	Crooked Lake	47	3		✓	10	
Ess Lake Forest Cpgd. 5 mi. NW of Hillman	Ess Lake	114	4		✓	5	
Jackson Lake Forest Cpgd. 6 mi. N of Atlanta	Jackson Lake	25	4		✓	5	
Avery Lake Forest Cpgd. 6 mi. SW of Atlanta	Avery Lake	254	1		✓	12	
Clear Lake State Park 9 mi. N of Atlanta	Clear Lake	133	1		✓	50	
Town Corner Lake Forest Cpgd. 9 mi. NW of Atlanta	Town Corner Lake	15	4		✓	5	

HURON-CLINTON METROPOLITAN AUTHORITY

	Body of water	Acres	Ramp class	Courtesy pier	Toilet	Parking spaces	Handicapper accessible
OGEMAW COUNTY							
Clear Lake 8 mi. W of Rose City	Clear Lake	171	2		✓	8	
Klacking Creek 1 mi. N of Selkirk	Rifle River		4			6	
Hardwood Lake 4 mi. NE of Skidway Lake	Hardwood Lake	172	2		✓	15	
Sage Lake 6 mi. E of Hale	Sage Lake	785	2	✓	✓	35	H
Horseshoe Lake 8 mi. W of Rose City	Horseshoe Lake	37	4			5	
George Lake 3 mi. SE of Lupton	George Lake	186	2			4	
Rifle River Forest Cpgd. 2 mi. N of Selkirk	Rifle River		4		✓	5	
Bush Lake Skidway Lake	Bush Lake	51	3			3	
Tee Lake 7 mi. SW of West Branch	Tee Lake	33	3		✓	4	
Lake George 5 mi. S of West Branch	Lake George	89	2		✓	6	
Peach Lake 4 mi. E of West Branch	Peach Lake	208	2		✓	15	
Au Sable Lake 5 mi. E of Lupton	Au Sable Lake	271	2		✓	8	
Kenneth Road 3 mi. NW of Skidway Lake	Rifle River		4		✓	8	
Rifle Lake 3 mi. SE of Lupton	Rifle Lake	183	2		✓	3	
Little Long Lake 4 mi. N of Skidway	Little Long Lake	20	4			4	
Ambrose Lake Forest Cpgd. 7 mi. W of Rose City	Ambrose Lake	44	4		✓	8	
Grousehaven Lake 1 mi. S of Lupton	Grousehaven Lake	95	1		✓	10	
Devoe Lake 2 mi. S of Lupton	Devoe Lake	130	1		✓	10	
Grebe Lake 2 mi. SE of Lupton	Grebe Lake	85	4			2	
Lodge Lake 2 mi. S of Lupton	Lodge Lake	40	4			5	
The Ranch 3 mi. S of Lupton	Rifle River		4		✓	10	
OSCODA COUNTY							
Tea Lake 3 mi. S of Lewiston	Tea Lake	216	2		✓	4	

	Body of water	Acres	Ramp class	Courtesy pier	Toilet	Parking spaces	Handicapper accessible
McCollum Lake Forest Cpgd. 8 mi. NE of Fairview	McCollum Lake	224	2		✓	6	
Parmalee Bridge Forest Cpgd. 2 mi. S of Red Oak	AuSable River		4		✓	5	
Whirlpool 3 mi. SE of Red Oak	AuSable River		4		✓	6	
Camp Ten Bridge 2 mi. NW of Mio	AuSable River		2	✓	✓	15	H
Mio Pond Forest Cpgd. Mio	Mio Pond	944	2		✓	10	
Comins Flat 4 mi. E of Mio	AuSable River		2		✓	30	
Muskrat Lake Forest Cpgd. 4 mi. NE of Red Oak	Muskrat Lake	86	4		✓	5	
M-33 Roadside Park Mio	AuSable River		2		✓	15	
McKinley 10 mi. E of Mio	AuSable River		4		✓	0	
OTSEGO COUNTY							
Dixon Lake 3 mi. SE of Gaylord	Dixon Lake	79	2	✓	✓	7	H
Big Lake 4 mi. E of Gaylord	Big Lake	126	3		✓	5	
Bradford Lake 1 mi. S of Waters	Bradford Lake	228	3		✓	10	
Lake Manuka 3 mi. W of Oak Grove	Lake Manuka	163	2		✓	4	
Heart Lake 1 mi. N of Waters	Heart Lake	65	3		✓	8	
Opal Lake 4 mi. E of Otsego Lake	Opal Lake	122	4		✓	8	
Big Bass Lake 4 mi. SW of Johannesburg	Big Bass Lake	70	3		✓	5	
Lake Twenty Seven 3 mi. E of Elmira	Lake Twenty Seven	112	4		✓	6	
Emerald Lake 4 mi. E of Otsego Lake	Emerald Lake	53	3		✓	5	
W. Twin Lake 3 mi. W of Lewiston	West Twin Lake	1313	3		✓	8	
Big Bear Lake Forest Cpgd. 1 mi. S of Vienna	Big Bear Lk.	435	3		✓	4	
Lake Marjory Forest Cpgd 1 mi. S of Waters	Lake Marjory	41	4		✓	6	
Pickerel Lake Forest Cpgd. 7 mi. E of Vanderbilt	Pickerel Lake	43	2		✓	6	
Otsego Lake Co. Park 1 mi. W of Oak Grove	Otsego Lake	1972	1	✓	✓	15	

	Body of water	Acres	Ramp class	Courtesy pier	Toilet	Parking spaces	Handicapper accessible
Otsego Lake St. Park 1 mi. S of Otsego Lake	Otsego Lake	1972	1	✓	✓	25	
PRESQUE ISLE COUNTY							
Lost Lake 4 mi. W of Hawks	Lost Lake	104	1		✓	11	
Long Lake 7 mi. E of Polaski	Long Lake	5652	3		✓	15	
Lake Emma 6 mi. SW of Hawks	Lake Emma	115	2		✓	25	
Lake Nettle 4 mi. W of Hawks	Lake Nettle	278	3		✓	10	
Little Tomahawk Lake 9 mi. S of Onaway	Little Tomahawk Lk.	23	4		✓	4	
Hammond Point 3 mi. E of Huron Beach	Lake Huron		4			6	
Townhall 4 mi. SE of Presque Isle	Grand Lake	5660	1		✓	30	
Lake Ferdelman 6 mi. SW of Hawks	Lake Ferdelman	33	3		✓	10	
Bear Den Lake 11 mi. S of Onaway	Bear Den Lake	29	3		✓	10	
Lake May 4 mi. SW of Hawks	Lake May	161	3		✓	5	
Shoepac Lake Forest Cpgd. 8 mi. S of Onaway	Shoepac Lake	45	2		✓	6	
Tomahawk Lake Forest Cpgd. 9 mi. S of Onaway	Tomahawk Lake	40	1		✓	5	
Onaway St. Park 6 mi. N of Onaway	Black Lake	10130	1		✓	20	
Rogers City Ramp Rogers City	Lake Huron		1	✓	✓	100	H
Hammond Bay 7 mi. NW of Huron Beach	Lake Huron		1	✓	✓	20	
Presque Isle 3 mi. N of Presque Isle	Lake Huron		1	✓	✓	30	
ROSCOMMON COUNTY							
Houghton Lake 2 mi. E of Houghton Lake	Houghton Lake	20004	1	✓	✓	50	H
Houghton Lake W. 1 mi. NW of Houghton Heights	Houghton Lake	20004	1	✓	✓	46	H
Houghton Lake E. 3 mi. N of Prudenville	Houghton Lake	20004	2	✓	✓	42	
Houghton Lake Forest Cpgd. 4 mi. S of Higgins Lake	Houghton Lake	20004	3		✓	15	
Lake St. Helen 1 mi. SW of St. Helen	Lake St. Helen	2400	1	✓	✓	27	

	Body of water	Acres	Ramp class	Courtesy pier	Toilet	Parking spaces	Handicapper accessible
S. Higgins Lake 4 mi. SW of Higgins Lake	Higgins Lake	9600	2		✓	55	H
S. Higgins Lake St. Park 4 mi. SE of Higgins Lake	Higgins Lake	9600	1	✓	✓	50	
Dead Stream Flooding 5 mi. NW of Houghton Heights	Dead Stream Fldg.	985	3		✓	15	

NORTHWEST

ANTRIM COUNTY

	Body of water	Acres	Ramp class	Courtesy pier	Toilet	Parking spaces	Handicapper accessible
Ellsworth Lake Ellsworth	Ellsworth Lake	120	1		✓	20	
Clam Lake 2 mi. SE of Clam River	Clam Lake	420	1		✓	15	
Deep Water Point 3 mi. N of Bellaire	Intermediate Lk.	1520	4		✓	5	
Graves Crossing Forest Cpgd. 9 mi. N of Mancelona	Jordan River		3		✓	5	
Noteware Landing 1 mi. S of Bellaire	Lake Bellaire	1775	4		✓	3	
Central Lake 1 mi. S of Central Lake	Intermediate Lk.	1520	3			5	
Openo Park 3 mi. N of Bellaire	Intermediate Lk.	1520	1	✓	✓	20	
St. Clair Lake Ellsworth	St. Clair Lake	64	3		✓	10	
Green Lake 3 mi. W of Antrim	Green Lake	40	4			10	
Lake of the Woods 6 mi. W of Mancelona	Lake of the Woods	185	4			3	
East Port Eastport	Torch Lake	18770	1	✓	✓	55	
Webster Bridge 4 mi. SE of East Jordan	Jordan River		4		✓	4	
Wilson Lake 3 mi. S of Ellsworth	Wilson Lake	106	3		✓	7	
Torch River Bridge 3 mi. NW of Rapid City	Torch Lake	18770	2			3	
Chestonia Bridge 7 mi. SE of East Jordan	Jordan River		4			3	
Elk Lake 3 mi. S of Kewadin	Elk Lake	7930	3		✓	8	
Steiner Road 2 mi. E of Clam River	Lake Bellaire	1775	4			5	
Birch Lake 1 mi. N of Kewadin	Birch Lake	326	3		✓	5	
Fisherman's Paradise 1 mi. S of Bellaire	Lake Bellaire	1775	2	✓	✓	64	H

	Body of water	Acres	Ramp class	Courtesy pier	Toilet	Parking spaces	Handicapper accessible
Elk Rapids Dock Elk Rapids	Grand Traverse Bay		1	✓	✓	50	
Elk Rapids Vil. Park Elk Rapids	Elk Lake	7930	2			15	
BENZIE COUNTY							
Veterans Mem. Park 3 mi. E of Honor	Platte River		4		✓	15	
Platte Lake 5 mi. NW of Honor	Platte Lake	2516	1	✓	✓	12	
Upper Herring Lake 4 mi. SE of Elberta	Upper Herring Lk.	565	2		✓	10	
Brooks Lake 5 mi. NW of Lake Ann	Brooks Lake	15	3		✓	5	
River Road 1 mi. W of Benzonia	Betsie River		4			4	
Turtle Lake 3 mi. W of Bendon	Turtle Lake	38	3		✓	10	
Lower Herring Lake 3 mi. S of Elberta	Lower Herring Lk.	450	2	✓		6	
Davis Lake 3 mi. N of Lake Ann	Davis Lake	34	3		✓	4	
Stevens Lake 3 mi. NW of Lake Ann	Stevens Lake	46	3		✓	3	
Herendeene Lake 1 mi. NW of Lake Ann	Herendeene Lake	37	3		✓	4	
Little Platte Lake 4 mi. NW of Honor	Little Platte Lk.	820	1	✓		20	H
Grass Lake Forest Cpgd. 3 mi. S of Bendon	Grass Lake	482	3		✓	10	
Lake Ann Forest Cpgd. 1 mi. SW of Lake Ann	Lake Ann	527	1		✓	6	
Platte River Forest Cpgd. 2 mi. SE of Honor	Platte River		4		✓	3	
Frankfort Mun. Ramp Frankfort	Betsie Lake	250	1	✓	✓	115	
Grace Road 2 mi. SW of Benzonia	Betsie River		4		✓	12	
Homestead Dam 2 mi. SE of Benzonia	Betsie River		4		✓	50	
US 31 1 mi. S of Benzonia	Betsie River		4		✓	25	
CHARLEVOIX COUNTY							
Susan Lake 4 mi. E of Charlevoix	Susan Lake	130	3		✓	5	
Six Mile Lake 4 mi. SW of East Jordan	Six Mile Lake	407	2		✓	4	

	Body of water	Acres	Ramp class	Courtesy pier	Toilet	Parking spaces	Handicapper accessible
Boyne Falls Mill Pond Boyne Falls	Boyne Falls Mill Pd.	3	4		✓	6	
Dutchmans Bay 3 mi. NW of East Jordan	Lake Charlevoix	17260	1	✓	✓	35	H
Alba Road 2 mi. S of East Jordan	Jordan River		4		✓	10	
Ironton Ironton	Lake Charlevoix	17260	1	✓	✓	44	
Deer Lake 3 mi. W of Boyne Falls	Deer Lake	490	3		✓	8	
Rogers Road Bridge 1 mi. S of East Jordan	Jordan River		3		✓	10	
Adams Lake 1 mi. W of Ironton	Adams Lake	48	3		✓	5	
Nowland Lake 2 mi. SW of Ironton	Nowland Lake	126	4		✓	5	
Nine Mile Point 2 mi. NW of Bay Shore	Lake Michigan		3		✓	10	
Young St. Park 2 mi. NW of Boyne City	Lake Charlevoix	17260	3		✓	3	
East Jordan Mun. Ramp East Jordan	Lake Charlevoix	17260	1		✓	31	
Boyne City Mun. Ramp Boyne City	Lake Charlevoix	17260	1	✓	✓	52	
Charlevoix Mun. Ramp 1 mi. NE of Charlevoix	Lake Charlevoix	17260	1	✓	✓	92	
CLARE COUNTY							
Long Lake 5 mi. N of Harrison	Long Lake	210	2	✓	✓	6	
Five Lakes 4 mi. N of Clare	Five Lakes	142	1	✓	✓	6	
Cranberry Lake 4 mi. NE of Harrison	Cranberry Lake	106	3		✓	6	
Windover Lake 3 mi. W of Lake George	Windover Lake	50	2	✓	✓	6	
Crooked Lake Lake	Crooked Lake	264	2	✓	✓	15	H
Little Long Lake 1 mi. NE of Harrison	Little Long Lake	43	2	✓	✓	9	
Perch Lake Lake	Perch Lake	50	3		✓	9	
Clam River 6 mi. W of Leota	Clam River		4		✓	3	
Lake George Lake George	Lake George	134	2		✓	10	
Nestor Lake 8 mi. SE of Harrison	Nestor Lake	15	2		✓	10	

	Body of water	Acres	Ramp class	Courtesy pier	Toilet	Parking spaces	Handicapper accessible
Lily Lake 3 mi. NE of Lake George	Lily Lake	209	2	✓	✓	10	
Mud Lake Forest Cpgd. 5 mi. NW of Lake	Mud Lake	219	4		✓	10	
Temple Forest Cpgd. 6 mi. NW of Lake George	Muskegon River		4		✓	5	
EMMET COUNTY							
Lake Paradise Carp Lake	Lake Paradise	1908	2	✓	✓	10	H
Round Lake 1 mi. W of Conway	Round Lake	333	2		✓	5	
Crooked Lake 3 mi. E of Conway	Crooked Lake	2400	2			8	
Wilderness St Park 7 mi. NW of Carp Lake	Lake Michigan		4		✓	10	
Petoskey Mun. Marina Petoskey	Lake Michigan		1	✓	✓	25	
Harbor Springs Ramp Harbor Springs	Lake Michigan		1	✓	✓	54	
GRAND TRAVERSE COUNTY							
Scheck's Place Forest Campground 4 mi. NE of Mayfield	Boardman River		4		✓	40	
Bowers Harbor 1 mi. W of Mapleton	Grand Traverse Bay		1	✓	✓	42	H
Arbutus Lake #5 4 mi. N of Mayfield	Arbutus Lake	395	3		✓	20	
Spider Lake Forest Cpgd. 3 mi. N of Mayfield	Spider Lake	459	2		✓	10	
River Road 4 mi. NW of Mayfield	Boardman River		4		✓	10	
Fish Lake 4 mi. S of Monroe Center	Fish Lake	18	3		✓	4	
Silver Lake 3 mi. N of Grawn	Silver Lake	600	1	✓	✓	31	H
Ellis Lake 2 mi. NE of Interlochen	Ellis Lake	42	3			8	
Cedar Lake 7 mi. N of Interlochen	Cedar Lake	50	3		✓	10	
Lake Skegemog 4 mi. NE of Williamsburg	Lake Skegemog	1460	1	✓	✓	30	
Fife Lake Fife Lake	Fife Lake	617	2	✓	✓	10	
Bass Lake N. 3 mi. NW of Grawn	Bass Lake	343	1	✓	✓	6	

	Body of water	Acres	Ramp class	Courtesy pier	Toilet	Parking spaces	Handicapper accessible
Bass Lake S. 2 mi. NW of Karlin	Bass Lake	89	3		✓	6	
Green Lake 1 mi. N of Karlin	Green Lake	1987	1	✓	✓	25	H
Cedar Hedge Lake 2 mi. NW of Interlochen	Cedar Hedge Lake	195	2		✓	15	
Arbutus Lake # 4 Forest Cpgd. 3 mi. N of Mayfield	Arbutus Lake	395	3		✓	15	
Forks Forest Cpgd. 7 mi. NE of Mayfield	Boardman River		4		✓	5	
Lake Dubonnet Forest Cpgd. 3 mi. NW of Interlochen	Lake Dubonnet	645	3		✓	24	
Whitewater Twp. Park 3 mi. N of Williamsburg	Elk Lake	7930	1	✓	✓	56	
Spring Lake Forest Cpgd. 1 mi SW of Fife Lake	Spring Lake	19	3		✓	30	
Interlochen St Park 1 mi. S of Interlochen	Duck Lake	1930	2		✓	20	
Interlochen St. Park 1 mi. S of Interlochen	Green Lake	1987	2		✓	10	
Clinch Mem. Ramp Traverse City	Grand Traverse Bay		1		✓	54	
East Arm 4 mi. NE of Traverse City	Grand Traverse Bay		2	✓	✓	32	
KALKASKA COUNTY							
East Lake 6 mi. E of S. Boardman	East Lake	91	2		✓	20	
Big Blue Lake 8 mi. E of Darragh	Big Blue Lake	114	2		✓	6	
Pickerel Lake Forest Cpgd. 4 mi. NE of Darragh	Pickerel Lake	100	3		✓	15	
Starvation Lake 7 mi. NE of Darragh	Starvation Lake	134	2		✓	8	
Bear Lake 11 mi. NW of Grayling	Bear Lake	317	2		✓	6	H
Freedom Park Rapid City	Rapid River		4		✓	15	
Torch River 2 mi. W of Rapid City	Torch River		1	✓	✓	30	
Cub Lake 12 mi. W of Grayling	Cub Lake	55	3		✓	4	
Indian Lake 7 mi. NE of Darragh	Indian Lake	69	2		✓	5	
Big Twin Lake 5 mi. E of Darragh	Big Twin Lake	215	2		✓	5	
Rainbow Jim Bridge 5 mi. W of Smithville	Manistee River		2		✓	6	

	Body of water	Acres	Ramp class	Courtesy pier	Toilet	Parking spaces	Handicapper accessible
CCC Bridge Forest Cpgd. 4 mi. NE of Sharon	Manistee River		4	✓	✓	20	
Guernsey Lake Forest Cpgd. 5 mi. N of S. Boardman	Guernsey Lake	31	3		✓	6	
Three Mile Bend 3 mi. E of Sharon	Manistee River		4			5	
Smithville Smithville	Manistee River		2		✓	20	
Sand Banks 2 mi. NE of Smithville	Manistee River		4		✓	15	
Cranberry Lake 2 mi. W of Grayling	Cranberry Lake	13	4		✓	4	
LAKE COUNTY							
Wagon Wheel 1 mi. SW of Baldwin	Baldwin Creek		4		✓	15	
Upper Branch 2 mi. SE of Branch	Pere Marquette R.		3		✓	6	
Roller Bridge 5 mi. E of Baldwin	Pere Marquette R.		4		✓	10	
Meadow Brook Bridge 3 mi SW of Bristol	Pine River		4			10	
Fox Bridge 3 mi. SW of Irons	Little Manistee R.		4			4	
Coe Creek 3 mi. SW of Bristol	Pine River		4		✓	40	
Edgetts Bridge 3 mi. S of Bristol	Pine River		4		✓	4	
Lincoln Bridge Forest Campground 6 mi. W of Bristol	Pine River		4			10	
Weavers 4 mi. S of Baldwin	Pere Marquette R.		4		✓	5	
Big Star Lake 7 mi. SE of Baldwin	Big Star Lake	912	1	✓	✓	49	H
Skookum S. Bank 4 mi. SW of Bristol	Pine River		4		✓	10	
Skookum N. Bank 3 mi. SW of Bristol	Pine River		4		✓	5	
Rockey 3 mi. NE of Baldwin	Baldwin Creek		4		✓	4	
Harper Lake 2 mi. W of Irons	Harper Lake	254	2		✓	5	
Switzer Lake 4 mi. E of Baldwin	Switzer Lake	10	4		✓	3	
M-37 Bridge 2 mi. S of Baldwin	Pere Marquette R.		4		✓	15	

	Body of water	Acres	Ramp class	Courtesy pier	Toilet	Parking spaces	Handicapper accessible
The Forks 3 mi. S of Baldwin	Pere Marquette R.		4		✓	10	
Indian Bridge 3 mi. S of Irons	Little Manistee R.		4		✓	20	
Spencer Bridge 5 mi. S of Irons	Little Manistee R.		4		✓	20	
Reed Lake 6 mi. SE of Branch	Reed Lake	45	3		✓	15	
Paradise Lake 3 mi. E of Baldwin	Paradise Lake	39	2		✓	15	
Baldwin Hatchery Baldwin	Baldwin River		4			8	
Big Leverentz Lake 2 mi. NE of Baldwin	Big Leverentz Lk.	20	3		✓	4	
Silver Creek Forest Cpgd. 5 mi. W of Bristol	Pine River		4		✓	50	
Big Bass Lake 5 mi. SW of Irons	Big Bass Lake	290	1	✓	✓	10	
Rainbow Rapids 6 mi. W of Baldwin	Pere Marquette R.		3		✓	0	
Gleason's Landing 2 mi. S of Baldwin	Pere Marquette R.		4		✓	0	
Upper Branch 9 mi. W of Baldwin	Pere Marquette R.		4		✓	0	
Bowman Bridge 5 mi. W of Baldwin	Pere Marquette R.		4		✓	0	
Olga Lake 4 mi. N of Bristol	Olga Lake	76	4		✓	0	
Elbow Lake 3 mi. W of Irons	Elbow Lake	50	3			0	
Sand Lake 2 mi. NW of Irons	Sand Lake	49	2		✓	0	
LEELANAU COUNTY							
Lake Leelanau W. 6 mi. NE of Cedar	Lake Leelanau	8219	3		✓	5	
Lake Leelanau E. 1 mi. W of Bingham	Lake Leelanau	8219	2	✓	✓	20	H
Lake Leelanau S. 1 mi. NW of Lake Leelanau	Lake Leelanau	8219	4		✓	10	
Lake Leelanau N. 2 mi. NE of Leland	Lake Leelanau	8219	2		✓	8	
Cedar Lake 2 mi. NW of Traverse City	Cedar Lake	252	2	✓	✓	15	
Glen Lake 5 mi. NE of Empire	Glen Lake	6285	2	✓	✓	20	
Lime Lake 2 mi. N of Maple City	Lime Lake	670	2	✓	✓	6	

	Body of water	Acres	Ramp class	Courtesy pier	Toilet	Parking spaces	Handicapper accessible
Carp River Leland	Lake Leelanau	8219	1			6	
Armstrong Lake 5 mi. SW of Maple City	Armstrong Lake	31	3		✓	3	
Solon Township Park 1 mi. E of Cedar	Cedar River		2			8	
West Arm Grand Traverse Bay 3 mi. NE of Bingham	Grand Traverse Bay		1	✓	✓	36	
The Narrows Lake Leelanau	Lake Leelanau	8219	1	✓	✓	28	
Leland Ramp Leland	Lake Michigan		1	✓	✓	44	
Elmwood Twp. Marina 3 mi. NW of Traverse City	Grand Traverse Bay		1	✓	✓	182	
Suttons Bay Ramp Suttons Bay	Grand Traverse Bay		1	✓		30	
Northport Ramp Northport	Grand Traverse Bay		1	✓	✓	41	
MANISTEE COUNTY							
Healy Lake Forest Cpgd. 4 mi. N of Kaleva	Healy Lake	40	3		✓	4	
Bear Lake 2 mi. NW of Bear Lake	Bear Lake	1869	1	✓	✓	32	
Nine Mile Bridge 8 mi. SW of Wellston	Little Manistee R.		4			3	
Portage Lake 3 mi. W of Onekama	Portage Lake	2164	2	✓	✓	70	
Onekama Park Onekama	Portage Lake	2164	1	✓	✓	40	
Canfield Lake 3 mi. S of Manistee	Canfield Lake	28	3			6	
Glovers Lake 8 mi. W of Copemish	Glovers Lake	20	3		✓	5	
Tippy Dam Campground 3 mi. N of Wellston	Tippy Dam Pond	1220	4		✓	41	
Tippy Dam 3 mi. N of Wellston	Manistee River		2		✓	226	
Stronach Stronach	Manistee Lake	930	1	✓	✓	157	H
East Lake Vil. Park East Lake	Manistee Lake	930	1	✓	✓	50	
First Street Ramp 1 mi. W of Manistee	Manistee River		1	✓	✓	290	
Arthur Street Ramp Manistee	Manistee Lake	930	1		✓	40	
Arcadia Dock Arcadia	Arcadia Lake	275	1			24	

	Body of water	Acres	Ramp class	Courtesy pier	Toilet	Parking spaces	Handicapper accessible
Bear Creek 4 mi. W of Brethren	Manistee River		2		✓	0	
Blacksmith Bayou 3 mi. S of Brethren	Manistee River		3		✓	0	
Rainbow Bend 6 mi. W of Brethren	Manistee River		2		✓	0	
High Bridge 3 mi. S of Brethren	Manistee River		2		✓	0	
Red Bridge 5 mi. NE of Wellston	Manistee River		2		✓	0	
Pine Lake 2 mi. SW of Wellston	Pine Lake	159	3		✓	0	
Dorner Lake 1 mi. SE of Wellston	Dorner Lake	50	3		✓	0	
Six Mile Bridge 5 mi. E of Stronach	Little Manistee R.		4			0	
Old Stronach Bridge 1 mi. E of Stronach	Little Manistee R.		4			0	
MASON COUNTY							
Gun Lake 2 mi. N of Fountain	Gun Lake	242	3		✓	4	
Upper 4 mi. NE of Fountain	Big Sable River		4			10	
Ford Lake 3 mi. E of Fountain	Ford Lake	208	2	✓	✓	5	H
Walhalla Road Bridge 1 mi. N of Walhalla	Pere Marquette R.		4		✓	12	
Ruby Creek 7 mi. S of Branch	Pere Marquette R.		4		✓	8	
Hackert Lake 3 mi. NW of Scottville	Hackert Lake	125	1	✓	✓	23	
Tallman Lake Tallman	Tallman Lake	170	4			1	
Pliness Lake 7 mi. S of Scottville	Pliness Lake	81	4		✓	5	
St. Mary's Lake 9 mi. S of Scottville	St. Mary's Lake	100	3		✓	10	
US-31 3 mi. SE of Ludington	Pere Marquette R.		2		✓	10	
Ludington St. Park 6 mi. NW of Ludington	Hamlin Lake	4750	1	✓	✓	15	
Scottville River Park Scottville	Pere Marquette R.		2	✓	✓	44	
Loomis Street Ramp Ludington	Lake Michigan		1	✓	✓	200	
Copeyon Park 1 mi. N of Ludington	Pere Marquette Lk.	554	1	✓	✓	82	

	Body of water	Acres	Ramp class	Courtesy pier	Toilet	Parking spaces	Handicapper accessible
Indian Bridge	Pere Marquette R.		2		✓	0	
2 mi. SE of Custer							
Hamlin Lake	Hamlin Lake	4750	3			0	
9 mi. NE of Ludington							
Hoags Lake	Hoags Lake	27	4			0	
6 mi. SE of Manistee							
MISSAUKEE COUNTY							
Lucas Road	Manistee River		3		✓	10	
12 mi. N of Jennings							
Lake Sapphire	Lake Sapphire	264	2	✓	✓	4	H
2 mi. SE of Jennings							
Goose Lake Forest Cpgd.	Goose Lake	100	3		✓	4	
2 mi. NW of Lake City							
Long Lake Forest Cpgd.	Long Lake	61	3		✓	1	
2 mi. NW of Lake City							
Reedsburg Dam Forest							
Campground	Dead Stream Fldg.	985	1		✓	20	
5 mi. NE of Merritt							
MUSKEGON COUNTY							
Fruitport	Spring Lake	1251	1	✓	✓	20	H
Fruitport							
Mona Lake Park	Mona Lake	695	1	✓	✓	22	
5 mi. S of Muskegon							
Muskegon St. Park	Muskegon Lake	4150	2		✓	35	
5 mi. W of Muskegon							
Muskegon St. Pk. - Snug Harbor	Muskegon Lake	4150	2		✓	25	
5 mi. W of Muskegon							
Hartshorn Mun. Marina	Muskegon Lake	4150	1	✓	✓	50	
Muskegon							
Giddings Street Ramp	Muskegon Lake	4150	1	✓	✓	315	
Muskegon							
Montague	White Lake	2571	1	✓	✓	100	
Montague							
Duck Lake St. Park	Duck Lake	112	2			0	
6 mi. SW of Whitehall							
Cottage Grove	Muskegon Lake	4150	1			26	
Muskegon							
Deremo Park	Big Blue Lake	330	1		✓	10	
8 mi. E of Montague							
Moore Park	Half Moon Lake	150	3		✓	6	
1 mi. S of Bailey							
Twin Lake Park	Twin Lake	125	3		✓	10	
Twin Lake							

	Body of water	Acres	Ramp class	Courtesy pier	Toilet	Parking spaces	Handicapper accessible
NEWAYGO COUNTY							
Brooks Lake 2 mi. SE of Newaygo	Brooks Lake	293	2		✓	22	
Pickerel Lake 3 mi. N of Newaygo	Pickerel Lake	318	2		✓	8	
Newaygo 1 mi. W of Newaygo	Muskegon River		2		✓	53	
Hess Lake 2 mi. S of Newaygo	Hess Lake	1125	2		✓	16	H
Ransom Lake 7 mi. SE of Newaygo	Ransom Lake	31	4			5	
Bills Lake 7 mi. E of Newaygo	Bills Lake	204	3		✓	20	
Englewright Lake 2 mi. SE of Engle Lake	Englewright Lake	54	4			5	
High Rollway 4 mi. E of Newaygo	Muskegon River		2		✓	75	
Anderson's Flats 3 mi. SW of Newaygo	Muskegon River		2		✓	25	
Pine Street 6 mi. E of Newaygo	Muskegon River		2		✓	81	
Marl Pit Creek 1 mi. NE of Bridgeton	Muskegon River		4			4	
Maple Island 5 mi. SW of Bridgeton	Muskegon River		2		✓	25	
Henning Park Newaygo	Muskegon River		2	✓	✓	96	
Highbank Lake 2 mi. W of Lilley	Highbank Lake	21	4		✓	0	
Nichols Lake 3 mi. SW of Bitely	Nichols Lake	143	2		✓	0	
Nichols Lake 2 mi. W of Woodland Park	Nichols Lake	143	3		✓	0	
Benton Lake 4 mi. W of Brohman	Benton Lake	31	3		✓	0	
Twinwood Lake 4 mi. N of Newaygo	Twinwood Lake	34	3			0	
Shelly Lake 3 mi. E of Woodland Park	Shelly Lake	13	3			0	
Brush Lake 2 mi. S of Woodville	Brush Lake	19	3		✓	0	
Hungerford Lake 7 mi. W of Big Rapids	Hungerford Lake	36	3			0	
Indian Lake 1 mi. S of Brohman	Indian Lake	34	3			0	
Diamond Lake 4 mi. NW of White Cloud	Diamond Lake	181	3		✓	20	

Public Boat Launches

	Body of water	Acres	Ramp class	Courtesy pier	Toilet	Parking spaces	Handicapper accessible
Robinson Lake 4 mi. W of White Cloud	Robinson Lake	137	3		✓	12	
Newaygo St. Park 2 mi. NE of Oxbow	Hardy Dam Pond	3750	2	✓	✓	10	
OCEANA COUNTY							
Crystal Lake 3 mi. N of Shelby	Crystal Lake	74	3			10	
McLaren Lake 4 mi. N of Hesperia	McLaren Lake	271	2	✓	✓	20	
Silver Lake St. Park 6 mi. W of Shelby	Silver Lake	690	2			3	
Pines Point 9 mi. W of Fremont	White River		3		✓	0	
Diamond 7 mi. E of Rothbury	White River		4			0	
OSCEOLA COUNTY							
Rose Lake Co. Park 2 mi. SW of Dighton	Rose Lake	370	1	✓	✓	5	
Hicks Lake 9 mi. E of LeRoy	Hicks Lake	155	2	✓	✓	7	
McCoy Lake 2 mi. S of LeRoy	McCoy Lake	12	3		✓	4	
Sunrise Lake Forest Cpgd. 6 mi. E of LeRoy	Sunrise Lake	120	2		✓	50	
Wells Lake 3 mi. SE of LeRoy	Wells Lake	48	3		✓	6	
Big Lake 2 mi. S of Sears	Big Lake	218	2	✓	✓	21	
Todd Lake 3 mi. SE of Ashton	Todd Lake	76	2		✓	8	
Diamond Lake 2 mi. SW of Tustin	Diamond Lake	62	3		✓	8	
Evart Riverside Park Evart	Muskegon River		2		✓	18	
Crawford Park 4 mi. NE of Sears	Muskegon River		2		✓	6	
WEXFORD COUNTY							
Berry Lake 3 mi. SE of Cadillac	Berry Lake	68	1	✓	✓	12	H
Harvey Bridge 5 mi. S of Buckley	Manistee River		3		✓	4	
Baxter Bridge 7 mi. E of Buckley	Manistee River		2		✓	6	
Long Lake Forest Cpgd. 5 mi. N of Cadillac	Long Lake	187	4	✓	✓	5	

	Body of water	Acres	Ramp class	Courtesy pier	Toilet	Parking spaces	Handicapper accessible
Mitchell St. Park 3 mi. SW of Cadillac	Lake Cadillac	1235	1	✓	✓	3	
Kenwood Park 2 mi. W of Cadillac	Lake Cadillac	1235	1	✓	✓	80	
Hemlock 5 mi. W of Cadillac	Lake Mitchell	2600	3		✓	0	
Dobson Bridge 2 mi. W of Hoxeyville	Pine River		4		✓	0	
Peterson Bridge 4 mi. W of Hoxeyville	Pine River		4		✓	5	

UPPER PENINSULA

ALGER COUNTY

	Body of water	Acres	Ramp class	Courtesy pier	Toilet	Parking spaces	Handicapper accessible
Forest Lake Forest Cpgd. 4 mi SE of Chatham	AuTrain R. Basin	1022	1		✓	25	
Anna River Mouth 1 mi. NE of Munising	Lake Superior		1		✓	62	
Nawakwa Lake 9 mi. S of Grand Marais	Nawakwa Lake	399	2	✓	✓	9	H
Whitefish River 8 mi. NW of Trenary	Whitefish River		4		✓	10	
Kingston Lake Forest Cpgd. 13 mi. NE of Melstrand	Kingston Lk.	250	1		✓	6	
Au Train Bay 2 mi. W of Au Train	Lake Superior		1	✓	✓	18	
Grand Marais Harbor Grand Marais	Lake Superior		1	✓		20	
Munising Mun. Ramp Munising	Lake Superior		1	✓		71	
Ackerman Lake 2 mi. E of Forest Lake	Ackerman Lake	14	3		✓	3	
Au Train Lake 2 mi. S of Au Train	Au Train Lake	830	2		✓	6	
Tish Lake 9 mi. W of Steuben	Tish Lake	60	3		✓	6	
Irwin 10 mi. W of Steuben	Irwin Lake	10	2		✓	4	

BARAGA COUNTY

	Body of water	Acres	Ramp class	Courtesy pier	Toilet	Parking spaces	Handicapper accessible
Vermillac Lake 2 mi. E of Covington	Vermillac Lake	622	1		✓	15	
King Lake Forest Cpgd. 6 mi. E of Covington	King Lake	498	1		✓	4	
Ruth Lake 1 mi. NW of Three Lakes	Ruth Lake	192	2		✓	4	
Silver River 5 mi. SW of Skanee	Huron Bay		2		✓	20	

	Body of water	Acres	Ramp class	Courtesy pier	Toilet	Parking spaces	Handicapper accessible
Sturgeon River 6 mi. W of Baraga	Sturgeon River		4		✓	6	
Keewaydin Lake 4 mi. N of Michigamme	Keewaydin Lake	171	1	✓	✓	5	
Beaufort Lake Forest Cpgd. 1 mi. E of Three Lakes	Beaufort Lake	462	1		✓	5	
Parent Lake 5 mi. NE of Covington	Parent Lake	170	1	✓	✓	7	H
Roland Lake 4 mi. SE of Skanee	Roland Lake	41	3		✓	12	
Six Mile Creek Trout Pond 6 mi. SW of Baraga	Six Mile Ck. Trout Pd.	12	4		✓	4	
Arvon Township Park 1 mi. N of Skanee	Huron Bay		1	✓	✓	58	
Big Lake Forest Cpgd. 5 mi. N of Watton	Big Lake	138	4		✓	6	
Baraga St. Park 1 mi. S of Baraga	Keweenaw Bay		2		✓	15	
Net River Flooding 7 mi. N of Covington	Net River		1		✓	8	
Michigamme Twp. Park 1 mi. SW of Michigamme	L. Michigamme	4260	1	✓	✓	10	
L'Anse Vil. Dock L'Anse	Keweenaw Bay		2			65	
CHIPPEWA COUNTY							
Frenchman Lake 1 mi. SE of Trout Lake	Frenchman Lake	197	2		✓	6	
Old Eckerman Trout Pond Eckerman	Tahquamenon R.		4		✓	10	
De Tour Passage 1 mi. S. of De Tour Village	Lake Huron		1	✓	✓	17	H
Potagannissing Flooding 5 mi. E of Drummond	Potagannissing Fldg.	2200	3			30	
Sugar Island 10 mi. E of Sault Ste. Marie	St. Marys River		1		✓	7	
Caribou Lake 5 mi. W of De Tour Village	Caribou Lake	825	1	✓	✓	10	
Tahquamenon Falls Tahquamenon Falls R. Mouth Cpgd. 4 mi. S of Paradise	Tahquamenon River		1	✓		10	
Trout Lake Twp Park 1 mi. W of Trout Lake	Carp Lake	560	1		✓	31	
Andrus Lake Forest Cpgd. 6 mi. W of Whitefish Point	Andrus Lake	31	2		✓	5	
Shelldrake Dam Forest Cpgd. 6 mi. SW of Whitefish Point	Shelldrake Dam Imp.	850	1		✓	10	

	Body of water	Acres	Ramp class	Courtesy pier	Toilet	Parking spaces	Handicapper accessible
Maxton Bay Forest Cpgd. 3 mi. NE of Drummond	Lake Huron		1			20	
Munuscong River Forest Cpgd. Kelden	Munuscong River		1	✓	✓	19	
Brimley St. Park 1 mi. NE of Brimley	Whitefish Bay		2		✓	15	
Cranberry Flooding 6 mi. W of De Tour Village	Cranberry Lake	75	4			6	
Raber Township Park Raber	St. Marys River		1	✓	✓	15	
Sault Ste. Marie Mun. Marina 3 mi. SE of Sault Ste. Marie	St. Marys River		1		✓	10	
Tahquamenon Falls St. Park 6 mi. S of Paradise	L. Superior		2		✓	13	
Whitefish Point Harbor Whitefish Point	Lake Superior		1	✓	✓	29	
Dunbar 3 mi. NE of Barbeau	Charlotte River		1	✓	✓	18	
DELTA COUNTY							
Ford River Mouth Ford River	Green Bay		1	✓	✓	52	H
Burnt Camp 1 mi. E of Cornell	Escanaba River		4		✓	5	
Sandy Point Escanaba	Little Bay de Noc		1	✓	✓	25	
Garden Bay 1 mi. S of Garden	Big Bay de Noc		1	✓	✓	10	
Kipling 1 mi. N of Gladstone	Little Bay de Noc		1	✓	✓	46	H
Portage Point 3 mi. S of Escanaba	Lake Michigan		4			10	
Dam 3 Impoundment 3 mi. W of Gladstone	Dam 3 Impound.	187	1		✓	7	
Little Fish Dam River 2 mi. E of Isabella	Big Bay de Noc		1	✓	✓	67	
Rapid River Mouth 1 mi. S of Rapid River	Little Bay de Noc		1	✓	✓	75	
Portage Bay Forest Cpgd. 6 mi. E of Fayette	Lake Michigan		4		✓	5	
Fayette St. Park Fayette	Big Bay de Noc		3	✓	✓	5	
Gladstone Marina Gladstone	Little Bay de Noc		1	✓	✓	50	
Camp 7 Lake 9 mi. SW of Steuben	Camp 7 Lake	60	2		✓	8	
Chicago Lake 9 mi. N of Isabella	Chicago Lake	164	3			2	

	Body of water	Acres	Ramp class	Courtesy pier	Toilet	Parking spaces	Handicapper accessible
Corner Lake 8 mi. W of Steuben	Corner Lake	156	2		✓	4	
Dana Lake 10 mi. SW of Steuben	Dana Lake	95	3		✓	3	
Gooseneck Lake 10 mi. S of Steuben	Gooseneck Lake	139	3			2	
Jackpine Lake 6 mi. S of Steuben	Jackpine Lake	63	3			2	
Lyman Lake 9 mi. S of Steuben	Lyman Lake	69	3			3	
DICKINSON COUNTY							
Mary Lake 2 mi. S of Loretto	Mary Lake	86	2		✓	5	
Pickerel Lake 2 mi. SW of Ralph	Pickerel Lake	71	3		✓	3	
Hamilton Lake 2 mi. SE of Loretto	Hamilton Lake	75	1		✓	10	
Norway Reservoir 3 mi. SW of Loretto	Norway Res.	300	1	✓	✓	17	H
Silver Lake 6 mi. NE of Channing	Silver Lake	118	1		✓	5	
Bergen Backwater 2 mi. N. of Waucedah	Bergen Backwater	248	2		✓	15	
Rock Lake 6 mi. E of Merriman	Rock Lake	76	4		✓	4	
Solberg Lake 6 mi. W of Felch	Solberg Lake	21	3		✓	6	
Edey Lake 4 mi. NE of Channing	Edey Lake	79	1		✓	5	
Six Mile Lake 3 mi. W of Felch	Six Mile Lake	96	1		✓	10	
Stromberg Park 1 mi. NE of Hardwood	Sturgeon River		1		✓	30	
W. Branch Forest Cpgd. 6 mi. N of Ralph	Escanaba River		4		✓	16	
Lower Dam Forest Cpgd. 8 mi. NE of Ralph	Escanaba River		4		✓	5	
Carney Lake Forest Cpgd. 6 mi. E of Merriman	Carney Lake	105	1		✓	9	
Gene's Pond Forest Cpgd. 5 mi. SW of Ralph	Gene's Pond	734	1		✓	25	
Lake Antoine Co. Park 3 mi. NE of Iron Mountain	Lake Antoine	748	1	✓	✓	81	
Bodelin Access Site 3 mi. NW of Iron Mountain	Menominee River		1	✓	✓	10	
Cowboy Lake Kingsford	Cowboy Lake	34	1	✓	✓	15	

	Body of water	Acres	Ramp class	Courtesy pier	Toilet	Parking spaces	Handicapper accessible
Hanbury Lake W. of Vulcan	Hanbury Lake	89	1	✓		8	
W. Branch Sturgeon River 6 mi. SW of Foster City	Sturgeon River		2		✓	10	
GOGEBIC COUNTY							
Cisco Lake 13 mi. W of Watersmeet	Cisco Lake	506	1		✓	5	
Dinner Lake 5 mi. S of Watersmeet	Dinner Lake	110	1		✓	8	
Duck Lake 5 mi. S of Watersmeet	Duck Lake	616	1		✓	4	
Thousand Island Lake 10 mi. W of Watersmeet	Thousand Island L.	1079	1	✓	✓	10	H
Lac Vieux Desert 8 mi. S of Watersmeet	Lac Vieux Desert	4260	1	✓	✓	17	
Chaney Lake 12 mi. S of Wakefield	Chaney Lake	520	1		✓	6	
Beatons Lake 9 mi. NW of Watersmeet	Beatons Lake	330	4			0	
Clearwater Lake 11 mi. W of Watersmeet	Clearwater Lake	185	1		✓	8	
Black River Lake 10 mi. S of Bessemer	Black River Lake	68	1		✓	8	
Lake Gogebic St. Park 8 mi. NE of Marenisco	Lake Gogebic	14781	1	✓	✓	5	
Oman Creek 18 mi. NW of Ironwood	Lake Superior		1	✓	✓	25	
Imp Lake 6 mi. SE of Watersmeet	Imp Lake	84	1		✓	8	
Clark Lake 7 mi. W of Watersmeet	Clark Lake	820	3		✓	35	
Crooked Lake 6 mi. W of Watersmeet	Crooked Lake	566	1		✓	54	
Little Duck Lake 4 mi. S of Watersmeet	Little Duck Lake	42	3		✓	6	
Moon Lake 5 mi. S of Watersmeet	Moon Lake	93	1		✓	8	
Allen Lake 3 mi. S of Watersmeet	Allen Lake	79	1		✓	7	
Grass Lake 7 mi. S of Watersmeet	Grass Lake	40	4			3	
Marion Lake NW 4 mi. E of Watersmeet	Marion Lake	318	3			6	
Marion Lake NE 4 mi. E of Watersmeet	Marion Lake	318	1		✓	10	
Taylor Lake 6 mi. E of Watersmeet	Taylor Lake	110	3		✓	7	

	Body of water	Acres	Ramp class	Courtesy pier	Toilet	Parking spaces	Handicapper accessible
Black River Harbor 14 mi. N of Bessemer	Black River		1		✓	20	
Elbow Lake 5 mi. SW of Marenisco	Elbow Lake	26	1		✓	3	
Redboat Lake 5 mi. SW of Marenisco	Redboat Lake	28	2		✓	5	
Henry Lake 7 mi. SW of Marenisco	Henry Lake	50	1		✓	5	
Thrush Lake 7 mi. SW of Marenisco	Thrush Lake	17	2		✓	4	
Moraine Lake 8 mi. SW of Marenisco	Moraine Lake	67	3		✓	5	
Bobcat Lake 2 mi. SE of Marenisco	Bobcat Lake	76	3		✓	5	
Little Oxbow Lake 9 mi. SE of Marenisco	Little Oxbow Lake	90	3		✓	5	
Ormes Lake 9 mi. SE of Marenisco	Ormes Lake	49	2		✓	5	
Dawn Lake 11 mi. SE of Marenisco	Dawn Lake	18	4			0	
Moosehead Lake 12 mi. SE of Marenisco	Moosehead Lake	54	1		✓	6	
Pomeroy Lake 10 mi. SE of Marenisco	Pomeroy Lake	314	2		✓	6	
Langford Lake 3 mi. S of Thayer	Langford Lake	481	2		✓	6	
Long Lake 8 mi. W of Watersmeet	Long Lake	168	3		✓	12	
McDonald Lake 6 mi. S of Bessemer	McDonald Lake	485	3		✓	5	
Eel Lake 8 mi. SW of Marenisco	Eel Lake	52	2		✓	5	
Presque Isle River 2 mi. S of Marenisco	Presque Isle River		2		✓	5	
HOUGHTON COUNTY							
Otter Lake 2 mi. E of Tapiola	Otter Lake	935	3		✓	6	
Clear Lake 4 mi. S of Twin Lakes	Clear Lake	24	1		✓	9	
Emily Lake Forest Cpgd. 3 mi. S of Twin Lakes	Emily Lake	54	3		✓	12	
Bootjack 6 mi. NW of Jacobsville	Portage Lake	10970	2		✓	6	
Prickett Dam Backwaters 5 mi. SE of Nisula	Prickett Dam Bkwtrs.	826	1		✓	10	
Sandy Lake 4 mi. S of Twin Lakes	Sandy Lake	101	3		✓	4	

	Body of water	Acres	Ramp class	Courtesy pier	Toilet	Parking spaces	Handicapper accessible
Swedetown Creek 2 mi. NW of Hancock	Portage Ship Canal		4			10	
Rice Lake 6 mi. E of Lake Linden	Rice Lake	680	1		✓	10	
Pike Lake 4 mi. S of Twin Lakes	Pike Lake	80	3		✓	8	
Boston Pond 1 mi. S of Boston	Boston Pond	140	2		✓	20	
Lake Linden Vil. Park 1 mi. NE of Lake Linden	Torch Lake	1178	1		✓	10	
Twin Lakes St. Park Twin Lakes	Lake Roland	292	1		✓	8	
White City 1 mi. W of Jacobsville	Portage River		1		✓	20	
Sturgeon River Sloughs 2 mi. SE of Chassell	Portage River		1		✓	8	
Grand Traverse Bay Harbor 8 mi. E of Lake Linden	Lake Superior		1	✓	✓	18	
Hancock Mun. Park 2 mi. NW of Hancock	Portage Lake	10970	1	✓	✓	29	
Lily Pond Ramp 4 mi. NW of Boston	Lake Superior		1	✓	✓	20	H
Elm River Township Ramp Twin Lakes	Lake Roland	292	1			6	
Otter Lake Dam 3 mi. E of Tapiola	Otter Lake	935	1		✓	8	
Chassell Chassell	Portage Lake	10970	1	✓	✓	10	
Old Sandy Dollar Bay	Portage Lake	10970	1	✓	✓	x	
S. Portage Entry 1 mi. W of Jacobsville	Portage Lake	10970	1	✓	✓	8	
Bob Lake 13 mi. N of Kenton	Bob Lake	133	3		✓	6	
Kunze Lake 5 mi. S of Sidnaw	Kunze Lake	13	4			3	
Hager Lake 3 mi. S of Sidnaw	Hager Lake	41	4			3	
Estes Lake 5 mi. N of Sidnaw	Estes Lake	23	4			3	
Crystal Lake 2 mi. W of Sidnaw	Crystal Lake	17	4			3	
Lower Dam Lake 5 mi. SW of Sidnaw	Lower Dam Lake	80	4		✓	6	
Stanton Township Park 9 mi. NW of Sidnaw	Lake Superior		2		✓	20	
Perrault Lake 3 mi. SW of Painesdale	Perrault Lake	39	3		✓	10	

	Body of water	Acres	Ramp class	Courtesy pier	Toilet	Parking spaces	Handicapper accessible
IRON COUNTY							
Tamarack Lake 12 mi. NW of Beechwood	Tamarack Lake	325	1		✓	5	
Lake Ellen Forest Cpgd. 10 mi. NE of Crystal Falls	Lake Ellen	144	2		✓	7	
Stanley Lake 3 mi. W of Caspian	Stanley Lake	310	1	✓	✓	8	
Emily Lake 7 mi. E of Iron River	Emily Lake	320	1		✓	5	
Holmes Lake 10 mi. E of Crystal Falls	Holmes Lake	28	3		✓	5	
Fire Lake 3 mi. SW of Amasa	Fire Lake	128	1		✓	4	
Indian Lake 5 mi. W of Alpha	Indian Lake	196	1		✓	8	
Cable Lake 10 mi. NW of Amasa	Cable Lake	320	3		✓	5	
Camp Lake 5 mi. W of Caspian	Camp Lake	101	2		✓	5	
Deer Lake Forest Cpgd. 9 mi. NE of Amasa	Deer Lake	81	2		✓	4	
Swan Lake 5 mi. NW of Crystal Falls	Swan Lake	163	3		✓	8	
Lake Mary 6 mi. SE of Crystal Falls	Lake Mary	265	1	✓	✓	5	H
Long Lake 6 mi. W of Crystal Falls	Long Lake	66	1		✓	6	
Erickson's Landing 4 mi. NW of Crystal Falls	Paint River		3		✓	10	
Carney Dam 2 mi. W of Stager	Brule River		3		✓	7	
The Wide Waters 8 mi. NW of Amasa	Net River		3		✓	5	
Snake Rapids 7 mi. W of Amasa	Net River		3		✓	10	
Glidden Lake Forest Cpgd. 5 mi. SE of Crystal Falls	Glidden Lake	29	3		✓	8	
Bewabic St. Park 4 mi. W of Crystal Falls	First Fortune Lk.	199	1	✓	✓	11	
Pentoga Co. Park 6 mi. W of Alpha	Chicagon Lake	1100	1	✓	✓	10	
Paint River Bridge 1 mi. E of Crystal Falls	Paint River		4		✓	15	
Bates Township Park 3 mi. NE of Iron River	Sunset Lake	545	1		✓	21	
Mastadon Township Park 1 mi. SE of Stager	Stager Lake	112	1		✓	6	

Launch	Body of water	Acres	Ramp class	Courtesy pier	Toilet	Parking spaces	Handicapper accessible
Robinson Lake 9 mi. S of Kenton	Robinson Lake	76	4			0	
Tepee Lake 7 mi. S of Kenton	Tepee Lake	115	3		✓	10	
James Lake 8 mi. NW of Beechwood	James Lake	212	3		✓	5	
Golden Lake 6 mi. W of Beechwood	Golden Lake	285	1		✓	12	
Brule Lake 8 mi. SW of Beechwood	Brule Lake	250	2		✓	8	
Hagerman Lake 5 mi. SW of Iron River	Hagerman Lake	584	2		✓	40	
Bass Lake 5 mi. SW of Iron River	Bass Lake	96	3		✓	5	
Lake Ottawa 4 mi. SW of Iron River	Lake Ottawa	551	1		✓	20	
Chamberlain Lake 12 mi. SW of Sidnaw	Chamberlain Lake	37	3		✓	6	
Winslow Lake 12 mi. S of Sidnaw	Winslow Lake	255	3		✓	8	
Hannah Webb Lake 11 mi. S of Sidnaw	Hannah Webb Lk.	64	3		✓	5	
Perch Lake 10 mi. S of Sidnaw	Perch Lake	994	3		✓	15	
Marten Lake 8 mi S of Sidnaw	Marten Lake	176	4			4	
Lake Ste. Kathryn 8 mi. S of Sidnaw	Lake Ste. Kathryn	151	3		✓	15	
Norway Lake 7 mi. S of Sidnaw	Norway Lake	53	3		✓	15	
Killdeer Lake 12 mi. SW of Kenton	Killdeer Lake	9	3		✓	3	
KEWEENAW COUNTY							
Lake Medora 9 mi. E of Copper Harbor	Lake Medora	695	1	✓	✓	5	
Gratiot Lake 4 mi. S of Delaware	Gratiot Lake	1438	1	✓	✓	8	
Lake Bailey 3 mi. E of Eagle Harbor	Lake Bailey	204	3		✓	20	
Thayers Lake 5 mi. E of Fulton	Thayers Lake	13	3			8	
Lac La Belle Dock Lac La Belle	Lake Superior		1	✓	✓	44	H
Fort Wilkins St. Park 1 mi. E of Copper Harbor	Lake Fanny Hooe	231	3	✓	✓	15	
Copper Harbor Copper Harbor	Lake Superior		1		✓	30	

	Body of water	Acres	Ramp class	Courtesy pier	Toilet	Parking spaces	Handicapper accessible
Eagle Harbor	Lake Superior		1	✓	✓	16	
Eagle Harbor							
LUCE COUNTY							
Manistique Lake	Manistique Lake	10130	1	✓	✓	14	
9 mi. SW of McMillan							
Silver Creek Trout Pond	Silver Creek Trout Pd.	18	4		✓	15	
7 mi. NW of Dollarville							
Kak's Lake	Kak's Lake	42	2		✓	10	
3 mi. SW of Dollarville							
Natalie	Dollarville Dam Imp.	1400	1		✓	10	
2 mi. W of Dollarville							
County Line	Manistique Lake	10130	1		✓	5	
7 mi. S of McMillan							
Twin Lake	Twin Lake	103	1	✓	✓	14	H
3 mi. S of Dollarville							
Bass Lake Forest Cpgd.	Bass Lake	180	1		✓	5	
8 mi. N of McMillan							
Bodi Lake Forest Cpgd.	Bodi Lake	306	2		✓	9	
4 mi. E of Two Heart							
Blind Sucker # 1 Forest Cpgd.	Blind Sucker Fldg.	1050	2		✓	5	
7 mi. W of Deer Park							
Blind Sucker #2 Forest Cpgd.	Blind Sucker Fldg.	1050	3		✓	12	
7 mi. W of Deer Park							
Luce Co. Park	N. Manistique Lake	1722	3		✓	25	
5 mi. S of McMillan							
Perch Lake Forest Cpgd.	Perch Lake	125	2		✓	6	
3 mi. S of Deer Park							
Pike Lake Forest Cpgd.	Pike Lake	292	1		✓	5	
4 mi. S of Two Heart							
Mouth of Two Hearted	Two Hearted River		2		✓	31	
River Forest Cpgd.							
Two Heart							
Culhane Forest Cpgd.	Culhane Lake	98	1		✓	5	
3 mi. E of Two Heart							
Sixteen Creek Forest Cpgd.	Tahquamenon R.		2		✓	4	
4 mi. NE of Newberry							
Muskallonge Lake St. Park	Muskallonge Lake	786	1	✓	✓	5	
1 mi. W of Deer Park							
Third Creek Trout Pond	Third Ck. Trout Pd.	5	4			10	
8 mi. SE of Newberry							
Brockies Trout Pond	Brockies Trout Pd.	4	4			3	
6 mi. NW of Dollarville							
Bucky's Trout Pond	Bucky's Trout Pd.	6	4			3	
6 mi. NW of Dollarville							
Spring Creek Trout Pond	Spring Ck. Trout Pd.	2	4			3	
9 mi. NW of McMillan							

Body of water	Acres	Ramp class	Courtesy pier	Toilet	Parking spaces	Handicapper accessible
Little Lake Harbor 3 mi. E of Two Heart	Little Lake	90	1	✓	✓	10	
Dollarville Dam Dollarville	Dollarville Dam Imp.	1400	1		✓	8	
Dollarville Dam Dollarville	Below dam		2		✓	9	
MACKINAC COUNTY							
Milakokia Lake Forest Cpgd. 5 mi. W of Curtis	Milakokia Lake	1956	2		✓	14	
Curtis Curtis	Manistique Lake	10130	1	✓	✓	42	H
Dunkies Landing 3 mi. N of Curtis	S. Manistique Lake	4001	1	✓	✓	10	
Wolfe Bay 2 mi. SW of Curtis	S. Manistique Lake	4001	1		✓	5	
Millecoquins Lake 1 mi. NW of Millecoquins	Millecoquins Lake	1062	1		✓	20	
Cooks Bay 3 mi. W of Curtis	Manistique Lake	10130	2	✓	✓	15	
McAlpine Pond 9 mi. N of Engadine	McAlpine Pond	10	4			6	
Upper Millecoquins River 8 mi. N of Engadine	Trout Pond	4	4			6	
Carp River Mouth 10 mi. N of St. Ignace	Lake Huron		1	✓	✓	45	
S. Manistique Lake Forest Cpgd. 3 mi. SW of Curtis	S. Manistique Lake	4001	3		✓	12	
Cedarville Ramp 1 mi. S of Cedarville	Lake Huron		1	✓		38	
Little Brevoort L. S. Forest Cpgd. 1 mi. E of Brevort	Little Brevoort L.	144	3		✓	3	
Little Brevoort L. N. Forest Cpgd. 1 mi. E of Brevort	Little Brevoort Lake	144	3		✓	3	
Brevoort Lake 3 mi. W of Allenville	Brevoort Lake	4230	1	✓	✓	0	
Bay City Lake Forest Cpgd. 2 mi. N of Hessel	Bay City Lake	25	3		✓	8	
St. Ignace St. Ignace	Lake Huron		1	✓	✓	35	
Naubinway Marina Naubinway	Lake Michigan		1	✓	✓	40	
Hessel Marina Hessel	Lake Huron		1	✓	✓	25	
MARQUETTE COUNTY							
Big Shag Lake 1 mi SW of Princeton	Big Shag Lake	180	1		✓	15	

	Body of water	Acres	Ramp class	Courtesy pier	Toilet	Parking spaces	Handicapper accessible
Big Trout Lake 4 mi. N of Little Lake	Big Trout Lake	27	1		✓	4	
Pike Lake Forest Cpgd. 5 mi. W of Princeton	Pike Lake	88	1		✓	5	
Bass Lake 2 mi. SW of Little Lake	Bass Lake	266	1		✓	8	
Squaw Lake Forest Cpgd. 2 mi. NW of Witch Lake	Squaw Lake	247	1		✓	7	
Lake Michigamme 3 mi. E of Michigamme	Lake Michigamme	4260	1	✓	✓	20	
Engman's Lake 4 mi. N of Little Lake	Engman's Lake	53	1		✓	10	
Bass Lake Forest Cpgd. 6 mi. W of Princeton	Bass Lake	77	1		✓	10	
Wolf Lake 6 mi. NE of Champion	Wolf Lake	109	3		✓	6	
Sporley Lake 3 mi. N of Little Lake	Sporley Lake	68	1		✓	25	
Johnson Lake 1 mi. S of New Swanzy	Johnson Lake	78	1	✓	✓	26	H
Twin Lake 1 mi. W of Witch Lake	Twin Lake	22	4		✓	6	
Arfelin Lake 9 mi. NW of Champion	Arfelin Lake	67	1		✓	7	
Witch Lake Witch Lake	Witch Lake	209	1		✓	8	
Little Shag Lake 2 mi. SW of Princeton	Little Shag Lake	106	1		✓	8	
Dead River Basin N. 10 mi. NW of Negaunee	Dead River Basin	2704	1		✓	7	
Hoist Basin 8 mi. W of Marquette	Dead River Basin	2704	1		✓	15	
Sawmill Creek 8 mi. N of Watson	Escanaba River		4		✓	20	
Boney Falls Basin 7 mi. E of Watson	Boney Falls Basin	171	2		✓	10	
Forestville 4 mi. NW of Marquette	Dead River		1		✓	8	
McClure Storage Basin 7 mi. W of Marquette	McClure Basin	132	1		✓	4	
Schweitzer Creek Flowage 5 mi. S of Ishpeming	Schweitzer Ck. Flow.	250	1		✓	5	
Perch Lake 1 mi. SE of Republic	Perch Lake	47	1		✓	5	
Little Lake Forest Cpgd. Little Lake	Little Lake	454	1		✓	6	
Escanaba River 6 mi. NE of Watson	Escanaba River		4		✓	5	

	Body of water	Acres	Ramp class	Courtesy pier	Toilet	Parking spaces	Handicapper
Horseshoe Lake Forest Cpgd. 1 mi. NW of Witch Lake	Horseshoe Lake	127	3	3	3	8	
Van Riper St. Park 1 mi. N of Beacon	Lake Michigamme	4260	1	✓	✓	20	
Lake Le Vasseur 5 mi. N of Skandia	Lake Le Vasseur	190	1			8	
Greenwood Reservoir 8 mi. SW of Ishpeming	Greenwood Res.	1265	1		✓	17	
Big Bay Harbor of Refuge 1 mi. N of Big Bay	Lake Superior		1		✓	10	
Marquette City Ramp 2 mi. N of Marquette	Presque Isle Harbor		1	✓	✓	170	
Anderson Lake W. Forest Cpgd. 5 mi. S of Princeton	Anderson Lake	42	4		✓	6	
Anderson Lake E. 4 mi. S of Princeton	Anderson Lake	42	1		✓	10	
M-28 Bridge 1 mi. E of Harvey	Chocolay River		4		✓	23	
MENOMINEE COUNTY							
Cedar River Mouth Cedar River	Cedar River		1	✓	✓	25	H
Koss Landing 1 mi. SE of Longrie	Menominee River		1		✓	8	
Lake Ann 3 mi. SW of Swanson	Lake Ann	21	3		✓	7	
Lake Mary 2 mi. SW of Swanson	Lake Mary	35	3		✓	4	
Sturgeon Landing 4 mi. SW of Longrie	Menominee River		1		✓	10	
Railroad Dock 2 mi. SW of Marinette	Menominee River		1	✓	✓	25	
Sturgeon Bend Park 7 mi. W of Nathan	Menominee River		1		✓	20	
North Lake 6 mi. E of Stephenson	North Lake	1800	4			4	
Hayward Lake Flooding 7 mi. SE of Stephenson	Hayward L. Fldg.	175	4			4	
Gerald Welling Mem. 4 mi. W of Nathan	Menominee River		1		✓	25	
J.W. Wells State Park 1 mi. S of Cedar River	Lake Michigan		4		✓	10	
Menominee Mun. Marina 1 mi. SE of Menominee	Green Bay		1	✓	✓	20	
Cedar River N. Forest Cpgd. 5 mi. N of Cedar River	Cedar River		4		✓	15	
Scott Paper Co. Menominee	Menominee River		1			6	

Body of water	Acres	Ramp class	Courtesy pier	Toilet	Parking spaces	Handicapper accessible
Stoney Point 5 mi. N of Menominee	Green Bay		1		✓	20	
ONTONAGON COUNTY							
Bergland Dock Bergland	Lake Gogebic	14781	1		✓	35	H
County Line Lake 7 mi. SW of Paulding	County Line Lake	62	1		✓	8	
Ewen Ewen	Ontonagon River		4			6	
Porcupine Mtns. St. Park 3 mi. W of Silver City	Lake Superior		2	✓	✓	3	
Misery River Mouth 7 mi. E of 14 Mile Point	Misery River		1		✓	15	
Big Iron River Mouth Silver City	Big Iron River		1	✓	✓	30	
Ontonagon Mun. Ramp Ontonagon	Ontonagon River		1	✓	✓	109	
Steusser Lake 6 mi. S of Ewen	Steusser Lake	34	3			10	
Courtney Lake 7 mi. W of Nisula	Courtney Lake	34	3		✓	6	
Sudden Lake 7 mi. W of Nisula	Sudden Lake	35	3			6	
Deadman Lake 6 mi. NE of Watersmeet	Deadman Lake	45	3			7	
Paulding Pond 2 mi. S of Paulding	Paulding Pond	20	4		✓	7	
Robbins Pond 3 mi. SW of Paulding	Robbins Pond	3	4		✓	4	
SCHOOLCRAFT COUNTY							
Manistique Mun. Ramp Manistique	Manistique R.		1	✓		40	
Wagner Dam 10 mi. NW of Seney	Fox River		4		✓	8	
Kennedy Lake 3 mi. SE of Germfask	Kennedy Lake	131	4			5	
Stanley Lake Forest Cpgd. 13 mi. E of Melstrand	Stanley Lake	125	4		✓	3	
Dodge Lake 11 mi. N of Manistique	Dodge Lake	72	1		✓	8	
Dutch Fred Lake 9 mi. N of Seney	Dutch Fred Lake	27	3		✓	6	
McDonald Lake 2 mi. E of Gulliver	McDonald Lake	1440	1	✓	✓	15	H
Snyder Lake 10 mi. N of Seney	Snyder Lake	70	1		✓	6	

113

	Body of water	Acres	Ramp class	Courtesy pier	Toilet	Parking spaces	Handicapper accessible
Ashford Lake 13 mi. N of Manistique	Ashford Lake	13	4		✓	5	
Clear Creek Pond 8 mi. N of Seney	Clear Creek Pond	4	4			6	
Thompson Creek Thompson	Thompson Creek		4		✓	238	
Cusino Lake Forest Cpgd. 7 mi. E of Melstrand	Cusino Lake	140	4		✓	3	
Fox River Forest Cpgd. 5 mi. NW of Seney	Fox River		4		✓	4	
Seul Choix Pte. 7 mi. SE of Gulliver	Lake Michigan		1	✓	✓	13	
N. Gemini Lake Forest Cpgd. 6 mi. E of Melstrand	Gemini Lake	120	1		✓	3	
S. Gemini Lake Forest Campground 5 mi. E of Melstrand	Gemini Lake	120	4		✓	3	
Ross Lake Forest Cpgd. 7 mi. E of Melstrand	Ross Lake	184	1		✓	5	
Mead Creek Forest Cpgd. 5 mi. NW of Blaney Park	Manistique R.		3		✓	10	
Merwin Creek Forest Cpgd. 6 mi. NW of Gulliver	Manistique R.		3		✓	10	
West Branch 15 mi. N of Manistique	Manistique R.		4		✓	2	
Indian Lake St. Park S. 3 mi. N of Thompson	Indian Lake	8659	1	✓	✓	20	
Indian Lake St. Park W. 5 mi. N of Thompson	Indian Lake	8659	2		✓	40	
Palms Book St. Park 7 mi. NW of Thompson	Indian Lake	8659	2		✓	5	
Manistique River 1 mi. N of Manistique	Manistique R.		2			6	
Bass Lake 1 mi. S of Steuben	Bass Lake	293	3			2	
Boot Lake 4 mi. S of Shingleton	Boot Lake	121	3		✓	3	
Clear Lake 4 mi. N of Steuben	Clear Lake	109	3			2	
Colwell Lake 3 mi. N of Steuben	Colwell Lake	158	2		✓	8	
East Lake 2 mi. SE of Steuben	East Lake	54	3			2	
Iron Jaw Lake 5 mi. W of Steuben	Iron Jaw Lake	51	3			2	
Minerva Lake 3 mi. SW of Steuben	Minerva Lake	45	3			2	

	Body of water	Acres	Ramp class	Courtesy pier	Toilet	Parking spaces	Handicapper accessible
Nineteen Lake 4 mi. W of Steuben	Nineteen Lake	26	3			2	
Petes Lake 8 mi. NW of Steuben	Petes Lake	190	2		✓	5	
Steuben Lake 1 mi. NE of Steuben	Steuben Lake	150	3		✓	2	
Triangle Lake 2 mi. SW of Steuben	Triangle Lake	169	3		✓	2	

Chapter 5

CANOE LIVERIES

Canoeing provides one of the best ways to experience Michigan waters on winding seasonal creeks, tiny ponds, major rivers and large lakes. Depending on your mood, the weather, water conditions and location, you can paddle hard or relax, fish, drift with the current, reach remote areas or gain a different perspective on downtown city areas. Because the sections of most Michigan rivers served by liveries are generally easy-flowing, paddling usually is not strenuous, However, if you venture out for multi-day trips or choose more remote stretches, some portaging may be necessary due to log jams, dams, seasonally low water and other impediments.

Rental reservations are recommended, particularly for summer weekends and holidays. Check whether the operator charges an additional fee for dropping you off at the starting point or picking you up at the end. Some liveries charge lower rates for weekdays, and a majority offer group discounts. All rental canoes are required to undergo safety inspection and must be equipped with Coast Guard-approved safety cushions or life jackets. Before setting off, ask about picnic areas, campgrounds, toilets and drinking water along the route. Ask in advance what items you should bring, such as insect repellent, fishing tackle, suntan lotion, weather-appropriate clothing, hat and food.

If you're interested in buying a canoe, this chapter indicates those liveries that sell new ones. They and others may have used ones for sale as well.

Some liveries have rental kayaks, rafts or rowboats available as well as canoes. The listings indicate liveries that also offer tubes; for more details on tubing rentals, see Chapter 6 on tube float opportunities.

There is a Michigan company that offers canoe guide service for paddlers with physical, behavioral or cognitive disabilities. Quietwater Ventures Ltd. conducts one-day individual and small group trips along a winding stretch of the AuSable River in Huron National Forest between Comins Flats and Glennie. Participants have the option of paddling or riding as passengers in specially equipped canoes. There are stops along the route for photography, birdwatching, sightseeing and trout fishing. The outfitter provides adaptive paddles, portable toilets, a mobile radio and emergency medical supplies. Its guides are medical or rehabilitative professionals or paraprofessionals. Safety instructions are given before each trip begins. Cabins and a campground are available at the starting point. For more information, contact Quietwater Ventures, 601 Tawas St., East Tawas MI 48730. The phone number is (517) 362-3806.

For additional information on canoeing and liveries, write to the Recreational Canoeing Association, Box 668, Indian River MI 48749 or call (616) 238-7868.

CANOE LIVERIES

	Overnight/multiday trips	Kayaks	Rafts	Tubes'	Meal & trip packages	On-site camping	Sales
SOUTHEAST							
JACKSON COUNTY							
Twin Pines Campground & Canoe Livery						✓	✓
9590 Wheeler Road							
Hanover MI 49241							
(517) 524-6298							
Kalamazoo River							
May 1 - Nov. 1							
3-5 hours; 10-15 miles							
MONROE COUNTY							
River Raisin Canoe Livery	✓	✓	✓				✓
9300 Dixon Road							
Box 136							
Carleton MI 48117							
(313) 269-2004							
River Raisin							
Also rents paddleboats							
May - October							
2-8 hours; 6-25 miles							

	Overnight/multiday trips	Kayaks	Rafts	Tubes	Meal & trip packages	On-site camping	Sales
OAKLAND COUNTY							

Heavner Canoe Rental
2775 Garden Road
Milford MI 48381
(313) 685-2379
Huron River
Also at Island Lake State
Recreation Area
  April - October
  1-6 hours; 5-20 miles
	✓	✓					✓

Wolynski Canoe Rental
2300 Wixom Trail
Milford MI 48381
(313) 685-1851
Huron River
  May 1 - Oct. 31
  3-5 hours; 3-8 miles
	✓	✓					

WASHTENAW COUNTY							

Argo Canoe Livery
1055 Longshore Drive
Box 8647
Ann Arbor MI 48105
(313) 994-2778
Off-season (313) 994-2780
Huron River
Also rents rowboats
  April - October
  1½-5 hours; 4-17 miles
	✓						

Canoesport 940 N. Main St. Ann Arbor MI 48104 (313) 996-1393 Huron River Year round						✓	

119

	Overnight/multiday trips	Kayaks	Rafts	Tubes	Meal & trip packages	On-site camping	Sales
Gallup Canoe Livery 3000 Fuller Road Box 8647 Ann Arbor MI 48104 (313) 994-2778 Off-season (313) 994-2780 Huron River Also rents paddleboats April - October 1½-5 hours; 4-17 miles	✓						

SOUTHWEST

BERRIEN COUNTY

	Overnight/multiday trips	Kayaks	Rafts	Tubes	Meal & trip packages	On-site camping	Sales
Paw Paw River Campground & Canoe Livery 5355 M-140 Watervliet MI 49098 (616) 463-5454 Off-season (616) 463-3344 Paw Paw River Also rents rowboats January - November 1-24 hours	✓				✓	✓	

ST. JOSEPH COUNTY

	Overnight/multiday trips	Kayaks	Rafts	Tubes	Meal & trip packages	On-site camping	Sales
Mendon Country Inn 440 W. Main St. Box 98 Mendon MI 49072 (616) 496-8132 St. Joseph River & Nottawa Creek April - November 2-8 hours; 10-30 miles	✓						

	Overnight/multiday trips	Kayaks	Rafts	Tubes	Meal & trip packages	On-site camping	Sales

Three Rivers Canoe, Kayak & Tube Rental
55737 Buckhorn Road
Three Rivers MI 49093
(616) 279-9326
St. Joseph, Rocky, Portage, Prairie, Fawn
& White Pigeon Rivers
Also rents fishing boats
  Year round
  0-6 hours; 0-12 miles
	✓	✓		✓			

CENTRAL

BARRY COUNTY

	Overnight/multiday trips	Kayaks	Rafts	Tubes	Meal & trip packages	On-site camping	Sales

Indian Valley Campground & Canoe Livery
8200 108th St.
Middleville MI 49333
(616) 891-8579
Thornapple River
Also rents boats
  April 1 - Dec. 1
  2-6 hours; 9-18 miles
	✓	✓	✓	✓		✓	✓

Whispering Waters Campground & Canoe Livery
1805 N. Irving Road
Hastings MI 49058
(616) 945-5166
Thornapple River
  May - November
  2-8 hours; 5-20 miles
				✓		✓	

	Overnight/multiday trips	Kayaks	Rafts	Tubes	Meal & trip packages	On-site camping	Sales

IONIA COUNTY
Double "R" Ranch
M-44 & S. White Bridge Road
Smyrna MI 48887
(616) 794-0520
Flat River
  May - September
  2½-8 hours
						✓	

MECOSTA COUNTY
Sawmill Canoe & Tube Rental
230 Baldwin
Big Rapids MI 49307
(616) 796-6408
Muskegon River
  Year round
  1 hour - 7 days
	✓		✓	✓	✓		✓

NORTHEAST

	Overnight/multiday trips	Kayaks	Rafts	Tubes	Meal & trip packages	On-site camping	Sales

ALCONA COUNTY
Alcona Canoe Rentals Inc.
6351 Bamfield Road
Glennie MI 48737
(517) 735-2973; (800) 526-7080
AuSable River
Also rents rowboats
  April 1 - Oct. 1
  2½-7 hours; 12-32 miles
	✓		✓			✓	

	Overnight/multiday trips	Kayaks	Rafts	Tubes	Meal & trip packages	On-site camping	Sales
ARENAC COUNTY							
Cedar Springs Campground & Canoe Rental 334 Melita Road Sterling MI 48659 (517) 654-3195 Rifle River April 1 - Oct. 15 2½-6 hours; 11-36 miles	✓			✓		✓	
Rifle River AAA Canoe Rental & Campground 5825 W. Townline Road Sterling MI 48659 (517) 654-2556 Off-season (517) 654-2333 Rifle River iles April 1 - Nov. 1 2½-8 hours; 18-36 miles	✓			✓		✓	
Riverbend Campground & Canoe Rental 864 N. Main Omer MI 48749 (517) 653-2576 Rifle River May 1 - Oct. 30 3-6 hours; 10-30 miles				✓		✓	
Russell Canoes & Campgrounds 146 Carrington St. Omer MI 48749 (517) 653-2644 Rifle River April - October 2 hours-5 days; 7-110 miles	✓			✓		✓	

	Overnight/multiday trips	Kayaks	Rafts	Tubes	Meal & trip packages	On-site camping	Sales

White's Canoe Livery
400 Old M-70
Sterling MI 48659
(517) 654-2654
Rifle River
  April 15 - Oct. 15
  2½-7; 17-40 miles
	✓			✓		✓	

CHEBOYGAN COUNTY
Partners Canoe Rental
S. Black River Road
Onaway MI 49765
(517) 733-2877
Black River
  May 15 - Sept. 30
  1 hour-3 days
	✓	✓				✓	

Sturgeon & Pigeon River
  Outfitters
4271 S. Straits Highway
Indian River MI 49749
(616) 238-8181
Sturgeon & Pigeon Rivers
Also rents windsurfers
  May 1 - mid October
  1-8 hours; 3-24 miles
	✓	✓		✓	✓	✓	✓

Tomahawk Trails Canoe Liv.
E. M-68 at I-75
Box 814
Indian River MI 49749
(616) 238-8703
Sturgeon & Pigeon Rivers
  May 1 - Nov. 1
  1-8 hours; 2-28 miles
	✓	✓		✓	✓		

	Overnight/multiday trips	Kayaks	Rafts	Tubes	Meal & trip packages	On-site camping	Sales
CRAWFORD COUNTY							
AuSable Canoes 217 Alger Grayling MI 49738 (517) 348-5851 AuSable River April 1 - Oct. 15 2-5½ hours; 10-25 miles	✓				✓		
Carlisle Canoes 110 State St. Grayling MI 49738 (517) 348-2301 AuSable River April 1 - Oct. 15 2-5½ hours; 10-25 miles	✓				✓		
Penrod's AuSable Canoe Trips 100 Maple St. Box 432 Grayling MI 49738 (517) 348-2910 AuSable River April - October 2-5½ hours; 10-25 miles	✓	✓					
Wyandotte Canoe & Outfitters Ltd. 1320 McMasters Bridge Road Grayling MI 49738 (517) 348-8354 AuSable River April 1 - Nov. 30 1-240 hours; 4-200 miles	✓	✓			✓	✓	

	Overnight/multiday trips	Kayaks	Rafts	Tubes	Meal & trip packages	On-site camping	Sales
GLADWIN COUNTY							

Cedar River Canoe Co.
1862 River Road
Beaverton MI 48612
(517) 426-7611
Cedar River
  May - September
  3-6 hours; 16-28 miles
						✓	

Paddle Brave Campground
 & Canoe Livery
10610 Steckert Bridge Road
Roscommon MI 48653
(517) 275-5273
AuSable River
  May - November
  1-6 hours; 8-26 miles
	✓			✓		✓	

OGEMAW COUNTY							

Troll Landing Canoe Base
 & Campground
2660 Rifle River Trail
636 W. Greenwood Road
Alger MI 48610
(517) 345-7260
Rifle River
  April - Oct. 1
  2½ hours-3 days; 11-75 mi.
	✓	✓		✓		✓	

OSCODA COUNTY							

Gott's Landing Inc.
M-33
Box 441
Mio MI 48647
(517) 826-3411
AuSable River
  April - Oct. 31
  2½-9 hours; 10-32 miles
	✓		✓	✓			✓

	Overnight/multiday trips	Kayaks	Rafts	Tubes	Meal & trip packages	On-site camping	Sales
Hinchman Acres AuSable River Canoe Rental 702 N. M-33 Mio MI 48647 (517) 826-3267 AuSable River April 15 - Oct. 15 2½-7 hours; 10-32 miles	✓			✓			✓
ROSCOMMON COUNTY Hiawatha Canoe Livery 1113 Lake St. (M-118) Roscommon MI 48653 (517) 275-5213; (800) 736-5213 AuSable River April 1 - Nov. 1 1½ hours-6 days	✓			✓			
Watters Edge Canoe Livery 10799 Dana Drive Roscommon MI 48653 AuSable River (517) 275-5568 May 1 - Sept. 30 1-10 hours; 8-45 miles	✓			✓			

NORTHWEST

	Overnight/multiday trips	Kayaks	Rafts	Tubes	Meal & trip packages	On-site camping	Sales
ANTRIM COUNTY Swiss Hideaway Inc. Box 269, Route 1 Mancelona MI 49659 (616) 536-2341 Jordan River May - October 1-3 hours; 5-15 miles		✓		✓			

	Overnight/multiday trips	Kayaks	Rafts	Tubes	Meal & trip packages	On-site camping	Sales
BENZIE COUNTY							

Betsie River Canoes & Campground
13598 Lindy Road
Thompsonville MI 49683
(616) 378-2386
Betsie River
  June - Labor Day
  2-5 hours
	✓			✓		✓	

Riverside Canoe Trips
M-22
5042 Scenic Highway
Honor MI 49640
(616) 325-5622
Platte River
Also rents boats
 & paddleboards
  May 1 - Oct. 15
  2-4 hours; 5-20
		✓		✓			

Vacation Trailer Park
2080 Benzie Highway
Benzonia MI 48616
(616) 882-5101
Betsie River
  May - Sept. 15
  1½ hours - 3 days
	✓					✓	✓

GRAND TRAVERSE COUNTY
Ranch Rudolf
6841 Brown Bridge Road
Traverse City MI 49684
(616) 947-9529
Boardman River
  May - November
  1½-3½ hours; 4-9 miles
				✓		✓	

	Overnight/multiday trips	Kayaks	Rafts	Tubes	Meal & trip packages	On-site camping	Sales
Traverse City Kayak Adventures 335 S. Airport Road Traverse City MI 49684 (800) YOU-RENT; (616) 941-8445 Also rents sailboards & catamarans Year round 2½-10 hours		✓		✓			
KENT COUNTY Grand Rogue Campground, Canoe & Tube Livery 6400 W. River Drive Belmont MI 49306 (616) 362-1053 Grand & Rogue Rivers May 1 - Oct. 15 2-4 hours; 8-16 miles				✓		✓	
LAKE COUNTY Baldwin Canoe Rental Box 269, South M-37 Baldwin MI 48304 (616) 745-4669 Pere Marquette & Pine Rivers April - Oct. 30 2-6 hours; 8-30 miles	✓	✓	✓			✓	

	Overnight/multiday trips	Kayaks	Rafts	Tubes	Meal & trip packages	On-site camping	Sales
Ivan's Canoe Rental M-37 at Pere Marquette River Box 787 Baldwin MI 49304 (616) 745-3361 Off-season: (616) 898-3062 Pere Marquette River May 1 - Oct. 15 3-8 hours; 15-40 miles	✓		✓	✓			
LEELANAU COUNTY Cedar Canoe Rental 8995 Kasson St. Box 56 Cedar MI 49621 (616) 228-6480 Cedar River May 1 - Sept. 30 1-4 hours							
Crystal River Canoe Livery 6052 Western Ave. Box 133 Glen Arbor MI 49636 (616) 334-3090 Crystal River April - November 1-2½ hours; 3-8½ miles		✓					
MANISTEE COUNTY Pine Creek Lodge & Canoe Rental 13544 Caberfae Highway Wellston MI 49689 (616) 848-4431 Little & Big Manistee Rivers April - October; 2-26 miles	✓			✓		✓	✓

	Overnight/multiday trips	Kayaks	Rafts	Tubes	Meal & trip packages	On-site camping	Sales
MISSAUKEE COUNTY Chippewa Landing 3241 W. Houghton Lake Rd. Lake City MI 49651 (616) 839-5511 Big Manistee River April 15 - Oct. 15	✓					✓	
MUSKEGON COUNTY Happy Mohawk Canoe Livery 735 Fruitvale Road Montague MI 49437 (616) 894-4209 White River May 1 - Oct. 15 1-12 hours	✓		✓	✓			✓
NEWAYGO COUNTY Croton Dam Float Trips 5355 Croton Drive Croton Dam MI 49337 (616) 652-6037 May 1 - Oct. 31 Big Muskegon River May 1 - Oct. 31 2-4 hours; 8-16 miles				✓		✓	
Vic's Canoes, Tubes & Rafts Salmon Run Campground R.R. 2 Grant MI 49327 (616) 834-5495 Muskegon River April 15 - Oct. 1 1½-8 hours; 5-30 miles	✓		✓	✓		✓	✓

	Overnight/multiday trips	Kayaks	Rafts	Tubes	Meal & trip packages	On-site camping	Sales
OCEANA COUNTY River's Edge Campground & Canoes 5425 Webster Road Box 189 Holton MI 49425 (616) 821-2735 Off-season: (517) 835-3454 White River May 1 - Oct. 1 3-12 hours; 8-35 miles	✓	✓		✓		✓	
OSCEOLA COUNTY Old Log Resort 1070 M-115 at Muskegon Riv. Marion MI 49665 (616) 743-2775 Muskegon River April - Dec. 31 3 hours-5 days	✓	✓				✓	
WEXFORD COUNTY Carl's Canoe Livery 7603 W. 50 Mile Rd. Cadillac MI 49601 (616) 862-3471 Pine River Also rents boats May - October 2-5 hours	✓	✓					
Chippewa Landing 3241 W. Houghton Lake Rd. Lake City MI 49651 (616) 839-5511 Big Manistee River April 15 - Oct. 15	✓					✓	

	Overnight/multiday trips	Kayaks	Rafts	Tubes	Meal & trip packages	On-camping	Sales
Famous Jarolim Canoe Rntl. M-37 R.R. 1 Wellston MI 49689 (616) 862-3475 Pine River April - Nov. 1 2-5½ hours	✓						
Horina Canoe Rental Highway M-37 R.R. 1 Wellston MI 49689 (616) 862-3470 Pine River April 15 - Oct. 30 2-6 hours; 10-30 miles	✓						
Marrik's Canoe Service 7603 West 50 Mile Road Cadillac MI 49601 (616) 862-3471 Pine River Also rents boats May - October 2-5 hours; 5-22 miles	✓	✓					
Sportsman's Port Canoes & Campground M-55 1/2 mi. E of M-37 R.R. 1 Wellston MI 49689 (616) 862-3571 Pine River May 1 - Oct. 15 1-5 hours	✓					✓	✓

	Overnight/multiday trips	Kayaks	Rafts	Tubes	Meal & trip packages	On-site camping	Sales
Wilderness Canoe Trips 6052 Riverview Road Mesick MI 49668 (616) 879-4121 Big Manistee River April 1 - Nov. 1 2-7 hours; 10-37 miles	✓						

UPPER PENINSULA

LUCE COUNTY

	Overnight/multiday trips	Kayaks	Rafts	Tubes	Meal & trip packages	On-site camping	Sales
Two Hearted Canoe Trips Inc. Co. Road 423 at Mouth of Two Hearted River Box 386 Newberry MI 49868 (906) 658-3357 Two Hearted River Also rents rowboats Mid April - November 1½-6 hours; 3-13 miles	✓				✓	✓	

MARQUETTE COUNTY

	Overnight/multiday trips	Kayaks	Rafts	Tubes	Meal & trip packages	On-site camping	Sales
Cope's Canoe Livery 2461 US 41 West Ishpeming MI 49849 (906) 486-4132 All Marquette County rivers May 15 - Oct. 15					✓		

SCHOOLCRAFT COUNTY

	Overnight/multiday trips	Kayaks	Rafts	Tubes	Meal & trip packages	On-site camping	Sales
Big Cedar Campground Route M-77, Box 7 Germfask MI 49836 Off-season: (904) 465-2810 Fox & Manistique Rivers May 1 - Oct. 1 2½-4 hours; 7-15 miles	✓					✓	

	Overnight/multiday trips	Kayaks	Rafts	Tubes	Meal & trip packages	On-site camping	Sales
Northland Outfitters M-77 Box 65 Germfask MI 49836 (906) 586-9801 Fox & Manistique Rivers May 1 - Oct. 15 2-8 hours; 8-30 miles	✓	✓				✓	

MICHIGAN DEPARTMENT OF NATURAL RESOURCES

Chapter 6
TUBING LIVERIES

Tubing provides a lazy, lolling way to enjoy some of Michigan's slow-moving rivers including the Rifle, the Rouge, the AuSable and the Sturgeon. Some outfitters set a minimum age for tubing. Some of those without minimums might require children to wear life jackets, possibly at extra cost. All provide transportation for you and your tubes to the put-in point or from the take-out point.

These liveries rent, and sometimes also sell, tubes. The listing does not include liveries without tube rentals.

Of course, you're free to use your own tubes -- either those specially designed for recreational use or tire inner tubes -- and go out on your own from public access sites. Although in most instances you'll have to plan or arrange for transportation from the take-out spot, there is an oxbow section of the South Branch of the White River near Hesperia that makes it possible to start and end at the same campground. It's located at Pines Point Campground in the Manistee National Forest and provides a 30-40-minute tube float trip.

SOUTHWEST

KENT COUNTY
Grand Rogue Campground, Canoe
 & Tube Livery
6400 W. River Drive
Belmont MI 49306
(616) 361-1053

Grand & Rogue Rivers
May 1 - Oct. 15
1-2 hours; 1-4 miles
No minimum age

ST. JOSEPH COUNTY
Three Rivers Canoe, Kayak
 & Tube Rental
55737 Buckhorn Road
Three Rivers MI 49093
(616) 279-9326
St. Joseph, Fawn, Portage, Prairie,
Rocky & White Pigeon Rivers

6 local rivers
Year round
0-29 hours; 0-20 miles
No minimum age

CENTRAL

BARRY COUNTY
Indian Valley Campground & Livery
8200 108th
Middleville MI 49333
(616) 891-8579

Thornapple River
Apr. 1 - Dec. 1
1-3 hours; 1-6 miles
Minimum age: 10

MECOSTA COUNTY
Sawmill Canoe & Tube Rental
230 Baldwin
Big Rapids MI 49307
(616) 796-6408

Big Muskegon River
Year round
2 hours
No minimum age

NORTHEAST

ALCONA COUNTY
Alcona Canoe Rental Inc
6351 Bamfield Road
Glennie MI 48737
(517) 735-2973

AuSable River
May 1 - Oct. 1
1-3 hours; 3-12 miles
No minimum age

ARENAC COUNTY
Cedar Springs Campground, Canoe
 & Tube Rental
334 Melita Road
Sterling MI 48659
(517) 654-3195

Rifle River
April 1 - Oct. 15
1.5-5 hours; 3-17 miles
No minimum age

Rifle River AAA Canoe Rental
 & Campground
5825 W. Townline Road
Sterling MI 48659
(517) 654-2556
Off-season (517) 654-2333

Rifle River
April 1 - Nov. 1
2-9 hours
No minimum age

Riverbend Campground
 & Canoe Rental
864 N. Main
Omer MI 48749
(517) 653-2576

Rifle River
Starts in May
1-6 hours; 1-10 miles
Minimum age: 5

Russell Canoes & Campground
146 Carrington St.
Omer MI 48749
(517) 653-2644

Rifle River
May - September
1.5-4 hours; 3.5-10 miles
No minimum age

White's Canoe Livery
400 Old M-70
Sterling MI 48659
(517) 654-2654

Rifle River
Apr. 15 - Oct. 15
1.5-6 hours; 3-12 miles
No minimum age

CHEBOYGAN COUNTY
Sturgeon & Pigeon River Outfitters
4271 S. Straits Highway
Indian River MI 49749
(616) 238-8181

Sturgeon River
May 1 - Labor Day
1-3 hours; .5-3 miles
No minimum age

Tomahawk Trails Canoe Livery
East M-68 at I-75
Box 814
Indian River MI 49749
(616) 238-8703

Sturgeon River
May 1 - Sept. 15
1.5-2.5 hours; 2-3 miles
Minimum age: 5

CRAWFORD COUNTY
Paddle Brave Campground
 & Canoe Livery
10610 Steckert Bridge Road
Roscommon MI 48653
(517) 275-5273

AuSable River
May - October
1-5 hours
No minimum age

OGEMAW COUNTY
Troll Landing Canoe Base
 & Campground
2660 Rifle River Trail
636 W. Greenwood Road
Alger MI 48610
(517) 345-7260

Rifle River
April 1 - Oct. 1
1-3 hours; 2-6 miles
Minimum age: 6

OSCODA COUNTY
Gott's Landing Inc.
Box 441
Mio MI 48647
(517) 826-3411

AuSable River
May - September
2.5-4.5 hours; 10-22 miles
No minimum age

Hinchman Acres AuSable River
 Canoe Rental
702 N. M-33
Mio MI 48647
(517) 826-3267

AuSable River
May 15 - Sept. 15
4-9 hours; 10-22 miles
Minimum age: 6

139

ROSCOMMON COUNTY

Watters Edge Canoe Livery
10799 Dana Drive
Roscommon MI 48653
(517) 275-5568

AuSable River
Memorial Day - Labor Day
1-10 hours
No minimum age

NORTHWEST

ANTRIM COUNTY

Swiss Hideaway Inc.
Box 269, Route 1
Mancelona MI 49659
(616) 536-2341

Jordan River
May - August
1-3 hours; 5-10 miles
Minimum age: 8

BENZIE COUNTY

Betsie River Canoes & Campground
13598 Lindy Road
Thompsonville MI 49683
(616) 882-5622

Betsie River
June - Labor Day
2 hours
Minimum age: 5

Riverside Canoe Trips
M-22
5042 Scenic Highway
Honor MI 49640
(616) 325-5622

Platte River
May 1 - Oct. 15
1-2 hours; 1-3 miles
No minimum age

GRAND TRAVERSE COUNTY

Ranch Rudolf
6841 Brownbridge
Traverse City MI 49684
(616) 947-9529

Boardman River
June - October
1.5-3 hours; 2-4 miles
Minimum age: 8

MANISTEE COUNTY

Pine Creek Lodge & Canoe Rental
13544 Caberfae Highway
Wellston MI 49689
(616) 848-4431

Little & Big Manistee
April - October

MUSKEGON COUNTY

Happy Mohawk Canoe Livery
735 Fruitvale Road
Montague MI 49437
(616) 894-4209

White River
May 1 - Oct. 15
1-3 hours
No minimum age

NEWAYGO COUNTY

Croton Dam Float Trips
5355 Croton Drive
Croton Dam MI 49337
(616) 652-6037

Big Muskegon River
May 1 - Oct. 31
3-4 hours; 8 miles
Minimum age: 8

Vic's Canoes, Tubes & Rafts
Salmon Run Campground
R.R. 2
Grant MI 49327
(616) 834-5494

Muskegon River
Apr. 15 - Oct. 1
3 hours; 5 miles
No minimum age

OCEANA COUNTY

River's Edge Campground & Canoes
5425 Webster Road
Box 189
Holton MI 49425
(616) 821-2735

White River
June 15 - Sept. 15
1-3 hours; 2-10 miles
No minimum age

Chapter 7

WILD, SCENIC
& NATURAL RIVERS

Two programs -- one federal, the other state -- protect at least some of Michigan's approximately 120 rivers from development, economic exploitation and environmental degradation. These efforts help safeguard irreplaceable resources for recreational uses such as canoeing, kayaking, fishing and swimming. About 2,700 miles of river so far receive at least some type of governmental protection, hundreds of miles more are under consideration for inclusion in the programs. But the drive to protect them is not easy on either the federal or the state levels, with opposition coming from a variety of critics, including some adjoining property owners, developers and timber industry interests.

For recreational users, it's vital to remember that protected status from the government does not eliminate the private ownership rights of adjacent landowners. That means you must obtain the owners' permission for access.

WILD AND SCENIC RIVERS SYSTEM

Portions of the Pere Marquette and Au Sable Rivers in the northern part of the Lower Peninsula were the first in Michigan to be designated by Congress as part of the Wild and Scenic River system. Then in early 1992, following a two-year legislative battle, Congress added sections of 14 others. Among the additions, 520 miles are permanently wild and scenic; the other 472 miles are temporarily protected, and the U.S. Forest Service must decide within three years whether to grant them permanent wild and scenic status. Together they give Michigan more federally protected river miles than any other state except Alaska and Oregon.

Congress created the national system in 1968. It now covers parts of 123 rivers in 33 states. Designation might not include an entire river but may cover its tributaries. Here's how the U.S. Department of the Interior classifies the rivers:

• Wild rivers: free of impoundments, with essentially primitive watersheds or shorelines and with unpolluted waters. Generally inaccessible.
• Scenic rivers: free of impoundments and have largely undeveloped shorelines and watersheds Accessible in spots by road.
• Recreational rivers: some shoreline development and may have undergone past impoundment or diversion. Readily accessible by road or railroad.

These rivers are now part of the wild and scenic system:

LOWER PENINSULA

Au Sable River
Bear Creek
Manistee River
Pere Marquette River
Pine River

UPPER PENINSULA

Black River
Carp River
Indian River
Ontonagon River
Paint River
Presque Isle River
Sturgeon River
Tahquamenon River
White Fish River
Yellow Dog River

The Forest Service study covers parts of the Presque Isle, Onto-nagon, Paint, Sturgeon, Brule, White Fish, Tahquamenon and Carp Rivers in the Upper Peninsula, and sections of the Little Manistee and White Rivers in the Lower Peninsula

MICHIGAN NATURAL RIVERS PROGRAM

Michigan's Natural Rivers program was established by the Legislature in 1970. Rivers designated by the state Natural Resources Commission, including selected tributaries, become subject to long-range management plans developed by municipal governments, local citizens and the Department of Natural Resources.

Regulation is carried out primarily by "natural river district" zoning, either by local governments along the shoreline or by the state. Zoning restrictions concern such matters as requiring a natural vegetation strip along the shore and setting minimum lot width and building setback requirements. They also prohibit commercial and industrial uses and forbid alteration of stream channels.

So far, the Natural Resources Commission has designated parts of 14 rivers in the Lower and Upper Peninsula as entitled to zoning protection. Portions of 25 other rivers have been proposed for the program.

Three classes of rivers are covered, and different parts of the same river may be in different categories. Each segment must be at least 10 miles long. Here's how DNR describes the classifications:

- **Wilderness rivers:** Free flowing, with primarily primitive and undeveloped land along their shores. Remote.

- **Wild-scenic river:** Wild, forested borders and located near development. Moderately accessible.

- **Country-scenic:** Located in agricultural areas with pastoral borders and homes nearby. Readily accessible.

The length of each river includes the protected tributaries, which also are listed.

**Protected
length**

SOUTHEAST/CENTRAL

Huron River   Washtenaw, Livingston Counties   39 miles

Tributaries: Davis Creek, Arms Creek & Mill Creek

SOUTHWEST

Rogue River   Kent County   132 miles

Tributaries: Spring Creek, Cedar Creek, Duke
Creek, Stegman Creek, Rum Creek, Shaw Creek
& Barkley Creek

Lower Kalamazoo River   Allegan County   55 miles

Tributaries: Rabbit River, Bear Creek, Sand
Creek, Swan Creek & Mann Creek

SOUTHWEST/CENTRAL

Flat River   Kent, Montcalm, Ionia Counties   109 miles

Tributaries: West Branch, Clear Creek, Coopers
Creek, Dickerson Creek & Wabasis Creek

NORTHEAST

Au Sable River   Crawford, Oscoda, Otsego
Roscommon, Montmorency,
Iosco & Alcona Counties   349 miles

Tributaries: Kolka Creek, Bradford Creek,

East Branch, South Branch, South Creek,
East Creek, Hudson Creek, Robinson Creek,
Beaver Creek, Douglas Creek, Thayer Creek,
North Branch, Chub Creek,Turtle Creek, West
Branch of Big Creek, East Branch of Big Creek,
Sohn Creek, Big Creek, Wolf Creek, Loud
Creek, Perry Creek, Comins Creek, Glennie
Creek, Nine Mile Creek & Blockhouse Creek

Pigeon River	Otsego, Cheboygan Counties	80 miles

Tributaries: All

Rifle River	Ogemaw, Arenac Counties	110 miles

Tributaries: Gamble Creek, Vaughn Creek,
Oyster Creek, Mayhue Creek, Houghton Creek
Wilkins Creek, Prior Creek, Klacking Creek,
Little Klacking Creek, Dedrich Creek, West Branch,
Eddy Creek, Silver Creek, Mansfield Creek
& Fritz Creek

NORTHWEST

Betsie River	Benzie, Manistee Counties	70 miles

Tributaries: Little Betsie River, Dair Creek

Boardman River	Grand Traverse Kalkaska Counties	88 miles

Tributaries: North Branch, South Branch, Beitner
Creek, Jaxson Creek, Swainston Creek, Jackson
Creek, East Creek, Parker Creek, Bancroft Creek,
Carpenter Creek, Twenty Two Creek, Taylor Creek,
Crofton Creek   & Failing Creek

Jordan River	Antrim, Charlevoix Counties	73 miles

Tributaries: Bennett Creek, Todd Creek,

147

Bartholomew Creek, Severance Creek, Webster
Creek, Lilak Creek, Martin Creek, Mill Creek,
Sutton Creek, Kocker Creek, Scott Creek, Tutstone
Creek, Green Creek, Stevens Creek, Landslide
Creek, Cascade Creek, Section 13 Creek, Six Tile
Creek, Five Tile Creek & all other tributaries
upstream of Rogers Bridge

Pere Marquette River   Lake, Mason, Oceana
                            Muskegon Counties   206 miles

Tributaries: Sweetwater Creek, Kinney Creek,
Danaher Creek, Baldwin River, Cole Creek,
North Branch of Cole Creek, South Branch of
Cole Creek, Bray Creek, Sandborn Creek,
Leverentz Creek, Middle Branch, Blood Creek,
Little South Branch, Swan Creek, Weldon Creek,
Big South Branch, Carr Creek, Cedar Creek
& Ruby Creek

White River   Oceana, Newaygo,
                           Muskegon Counties   163 miles

Tributaries: Mullen Creek, Five Mile Creek,
Flinton Creek, Wrights Creek, Mena Creek,
Martin Creek, East Branch of Heald Creek,
Braton Creek, Cushman Creek, Skeels Creek,
North Branch, Robinson Creek, Cobmoosa
Creek, Newman Creek, Knutson Creek, Sand
Creek, Carlton Creek, Mud Creek, Lanford Creek,
Silver Creek & Cleveland Creek

UPPER PENINSULA

Fox River   Schoolcraft, Luce
                           Alger Counties   109 miles

Tributaries: Casey Creek, West Branch, Little
Fox, Hudson Creek, East Branch, Clear Creek,
Camp Seven Creek, Cold Creek, Spring Creek,
Deer Creek & Bev Creek

Two Hearted River   Luce County   115 miles

Tributaries: North Branch, West Branch,
South Branch, Dawson Creek & East Branch

Chapter 8

FISHING

Fishing is big recreation and big business in Michigan. Each year, the Department of Natural Resources sells an average of 1.2 million annual fishing licenses to residents, nonresidents and seniors. More than 300,000 of those anglers also obtain trout stamps. In addition, each year DNR sells approximately 275,000 one-day permits and 70,000 sportsperson's licenses, which provide a combination of fishing and hunting privileges.

This chapter covers state fish hatcheries, commercial game fish breeders and the Department of Natural Resources Master Angler Program. See Chapter 11 for charter boat operators who cater to fishing parties.

STATE FISH HATCHERIES

The Department of Natural Resources operates six fish hatcheries that produce a variety of species for release, or planting, into Michigan's lakes and rivers. The hatcheries are an essential part of the state's commitment to quality fishing experiences for its residents and for visitors.

Hatcheries are open to the public for free self-guided tours from 8 a.m. to 4:30 p.m. Typically, you'll be able to see such fish-raising features as incubation rooms, indoor rearing tanks and outdoor rearing raceways. Depending on the time of your visit, you may also be able to watch the feeding process and the loading of fish from the raceways onto trucks by hand or by pump.

SOUTHWEST

VAN BUREN COUNTY
Wolf Lake State Fish Hatchery
34270 C.R. 652
Mattawan MI 49071   (616) 668-3388

Main species: northern pike, Atlantic salmon, rainbow trout, tiger muskellunge, chinook salmon, sturgeon, Montana grayling, muskellunge, walleye, brown trout, channel catfish. It produces 3.5 million fish a year.

The Wolf Lake facility includes a free museum that depicts the history of fisheries in Michigan, the commercial fishing industry, the sea lamprey invasion of the Great Lakes, fishing gear and some record-breaking specimens. The Michigan Room shows dioramas of various fish habitats in the state, such as warm water and trout streams. There are three-dimensional Great Lake charts. Also, there are audio-visual programs about fisheries management and hatcheries operations. The museum is closed Mondays and Tuesdays.

NORTHWEST

BENZIE COUNTY
Platte River State Fish Hatchery
15210 US 31
Beulah MI 49617   (616) 325-4611

Main species: Coho salmon, chinook salmon. The state's largest hatchery, it raises 7 million to 8 million young salmon each year.

EMMET COUNTY
Oden State Fish Hatchery
3377 1/2 Oden Road
Oden MI 49764   (616) 347-4689

Main species: Rainbow trout, brown trout. It produces 1 million to 2 million trout each year.

WEXFORD COUNTY
Harrietta State Fish Hatchery
6801 Thirty Mile Road
Harrietta MI 49638   (616) 389-2211

Main species: Rainbow trout, brown trout.

UPPER PENINSULA

MARQUETTE COUNTY
Marquette State Fish Hatchery
488 Cherry Creek Road
Marquette MI 49855   (906) 249-1611

Main species: Lake trout, brook trout, splake. It produces 1.7 million fish each year.

SCHOOLCRAFT COUNTY
Thompson State Fish Hatchery
Rte. 2, Box 2555
Manistique MI 49854   (906) 341-5587

Main species: Rainbow trout, brown trout, chinook salmon, walleye. It raises 1 million trout, 16 million walleye and 500,000 salmon each year.

GAME FISH BREEDERS

For a variety of reasons, aquaculture -- commercial fish farming -- is growing in popularity in Michigan. It provides a non-traditional alternative crop for some farmers, and researchers at Michigan State University, the U.S. Department of Agriculture's North Central Regional Aquaculture Center in East Lansing and elsewhere are working to develop new information to make such ventures more feasible, more professional and more economically profitable. In general, game fish breeders offer fee fishing, planting stock, dressed fish or a combination of such services. Some offer additional services, such as smoked fish.

In these listings, the county is the one where the breeder's principal ponds are located, even if the breeder's offices are elsewhere.

	Species	Fee fishing	Planting stock	Dressed fish

SOUTHEAST

LAPEER COUNTY

Imlay City Fish Farm Inc. 1442 N. Summers Road Imlay City MI 48444 (313) 724-2185	All species		✓	

OAKLAND COUNTY

James H. Cash 56555 11 Mile Road New Hudson MI 48165 (313) 437-1266	Bass, bluegill & sunfish		✓	

WASHTENAW COUNTY

Spring Valley Trout Farm 12190 Island Lake Road Dexter MI 48130 (313) 426-4772	Rainbow trout, bass, channel catfish & hybrid sunfish	✓	✓	✓

SOUTHWEST

BERRIEN COUNTY

Bob-a-Ron Campground 7650 Warren Woods Road Three Oaks MI 49128 (616) 469-3894	Bass, bluegill, perch & channel catfish	✓		
Jones Catfish Farms 9450 N. Branch Road Watervliet MI 49098 (616) 463-3575	Channel catfish, crappie, bluegill & sunfish	✓	✓	✓
Oronoko Lakes 1788 E. Snow Road Berrien Springs MI 49103 (616) 471-7389	Bass, bluegill, walleye & channel catfish	✓		

	Species	Fee fishing	Planting stock	Dressed fish
KALAMAZOO COUNTY				
Moose Miller's Hybrid Bluegills 5695 N. 2d St. Kalamazoo MI 49009 (616) 375-4308	Bluegill		✓	
OTTAWA COUNTY				
Bay Port Aquaculture Systems 16990 Croswell West Olive MI 49460 (616) 399-3520	Yellow perch		✓	✓
Jack's Fish Farm 14671 120th Ave. Grand Haven MI 49417 (616) 846-5844	Bass, bluegill, walleye, trout catfish, perch & northern pike		✓	✓
Robinson Trout Farm 12090 N. Cedar Grand Haven MI 49417 (616) 842-6976	Rainbow & brook trout	✓	✓	✓

CENTRAL

	Species	Fee fishing	Planting stock	Dressed fish
BAY COUNTY				
Gene's Fish and Bait Farm 1515 11 Mile Road Linwood MI 48634 (517) 879-5453	Rainbow trout, bass, northern pike, bluegill, perch & channel catfish	✓	✓	✓
Perch Research International 2301 W. Mt. Forest Road Bentley MI 48613 (517) 879-3522	Perch, bluegill, sunfish, fathead bullhead, rosie red, golden shiner & calico		✓	✓

	Species	Fee fishing	Planting stock	Dressed fish
MECOSTA COUNTY Aqua Springs 19465 200th Ave. Big Rapids MI 49307 (616) 796-2284	Rainbow, brook & brown trout; northern pike, yellow perch, walleye, bluegill bass, catfish	✓	✓	✓
MONTCALM COUNTY Springwater Trout Farms Inc. 6768 Whitefish Road Howard City MI 49329 (616) 937-5862	Brook trout		✓	✓

NORTHEAST

	Species	Fee fishing	Planting stock	Dressed fish
ALCONA COUNTY Cedarbrook Trout Hatchery & Farm 1543 Lakeshore Drive Harrisville MI 48740 (5170 724-5241	Rainbow, brook & brown trout	✓	✓	✓
CHEBOYGAN COUNTY Spring Valley Farm 17364 Trowbridge Road Wolverine MI 49799 (616) 525-8626	Rainbow trout		✓	
CRAWFORD COUNTY River Park Campground & Trout Pond Box 185 Grayling MI 49738 (616) 348-9092	Trout	✓		

	Species	Fee fishing	Planting stock	Dressed fish
GLADWIN COUNTY Blue Springs Fish Factory 3840 Buzzell Road Gladwin MI 48624 (517) 426-4352	Rainbow & brook trout	✓	✓	✓
IOSCO COUNTY The Fish Specialist Box 333 Tawas City MI 48764 (517) 362-5118	Bass, perch & bluegill	✓	✓	✓
OGEMAW COUNTY Berg's Fish Farm 675 Oyster Road Rose City MI 48654 (517) 685-2340	Rainbow, brook & brown trout; hybrid bluegill,, bass, northern pike & walleye	✓	✓	✓
Rose City Trout Farms 2646 Townline Road Rose City MI 48654 (517) 685-2200	Rainbow, brown & brook trout; walleye, bass & hybrid bluegill		✓	
West Branch Trout Farm 2585 Rau Road West Branch MI 48661 (517) 345-7219	Brook, brown & rainbow trout; & hybrid bluegill	✓	✓	✓

NORTHWEST

	Species	Fee fishing	Planting stock	Dressed fish
ANTRIM COUNTY Pleasant Valley Trout Farm Kidder Road, Box 274 East Jordan MI 49727 (6160 536-2681	Rainbow trout		✓	

	Species	Fee fishing	Planting stock	Dressed fish
KALKASKA COUNTY Flowing Well Trout Farm 1529 Flowing Well Road Kalkaska MI 49646 (616) 258-2888	Rainbow, brook & brown trout	✓	✓	✓
MASON COUNTY Branch Trout Fishing Resort 1851 N. Tyndall Branch MI 49402 (616) 898-3178	Rocky mountain rainbow trout	✓	✓	✓
MUSKEGON COUNTY Michillinda Trout Ranch 3251 Michillinda Road Whitehall MI 49461 (616) 894-6175	Brook, brown, rainbow trout; catfish, bass bluegill & walleye	✓	✓	✓
NEWAYGO COUNTY Stoney Creek Trout Farms 11073 Peach Ave. Grant MI 49327 (800) 448-3873	Rainbow, brook, brown trout; perch, walleye,, catfish, hybrid bluegill & bass		✓	
OSCEOLA COUNTY Forest Fish Farm 9560 N. River Road Evart MI 49631 (616) 734-3107	Trout	✓	✓	✓
WEXFORD COUNTY Harietta Hills Trout Farm 1681 S. 7 1/2 Road Harietta MI 49638 (616) 389-2514	Rainbow trout		✓	

	Species	Fee fishing	Planting stock	Dressed fish
Northern Trout & Wildlife Farms 1172 E. 14 Road Manton MI 49663 (616) 824-6396 (616) 824-6916	Brook, brown rainbow trout, Atlantic salmon & grayling	✓	✓	✓

UPPER PENINSULA

CHIPPEWA COUNTY

Barbeau Farms Kurtis Road Barbeau MI 49710 (906) 647-7721	Rainbow trout & kamaloop		✓	✓

GOGEBIC COUNTY

Watersmeet Trout Hatchery Box 216 Watersmeet MI 49969 (906) 358-4331	Rainbow, brook & brown trout	✓	✓	✓

MASTER ANGLER PROGRAM

The Department of Natural Resources operates a Master Angler program that awards certificates for catching state-record fish or one of the top five fish of its kind for the year. Fish must be weighed on inspected scales; the signature of two witnesses and pictures must be submitted. Winners receive arm patches.

Eligible species are: largemouth bass; smallmouth bass; white bass; rock bass; warmouth bass; green sunfish; bluegill; pumpkinseed sunfish; redear sunfish; hybrid sunfish; white crappie; black crappie; walleye; sauger; perch; Great Lakes muskellunge; northern muskellunge; tiger muskellunge; northern pike; channel catfish; flathead catfish; brown bullhead; black bullhead; yellow bullhead; burbot; gar; lake sturgeon; Atlantic salmon; chinook salmon; coho salmon;

pink salmon; rainbow trout (steelhead); smelt; largemouth buffalo; brown trout; brook trout; lake trout; splake; bowfin (dogfish); redhorse sucker; white sucker; longnose sucker; hog sucker; carpsucker; carp; freshwater drum; lake whitefish; Menominee whitefish; lake herring cisco; mooneye; and American eel.

Applications are available through DNR offices or the DNR Fisheries Division, Box 30028, Lansing MI 48909. The Fisheries Division can be reached at (517) 373-1280.

FISHING SHOWS

A number of combined boating and fishing shows are listed in Chapter 28, but the annual Greater Detroit Sportfishing Expo classifies itself as the largest "pure" fishing show in the state. Exhibitors include manufacturers, retailers, outfitters, guides and fishing lodges, and there are dozens of seminars, flyfishing demonstrations and other activities. The show takes place at the Palace of Auburn Hills in conjunction with the Oakland County Sportfishing Association.

For more information, write to the producer of the show, Expositions Inc., Box 550, Edgewater Branch, Cleveland OH 44107-0550 or call (216) 529-1300.

The Michigan Flyfishing Expo bills itself as the nation's largest flyfishing show. Its exhibits, collectibles and tackle manufacturers' displays are limited to flyfishing. It's held at the Southfield Civic Center

For more information, contact the sponsor, the Michigan Flyfishing Club, at Box 530113, Livonia MI 48153.

NATIONAL TROUT FESTIVAL

The small village of Kalkaska is home to the National Trout Memorial and host to the annual National Trout Festival. You'll find the memorial -- a 17-foot-high brook trout -- on US 131, along with a lighted fountain and Michigan exhibits. The Kalkaska area boasts 400 miles of rivers and trout streams and more than 165,000 acres of state land for public recreation.

For more information, write to the Kalkaska Chamber of Commerce, Box 291, Kalkaska MI 49646 or call (616) 258-9103.

FISHERIES RESEARCH

Michigan is a national leader in fisheries research for sport, commercial fishing and aquaculture. If you're interested in fisheries research, contact:

- Department of Fisheries and Wildlife, Natural Resources Building, Michigan State University, East Lansing MI 48834 or call (517) 355-4477.

  The department teaches courses and conducts research in wildlife ecology and management; conservation biology; fisheries ecology and management; aquaculture; and environmental toxicology.

- North Central Regional Aquaculture Center, U.S. Department of Agriculture, 13 Natural Resources Building, Michigan State University, East Lansing MI 48824 or call (517) 353-1222.

  The center serves 12 Midwest states as one of five regional centers across the country set up to promote the aquaculture industry. The center conducts an aquaculture extension program, conducts market and economic surveys, works on improving the culture technology for individual species of fish, coordinates regional conferences and issues publications.

- Michigan Sea Grant College Program has two locations: 334 Natural Resources Building, Michigan State University, East Lansing MI 48824 or call (517) 353-9568; and 2200 Bonisteel Blvd., University of Michigan, Ann Arbor MI 48109 or call (313) 764-1138.

  The Sea Grant Program supports university-based basic and applied research on biological, physical, societal and economic issues related to Great Lakes resources; provides outreach services to transfer research results and other information to coastal communities and businesses; and promotes marine education, including financial support for college students and development of marine curricula for public schools. Many of its activities involve recreational and commercial fishing, diving safety, commercial shipping, recreational boating and environmental protection.

- Institute for Fisheries Research, Department of Natural Resources, University Museums Annex, Ann Arbor MI 48109 or call (313) 663-3554.

  The institute conducts research on a variety of fisheries topics.

Chapter 9

SCUBA DIVING

Scuba diving is one of America's fastest-growing sports, and the Great Lakes region is an increasingly popular destination for divers, both from around the United States and abroad. For divers, the biggest attraction is the wealth of well-preserved shipwrecks in Lakes Michigan, Huron and Superior, together with old dock sites along the shores. Many of the known wrecks are located within Michigan's system of nine Great Lakes underwater preserves, which are detailed in the next chapter, Chapter 10.

The St. Clair River linking Lake St. Clair to Lake Huron is another favorite dive destination, especially along the stretch of river between Port Huron, Mich., and Sarnia, Ont. Divers also frequently explore the state's inland waters, including Higgins, Gull, Brockway, Murray, Heart and Baw Beese Lakes, Hardy Pond, Inland Quarry and the Boardman River. The waters around Isle Royale National Park in Lake Superior are the final resting area for a number of doomed ships.

And with the state's historic reliance on shipping and its strategic location along the Great Lakes, new discoveries are not unusual. Divers locate the previously unknown wrecks of ships in and out of the preserve areas. For example, there was the recent discovery in the East Arm of Grand Traverse Bay of lumber, pilings, railroad tracks, a wagon wheel and other artifacts from the Cobbs & Mitchell loading dock, which served the timbering industry from about 1885 to 1905. And the tug *Sport*, which sank in Lake Huron near Lexington in 1920, remained undiscovered until 1987.

All the dive shops listed in this chapter are open year-round unless otherwise indicated. They offer a variety of services including certified instruction, equipment rental and sales, air and dive-related trips and expeditions. Some also provide special activities, such as dive-ins, treasure hunts and presentations about wrecks, underwater safety and world travel. You'll find charter boats that cater to divers listed

	Air	Sales	Rentals	Repairs	Instruction	Offer charters	Arrange charters	Dive travel services
SOUTHEAST								
JACKSON COUNTY								
Divers Mast 2900 Lansing Ave. Jackson MI 49202 (517) 784-5862; (800) 52D-IVER	✓	✓	✓	✓	✓		✓	✓
MACOMB COUNTY								
Advanced Aquatics Diving Inc. 25020 E. Jefferson St. Clair Shores MI 48080 (313) 779-8777	✓	✓	✓	✓	✓		✓	✓
Bruno's Dive Shop Inc. 34740 Gratiot Mt. Clemens MI 48043 (313) 792-2040	✓	✓	✓	✓	✓	✓	✓	✓
Macomb Dive Shop Ltd. 28869 Bunert Warren MI 48093 (313) 774-0640	✓	✓	✓	✓	✓	✓	✓	✓
Sea-Side Dive Shop Inc. 28612 Harper St. Clair Shores MI 48081 (313) 772-7676	✓	✓	✓	✓	✓	✓	✓	✓
OAKLAND COUNTY								
Diver's Den 604 S. Lapeer Lake Orion MI 48362 (313) 693-9801	✓	✓	✓	✓	✓	✓	✓	✓

	Air	Sales	Rentals	Repairs	Instruction	Offer charters	Arrange charters	Dive travel services
Pro Scuba Center 4395 Dixie Highway Waterford MI 48329 (313) 674-3483	✓	✓	✓	✓	✓		✓	✓
Recreational Diving Systems Inc. 4424 N. Woodward Royal Oak MI 48073 (313) 549-0303	✓	✓	✓	✓	✓	✓	✓	✓
Underwater Outfitters 2579 Union Lake Road Commerce Township MI 48382 (313) 363-2224	✓	✓	✓	✓	✓		✓	✓
U.S. Scuba Center 3260 S. Rochester Road Rochester MI 48307 (313) 853-2800	✓	✓	✓	✓	✓		✓	✓
ST. CLAIR COUNTY Tom & Jerry Scuba 8655 Dixie Fair Haven MI 48023 (313) 725-1991	✓	✓	✓	✓	✓	✓	✓	✓
WASHTENAW COUNTY Divers Inc. 3380 Washtenaw Ave. Ann Arbor MI 48104 (313) 971-7770	✓	✓	✓	✓	✓		✓	✓
Ocean Technology Group 254 Wagner Rd. South Box 2797-HP Ann Arbor MI 48106 (313) 996-8888	✓	✓			✓		✓	✓

	Air	Sales	Rentals	Repairs	Instruction	Offer charters	Arrange charters	Dive travel services
Divers Incorporated 3380 Washtenaw Ave. Ann Arbor MI 48104 (313) 971-7770	✓	✓	✓	✓	✓		✓	✓
WAYNE COUNTY Divers Incorporated 42295 Ann Arbor Road Plymouth MI 48170 (313) 451-5430	✓	✓	✓	✓	✓		✓	✓
Don's Dive Shop Inc. 29480 W. 10 Mile Road Farmington Hills MI 48024 (313) 477-7333	✓	✓	✓	✓	✓		✓	✓
Michigan Underwater School of Diving 3280 Fort St. Lincoln Park MI 48146 (313) 388-1322	✓	✓	✓	✓	✓	✓		✓
Tom & Jerry Scuba & Sport 20318 Van Born Dearborn Heights MI 48127 (313) 278-1124	✓	✓	✓	✓	✓	✓	✓	✓

SOUTHWEST

ALLEGAN COUNTY

	Air	Sales	Rentals	Repairs	Instruction	Offer charters	Arrange charters	Dive travel services
Ocean Sands Scuba 780 S. Columbia Ave. Holland MI 49423 (616) 396-0068	✓	✓	✓	✓	✓	✓	✓	✓

	Air	Sales	Rentals	Repairs	Instruction	Offer charters	Arrange charters	Dive travel services
BERRIEN COUNTY Michiana Scuba 301 E. Main St. Niles MI 49120 (616) 683-4502	✓	✓	✓	✓	✓		✓	✓
Wolf's Divers Supply Inc. 250 W. Main St. Benton Harbor MI 49022 (616) 926-1068	✓	✓	✓	✓	✓			✓
CALHOUN COUNTY Sub-Aquatic Sports & Service 347 N. Helmer Rd. Battle Creek MI 49015 (616) 968-8551	✓	✓	✓	✓	✓		✓	✓
KALAMAZOO COUNTY Adventures in Diving 1411 Nassau Kalamazoo MI 49001 (616) 381-9220				✓	✓		✓	✓
Dive Site 9125 Portage Road Kalamazoo MI 49002 (616) 323-3700	✓	✓	✓	✓	✓	✓		✓
KENT COUNTY A & C Diving Academy 4280 Plainfield Ave. NE Grand Rapids MI 49505-1612 (616) 363-7711	✓	✓	✓	✓	✓		✓	✓
Great Lakes Dive Locker 4909 S. Division Ave. Wyoming MI 49548 (616) 531-9440	✓	✓	✓	✓	✓		✓	✓

	Air	Sales	Rentals	Repairs	Instruction	Offer charters	Arrange charters	Dive travel services
Skamt Shop 5055 Plainfield NE Grand Rapids MI 49505 (616) 364-8418	✓	✓	✓	✓	✓	✓		✓
OTTAWA COUNTY Spring Lake Divers' Den Inc. 915 W. Savidge Spring Lake MI 49456 (616) 842-4300	✓	✓	✓	✓	✓		✓	✓

CENTRAL

	Air	Sales	Rentals	Repairs	Instruction	Offer charters	Arrange charters	Dive travel services
BAY COUNTY Deep Six Scuba Schools 884 N. Pine Road Essexville MI 48732 (517) 892-2715	✓	✓	✓	✓	✓		✓	✓
GENESEE COUNTY The Dive Shop Inc. G-4020 Corunna Road Flint MI 48532 (313) 732-3900	✓	✓	✓	✓	✓		✓	✓
INGHAM COUNTY ZZ UnderWater World 1806 E. Michigan Ave. Lansing MI 48912 (517) 485-3894	✓	✓	✓	✓	✓		✓	✓
MIDLAND COUNTY Seaquatics Inc. 5027 Eastman Ave. Midland MI 48640 (517) 835-6391	✓	✓	✓	✓	✓	✓	✓	✓

	Air	Sales	Rentals	Repairs	Instruction	Offer charters	Arrange charters	Dive travel services
SANILAC COUNTY Four Fathoms Diving 7320 Main St. Box 219 Sandusky MI 48471 (313) 622-8013	✓	✓	✓	✓	✓		✓	✓

NORTHEAST

	Air	Sales	Rentals	Repairs	Instruction	Offer charters	Arrange charters	Dive travel services
ALPENA COUNTY Summit Sports 224 E. Chisholm Alpena MI 49707 (517) 356-1182	✓	✓	✓	✓	✓			
Thunder Bay Divers 160 E. Fletcher Alpena MI 49707 (517) 356-9336	✓	✓	✓	✓	✓	✓		✓

ROSCOMMON COUNTY
The Scuba Shack Inc.
9982 W. Higgins Lake Drive
Higgins Lake MI 48627
(517) 821-6477
  Open: Apr. 15 - Oct. 15
  Off-season: Box 213
  Higgins Lake MI 48627
	✓	✓	✓	✓	✓			✓

NORTHWEST

	Air	Sales	Rentals	Repairs	Instruction	Offer charters	Arrange charters	Dive travel services
GRAND TRAVERSE COUNTY Great Lakes Scuba 2187 N. US 31 South Traverse City MI 49684 (616) 946-1602	✓	✓	✓	✓	✓	✓		✓

	Air	Sales	Rentals	Repairs	Instruction	Offer charters	Arrange charters	Dive travel services
LEELANAU COUNTY Scuba North Inc. 13380 W. Bayshore Drive Traverse City MI 49684 (616) 947-2520	✓	✓	✓	✓	✓	✓	✓	✓
MASON COUNTY Rod's Reef 3134 W. Johnson Road Ludington MI 49431 (616) 843-8688	✓	✓	✓	✓	✓	✓		✓
MUSKEGON COUNTY West Michigan Dive Center Inc. 2367 W. Sherman Muskegon MI 49441 (616) 755-3771	✓	✓	✓	✓	✓		✓	✓

UPPER PENINSULA

	Air	Sales	Rentals	Repairs	Instruction	Offer charters	Arrange charters	Dive travel services
ALGER COUNTY Grand Island Charters 410 Mill St. Munising MI 49862 (906) 387-4477 Open: May - October	✓		✓		✓	✓		
CHIPPEWA COUNTY Superior Coast Inc. Box 39 Paradise MI 49768 (906) 492-3445 Open: May - November	✓							

	Air	Sales	Rentals	Repairs	Instruction	Offer charters	Arrange charters	Dive travel services
DELTA COUNTY								
Dive Shop of Escanaba	✓	✓	✓	✓	✓			
2220 6th Ave. N.								
Escanaba MI 49829								
(906) 786-3483								
DICKINSON COUNTY								
City Sales Co.	✓							
809 Lake Antoine Road								
Iron Mountain MI 49801								
(906) 774-3555								
HOUGHTON COUNTY								
Narcosis Corner Divers	✓	✓	✓	✓		✓		
474 Third St.								
Calumet MI 49913								
(906) 337-3156								
MACKINAC COUNTY								
Diver Down Scuba Shop Inc.	✓	✓	✓	✓	✓		✓	✓
717 N. Third								
Marquette MI 49855								
(906) 225-1699								
Straits Diving	✓	✓	✓	✓	✓	✓		
589 N. State St.								
St. Ignace MI 49781								
(906) 643-7009								
Open: June - September								
Off season:								
c/o Recreational Diving Systems								
4424 N. Woodward								
Royal Oak MI 48072								

	Air	Sales	Rentals	Repairs	Instruction	Offer charters	Arrange charters	Dive travel services
MENOMINEE COUNTY M & M Diving 1901 10th St. Box 74 Menominee MI 49858 (906) 863-7330 Open: May 1- Oct. 1	✓	✓	✓	✓	✓	✓		✓

in Chapter 11, and other scuba courses in Chapter 20.

This chapter also covers dive clubs across the state and two popular annual diving festivals.

DIVING CLUBS

STATEWIDE

Michigan Skin Diving Council   (313) 391-0728
2606 Holland
Lake Orion MI 48035

SOUTHEAST

MACOMB COUNTY
Michigan Aquatic Adventurers   (313) 752-7088
212 E. Washington
Romeo MI 48065

OAKLAND COUNTY
Christian Divers Association   (313) 628-3287
4455 Dogwood
Clarkston MI 48348

GM Underseas Scuba Club　　　　　　　(313) 776-3372
c/o Jennifer Aiken　　　　　　　　　　(313) 244-4628
Box 99008
Troy MI 48099-0008

Michigan Sea Snoopers
59259 Albert Lane
New Hudson MI 48165

Oakland Otters Diving Club　　　　　　(313) 363-2530
c/o Bernie Fling
3351 Oakleaf
West Bloomfield MI 48234

ST. CLAIR COUNTY
Club Poseidon　　　　　　　　　　　　(313) 364-8947
Box 610711
Port Huron MI 48061

WASHTENAW COUNTY
Michigan Moose Diving Club
c/o Ray Ravary Jr.
1940 Whittier
Ypsilanti MI 48197-1729

WAYNE COUNTY
Ford Seahorses Scuba Diving Club　　　(313) 561-8393
1841 N. Denwood
Dearborn MI 48123

Great Lakes Aquanauts　　　　　　　　(313) 420-2235
14953 Dogwood Drive
Plymouth MI 48170

SOUTHWEST

KENT COUNTY
Grand Valley Scuba Divers Inc.　　　　(616) 942-0415
c/o Rex Slingsby
1025 Argo S.E.
Grand Rapids MI 49546

CENTRAL

GENESEE COUNTY
Mid-Michigan U/W Divers   (313) 767-6323
G-4020 Corunna Road   (313) 732-3900
Flint MI 48532

INGHAM COUNTY
Capitol City Dive Club   (517) 349-8728
Box 1852   (517) 623-6868
East Lansing MI 48826

SAGINAW COUNTY
Saginaw Underwater Explorers   (517) 791-1707
c/o Dale Purchase   (517) 687-7681
4181 Wayside
Saginaw MI 48603

NORTHEAST

CHEBOYGAN COUNTY
Cheboygan Skin Diving Club   (616) 627-6673
Box 176
9576 M-33
Cheboygan MI 49721

SPECIAL DIVING EVENTS

Two of the major annual diving events in Michigan are the Great Lakes Shipwreck Festival in Dearborn and Diver's Showcase in Lansing:

Great Lakes Shipwreck Festival
This festival is sponsored by the Ford Seahorses Scuba Dive Club of Dearborn each February. It offers a variety of programs, underwater films and seminars on such topics as underwater resources and photography, underwater archeology and history, cave diving, shipwrecks, diving techniques and the bottomland preserve movement. Exhibitors include maritime museums and historical societies, col-

lectors of marine memorabilia and photographs, marine artists and underwater preserve groups. There also is an annual photo contest.

For more information, contact the Ford Seahorses at 1841 N. Denwood, Dearborn MI 48128 or call (313) 561-8393.

Diver's Showcase
Sponsored by the Michigan Bureau of History, Michigan Sea Grant Program, ZZ UnderWater World and the Capital City Dive Club each November, the showcase offers presentations, video and slide shows and entertainment. Subjects generally include diving techniques and technology, shipwreck exploration, popular dive areas, underwater archeology, bottomland preserves and shipwreck conservation.

For more information, contact ZZ UnderWater World at 1806 E. Michigan Ave., Lansing MI 48912 or call (517) 485-3894.

Chapter 10

UNDERWATER PRESERVES

After four years of legislative debate, Michigan lawmakers in 1980 approved a new program to preserve and protect shipwreck sites and artifacts in the Great Lakes bottomlands. Later, the law was bolstered by adding criminal penalties for vandalism and unauthorized removal or destruction of artifacts from bottomland preserves.

So far, the state Natural Resources Commission has designated seven preserves, covering 1,650 square miles in three of the Great Lakes: Huron, Superior and Michigan. They are jointly administered by the Secretary of State, which is responsible for historic preservation, and the Department of Natural Resources.

These preserves safeguard more than 100 known shipwrecks, many in excellent condition due to the cold waters which slow the destructive processes of rust and decay. There's a lot of information known about many of these ill-fated ships, their crews and cargo. For others, details including the precise dates of disaster, are unknown.

Most of these wrecks are deeply enough submerged that access is limited to sports divers. Some, however, are under 20 feet of water or less, making them visible with only a snorkel and mask.

For these ships -- and often for their crews -- the final voyages ended by violent gale or unexpected snowstorm, by ravaging fire or unseen reef, by fog-shrouded collision or submerged ice, or by human negligence. Whatever the cause, their remains provide sport to divers, insight to marine archeologists, shelter to fish -- and warning to boaters of the Great Lakes' furies, unpredictabilities and whims.

In addition to shipwrecks, these preserves feature unusual geologic formations, underwater cliffs and underwater caves.

Meanwhile, the National Oceanic and Atmospheric Administration, an arm of the U.S. Commerce Department, is considering a proposal to designate Thunder Bay in Lake Huron as a national marine sanctuary. The final decision could take several years. National sanctuaries are designated to manage and preserve distinctive areas of the marine environment for recreational, research, historic, educational, ecological, conservation or aesthetic values that give them special national significance. If approved, Thunder Bay would become the first national marine sanctuary in the Great Lakes.

The prospective sanctuary would encompass the state's current Thunder Bay Bottomland Preserve but would be larger, including wetlands and distinctive underwater limestone formations, with submerged terraces and scarps. Eighty-three identified shipwrecks have been located within the proposed zone. Four islands within the area are already protected as nature sanctuaries, two owned by the Michigan Island National Wildlife Refuge and two by the Michigan Nature Association.

See Chapter 9 for information about scuba diving elsewhere in Michigan.

Sources of additional information about the preserve program are:
- Michigan Underwater Preserve Council, c/o Mike Kohut, 4424 N. Woodward Ave., Royal Oak MI 48073.
- Michigan Underwater Salvage and Preserve Committee, Department of Natural Resources, Box 20028, Lansing MI 48909.
- Michigan Sea Grant Program, 334 Natural Resources Building, Michigan State University, East Lansing MI 48824-1222. Call (517) 353-9568.

NORTHEAST

Thunder Bay Bottomland Preserve   Lake Huron
289 square miles

Features include 22 major wrecks, limestone reefs and sinkholes, and a diver memorial 12 feet below the surface near Sulphur Island. Thunder Bay Island, Sugar Island and Crooked Island are wholly within the preserve, which also abuts Middle Island.

Wreck depths: 18 to 145 feet

Here are some of the wrecks popular among divers:

Schooner *E.B. Allen*, 112 feet long, lost southeast of Thunder Bay Island on Nov. 20, 1871. It's at 90-110 feet.

Steamer *Grecian*, 269 feet long, lost south-southeast of Thunder Bay Island Light on June 15, 1906. It's at 70-105 feet.

Schooner *Lucinda Van Valkenburg*, 128 feet long, lost north-northeast of Thunder Bay Island on June 1, 1887. It's at 70 feet.

Schooner *Molly T. Horner*, 130 feet long, lost between Bird Island

and Scarecrow Island in 1906. It's at 18 feet.

Steamer *Monohansett*, 164 feet long, lost west of Thunder Bay Light on Nov. 23, 1907. It's at 20 feet.

Sidewheel steamer *Montana*, 235 feet long, lost near Thunder Bay Island Light on Sept. 6, 1914. It's at 70 feet.

Schooner *Nellie Gardner*, 177 feet long, lost off Thunder Bay Island on Oct. 15, 1883. It's at 18 feet.

Steamer *Nordmeer*, 550 feet long, lost on Thunder Bay Shoal in Nov. 19, 1966. It's at 40 feet.

Steamer *Oscar T. Flint*, 240 feet long, lost east of Alpena on Nov. 25, 1909. It's at 30-35 feet.

Steamer *P.H. Birckhead*, 156 feet long, lost south of Alpena on Sept. 30, 1905. It's at 12 feet.

Freighter *Portsmouth*, 176 feet long, lost off Middle Island on Nov. 8, 1876. It's at 20-40 feet.

Barge *Scanlon*, lost between North Point and Whitefish Point. It's at 5-15 feet.

Steamer *W.P. Thew*, 132 feet long, lost northeast of Thunder Bay Island Light on June 22, 1909. It's at 90 feet.

**Sanilac Shores Bottomland Preserve   Lake Huron
160 square miles**

Features include 10 major wrecks.
Wreck depths: 15 - 100 feet
Here are some of the wrecks popular among divers:

Steamer *Charles A. Street*, 165 feet long, lost north of Port Sanilac on July 20, 1908. It's at 4-15 feet.

Steamer *Charles S. Price*, 504 feet long, lost southeast of Lexington on Nov. 12, 1913. It's at 35-60 feet.

Schooner *Colonel A. B. Williams*, 110 feet long, lost in 1864, northeast of Port Sanilac. It's at 75-85 feet.

Steamer *Eliza H. Strong*, 205 feet long, lost Oct. 25, 1904, east of Lexington. It's at 25-30 feet.

Barge *F.B. Gardner*, 177 feet long, lost northeast of Port Sanilac on Sept. 15, 1904. It's at 50-55 feet.

Steamer *North Star*, 300 feet long, lost southeast of Port Sanilac on Nov. 25, 1908. It's at 85-100 feet.

Steamer *Regina*, 250 feet long, lost northeast of Lexington on Nov. 11, 1913. It's at 55-80 feet.

Tug *Sport*, 57 feet long, lost east of Lexington on Dec. 13, 1920. It's at 30-50 feet.

Thumb Area Bottomland Preserve   Lake Huron
276 square miles

Features include 10 major wrecks, caves and discarded grindstones.
Wreck depths: 10 to 185 feet
Here are some wrecks popular among divers:
Steamer *Albany*, 267 feet long, lost northeast of Pte. Aux Barques Lighthouse on Nov. 7, 1893. It's at 135-145 feet.
Barge *Chickamauga*, 322 feet long, lost near Harbor Beach on Sept. 13, 1919. It's at 35 feet.
Schooner *Dunderburg*, 186 feet long, lost northeast of Harbor Beach in July 1868. It's at 150-160 feet.
Steamer *Enterprise*, 120 feet long, lost northeast of Pte. Aux Barques Lighthouse on Sept. 13, 1894. It's at 180-185 feet.
Steamer *Glenorchy*, 365 feet long, lost east-southeast of Harbor Beach on Oct. 28, 1924. It's at 110-120 feet.
Steamer *Governor Smith*, 240 feet long, lost northeast of Grindstone City on Aug. 19, 1906. It's at 180-190 feet.
Steamer *Iron Chief*, 212 feet long, lost northeast of Grindstone City on Oct. 3, 1904. It's at 125-140 feet.
Steamer *Philadelphia*, 236 feet long, lost northeast of Pte. Aux Barques Lighthouse on Nov. 7, 1893. It's at 120-130 feet.

NORTHWEST

Manitou Passage Bottomland Preserve   Lake Michigan
281 square miles

Features include 9 major wrecks and old docks. North Manitou Island and South Manitou Island, both part of Sleeping Bear Dunes National Lakeshore, are surrounded by the preserve.
Wreck depths: 10 to 160 feet
Here are some of the wrecks popular among divers:
Steamer *Congress*, 265 feet long, lost Oct. 4, 1904, in South Manitou Harbor. It's at 135-165 feet.
Steamer *Francisco Morazan*, 246 feet long, lost Nov. 29, 1960, off the south end of South Manitou Island. It's at 0-20 feet.

Schooner *H.D. Moore*, 103 feet long, lost Sept. 10, 1907, at north of Gull Point on South Island. It's at 20-25 feet.

Brig *James McBride*, 121 feet long, lost off Sleeping Bear Point on Oct. 19, 1857. It's at 5-15 feet.

Schooner *Josephine Dresden*, 95 feet long, lost off Crescent City Dock on North Manitou Island on Nov. 27, 1907. It's at 5-20 feet.

Freighter *J.S. Crouse*, 90 feet long, lost at Glen Haven on Nov. 15, 1919. It's at 12-15 feet.

Schooner *Montauk*, lost north of Vessel Point off North Manitou Island on Nov. 24, 1882. It's at 15-35 feet.

Steamer *P.J. Ralph*, 211 feet long, lost in South Manitou Harbor on Sept. 8, 1924 . It's at 16-40 feet.

Steamer *Rising Sun*, 133 feet long, lost off Pyramid Point on Oct. 29, 1917. It's at 7-12 feet.

Schooner *Supply*, lost east of Vessel Point off North Manitou Island in October 1862. It's at 12-15 feet.

Steamer *Walter L. Frost*, 235 feet long, lost at the south end of South Manitou Island on Nov. 4, 1903. It's at 25-30 feet.

Freighter *William T. Graves*, 207 feet long, lost Oct. 31, 1885, on North Manitou Shoal. It's at 15-20 feet.

UPPER PENINSULA

Alger Bottomland Preserve   **Lake Superior**
113 square miles

Features include 8 major wrecks, underwater caves and rock cliffs. The preserve borders on Pictured Rocks National Lakeshore, and surrounds Grand Island, which is now national forest. Wood and Williams Islands are also in the preserve.

Wreck depths: 12 to 100 feet

Here are some of the wrecks popular among divers:

Schooner *Burmuda*, lost at the south end of Grand Island on the east side of Murray Bay in November 1868. It's at 25-40 feet.

Schooner *George*, 203 feet long, lost north of Miners Castle off Pictured Rocks National Lakeshore on Oct. 24, 1893. It's at 25-40 feet.

Steamer *Herman H. Hettler*, 210 feet long, lost off the east end of Trout Point on Grand Island on Nov. 21, 1926. It's at 33 feet.

Steamer *Kiowa*, 251 feet long, lost south of Au Sable Point on Nov.

30, 1929.

Steamer *Manhattan*, 252 feet long, lost on the north side of the East Channel of Munising Bay, near the south end of Grand Island, on Oct. 26, 1903. It's at 20-30 feet.

Steamer *Sitka*, 272 feet long, lost on Au Sable Reef on Oct. 4, 1904. It's at 25-40 feet.

Steamer *Smith More*, 223 feet long, lost in the East Channel of Munising Bay on July 13, 1889. It's at 90-110 feet.

Sidewheel steamer *Superior*, lost off Pictured Rocks National Lakeshore on Oct. 29, 1856. It's at 25-40 feet.

Keweenaw Bottomland Preserve   Lake Superior
192 square miles

Features include 15 major wrecks. The preserve wraps around the tip of the Keweenaw Peninsula and includes Manitou Island.

Wreck depths: 10 to 105 feet.

Here are some of the major wrecks popular among divers:

Steamer *Altadoc*, 355 feet long, lost at Keweenaw Point on Dec. 8, 1927. It's at 15 feet.

Steamer *City of Bangor*, 444 feet long, lost at Keweenaw Point on Nov. 30, 1926. It's at 15 feet.

Steamer *City of Superior*, 190 feet long, lost near Copper Harbor Lighthouse on Nov. 11, 1857. It's at 15-35 feet.

Barge *City of St. Joseph*, 254 feet long, lost near Little Grand Marais Harbor on Sept. 22, 1942. It's at 10-35 feet.

Sidewheeler *Gazelle*, 158 feet long, lost off Eagle Harbor on Sept. 8, 1860. It's at 20-30 feet.

Steamer *James Pickands*, 232 feet long, lost at the mouth of Eagle River on Sept. 22, 1894. It's at 10 to 30 feet.

Brig *John Jacob Astor*, 78 feet long, lost at Copper Harbor on Sept. 21, 1844. It's at 20-35 feet.

Steamer *Langham*, 281 feet long, lost in Bete Grise Bay on Oct. 23, 1910. It's at 90-105 feet.

Steamer *Maplehurst*, 235 feet long, lost near Houghton on Dec. 1, 1922. It's at 15-20 feet.

Steamer *Scotia*, 231 feet long, lost at Keweenaw Point on Oct. 24, 1884. It's at 15 feet.

Steamer *Tioga*, 285 feet long, lost at Sawtooth Reef near the mouth of the Eagle River on Nov. 26, 1919. It's at 30-35 feet.

Barge *Transport*, 254 feet long, lost near Little Grand Marais Harbor on Sept. 22, 1942. It's at 10-35 feet.

Sidewheeler *Traveller*, 199 feet long, lost in Eagle Harbor on Aug. 17, 1865. It's at 20 feet.

Steamer *Wasaga*, 238 feet long, lost in Copper Harbor on Nov. 6, 1910. It's at 25-35 feet.

Steamer *William C. Moreland*, 580 feet long, lost at Sawtooth Reef near the mouth of the Eagle River on Oct. 18, 1910. It's at 35-45 feet.

Marquette Bottomland Preserve   Lake Superior
174 square miles

Features include 6 major wrecks and geological formations, divided into the Marquette and Huron Island units. The Huron Island unit includes Lighthouse and McIntyre Islands.

Wreck depths: 5 to 150 feet

Here are some of the wrecks popular among divers:

Sidewheeler steamer *Arctic*, 237 feet long, lost at Huron Island on May 28, 1860. It's at 5-150 feet.

Steamer *Charles J. Kershaw*, 223 feet long, lost at the mouth of the Chocolay River on Sept. 29, 1895. It's at 25-35 feet.

Steamer *D. Leutey*, 179 feet long, lost at Lighthouse Point on Oct. 31, 1911. It's at 25-30 feet.

Schooner-barge *George Nestor*, 207 feet long, lost at Huron Island on April 30, 1909. It's at 30-40 feet.

Schooner *George Sherman*, 140 feet long, lost east of Shot Point on Oct. 22, 1887. It's at 20-40 feet.

Schooner *Southwest*, 137 feet long, lost southeast of Huron Island on Sept. 18, 1898. It's at 90-110 feet.

Straits of Mackinac Bottomland Preserve   Lakes Huron
152 square miles   & Michigan

Features include 9 major wrecks and old docks. St. Helens Island, on the west side of the Straits, is surrounded by the preserve. It also abuts Mackinac and Bois Blanc Islands on the east side of the Straits.

Wreck depths: 40 to 145 feet

Here are some of the wrecks popular among divers:

Steamer *Cayuga*, 57 feet long, lost northwest of Sturgeon Bay in 1866. It's at 135 feet.

Steamer *Cedarville*, 588 feet long, lost east of Mackinaw City on May 7, 1965. It's at 35-110 feet.

Steamer *Eber Ward*, 213 feet long, lost April 19, 1909, west of the Straits of Mackinac. It's at 145 feet.

Brig *Henry Clay*, 87 feet long, lost near Point Nipigon Dec. 3, 1850. It's at 65-80 feet.

Bark *Maitland*, 137 feet long, lost west of McGulpin Point on June 11, 1871. It's at 80-90 feet.

Steamer *Minneapolis*, 226 feet long, lost northeast of McGulpin Point on April 4, 1894. It's at 115-130 feet.

Schooner *M. Stalker*, 135 feet long, lost northwest of Mackinaw City on Nov. 5, 1886. It's at 80-90 feet.

Schooner *Northwest*, 223 feet long, lost west of McGulpin Point on April 6, 1898. It's at 70-75 feet.

Schooner *Richard Winslow*, 216 feet long, lost northwest of Waugoshance Point on Sept. 5, 1898. It's at 25 feet.

Brig *Sandusky*, 110 feet long, lost northwest of McGulpin Point on Sept. 18, 1856. It's at 80-90 feet.

Steamer *William H. Barnum*, 218 feet long, lost northeast of Freedom on April 3, 1894. It's at 70-75 feet.

Whitefish Point Bottomland Preserve   Lake Superior
375 square miles

Features include 17 major wrecks, some of which are too deep for sport diving in safety.

Wreck depths: 15 to 270 feet

Here are some of the wrecks popular among divers:

Schooner-barge *Eureka*, 138 feet long, lost north of Vermilion on Oct. 20, 1886. It's at 50 feet.

Steamer *Indiana*, 146 feet long, lost north of Crisp Point on June 6, 1858. It's at 110-120 feet.

Steamer *John B. Cowle*, 420 feet long, lost northwest of Whitefish Point on July 12, 1909. It's at 200-220 feet.

Propeller *John Mitchell*, 420 feet long, lost west-northwest of Whitefish Point on July 10, 1911. It's at 140-150 feet.

Schooner-barge *Miztec*, 194 feet long, lost west-northwest of Whitefish Point on May 13, 1921. It's at 50 feet.

Steamer *M.M. Drake*, 201 feet long, lost north of Vermilion Point on Oct. 2, 1901. It's at 50 feet.

Lumber hooker *Myron*, 186 feet long, lost west-northwest of White-fish Point on Nov. 22, 1919. It's at 45-50 feet.

Steamer *Neshoto*, 284 feet long, lost northeast of Crisp Point on Sept. 27, 1908. It's at 15 feet.

Schooner-barge *Niagara*, 205 feet long, lost off Vermilion Point on Sept. 7, 1887. It's at 100-120 feet.

Steamer *Panther*, 243 feet long, lost off Parisienne Island on June 26, 1916. It's at 100-110 feet.

Steamer *Samuel Mather*, 246 feet long, lost north of Point Iroquois on Nov. 22, 1891. It's at 170-180 feet.

Steamer *Vienna*, 191 feet long, lost southeast of Whitefish Point on Sept. 17, 1892. It's at 140-145 feet.

Chapter 11

BOAT CHARTERS

It was a captain from northern Michigan, George Raff, who is credited with starting the region's sports charter fishing industry in the early 1920s by discovering that lake trout could be caught by trolling in Grand Traverse Bay. Now hundreds of charter boats service Michigan's Great Lakes, rivers and inland lakes. For most captains, fishing charters constitute their primary business, while others specialize in scuba diving charters or excursions. Many captains offer multiple services.

All 250 boats listed in this chapter are licensed and inspected by either the state Department of Natural Resources or the U.S. Coast Guard, and all use Coast Guard-licensed captains. Excluded from the list are DNR-licensed charter boats which did not report a primary or secondary port in the state, such as those that operate from Michigan City, Ind.

The listing also indicates those boats deemed handicapper-accessible by the charter operator. However, that definition varies from operator to operator, so check in advance to ensure that the boat will meet your needs.

Before you go, ask what equipment and other items you're responsible for, such as Michigan fishing license and trout stamp, fishing and diving gear, food and beverages. Generally, one-day licenses can be purchased from the operator. Most charter operators recommend that you bring soft-soled shoes, camera, sunscreen, sun glasses, rain gear, jacket, lunch and -- for a fishing excursion -- a cooler to haul back your catch. The cost of cleaning and bagging your fish is usually included in the charter fee, and some operators even provide a free snapshot. Check into pre-season, post-season and weekday discounts. If you're traveling from out of town, the charter company can recommend or arrange motel or camping reservations.

From a consumer's perspective, it's important to ask in advance about cancellation policies, reservation deadlines and deposit refunds if you or the operator cancel due to sickness or bad weather. When you make reservations: verify whether you'll be charged per passenger or a flat rate; ask whether you can remain on the water for the full charter period even if you catch your limit; and check on the suggested amount of tips for the crew members. Incidentally, on a fishing charter some operators promise to refund your fee if you don't catch anything.

Charter listings are separated by region, then arranged alphabetically by primary port or home base, not by county. Operators' secondary ports, if any, are listed below their phone numbers.

	Lake fishing	River fishing	Scuba	Cruises & excursions	Handicapper accessible
SOUTHEAST					
ALGONAC					
(St. Clair County)					
Bob's Charter Service	✓	✓	✓	✓	H
8997 Anchor Bay Drive Above Average - 32'					
Fair Haven MI 48023					
(313) 794-3854					
Mt. Clemens, Port Huron, Port					
Sanilac, Rogers City, Presque					
Isle, Rockport, Harrisville					
Gattor Charter	✓	✓	✓	✓	H
9345 Weber Road Gattor II - 26'					
Richmond, MI 48062 Gattor III - 24'					
(313) 727-9410					
Alpena					
Jim's Sport Fishing Charters	✓	✓	✓	✓	H
34846 Jerome					
New Baltimore MI 48047 Fishin' Machine - 27'					
(313) 725-4020					
Alpena, Rogers City,					
Port Huron					

	Lake fishing	River fishing	Scuba	Cruises & excursions	Handicapper accessible
ANCHOR BAY **(St. Clair County)** North Bay Charters 49777 Vercshave New Baltimore MI 48047 (313) 725-8233 Lexington, Port Sanilac North Bay - 26'	✓		✓	✓	H
BOLLES HARBOR **(Monroe County)** Le Chasseur Sport Fishing Charters 5131 Evergreen Monroe MI 48161 (313) 242-5721 Le Chasseur - 27'	✓				H
Trade Winds Charter Service Box 141 LaSalle MI 48145 (313) 243-2319 Trade Winds I - 30' Trade Winds II - 30'	✓		✓	✓	H
DETROIT RIVER **(Wayne County)** Albacore Fishing Charters 3233 Los Angeles Warren MI 48091 (313) 756-3711 Saginaw Bay Albacore - 21'	✓				
FAIR HAVEN **(St. Clair County)** Sportsmen's Charter 7103 St. Clair Ave. Fair Haven MI 48023 (313) 725-3678 Lexington, Port Sanilac SeaWeed - 25'	✓	✓		✓	H

	Lake fishing	River fishing	Scuba	Cruises & excursions	Handicapper accessible
HURON POINT **(Macomb County)** Smok'n Lou's Charter Service 29401 S. Seaway Court Smok'n Lou - 26' Mt. Clemens MI 48045 (313) 469-0669	✓	✓		✓	H
KENSINGTON LAKE **(Oakland County)** Kensington Metropark 2240 W. Buno Road Island Queen - 58' Milford MI 48380 (313) 685-1561				✓	H
LA SALLE (Monroe County) Tom's Sportfishing Charters 123 Highland Sweet Lene - 25' Jackson MI 49201 (517) 522-8828	✓				H
LEXINGTON **(Sanilac County)** Just In Time Industries 7893 Lakeview Model T - 28' Lexington MI 48450 (313) 359-8910 Port Sanilac	✓				H
Lakeshore Charters & Marine Exploration Inc. 4658 S. Lakeshore Sand Dollar - 27' Lexington MI 48450 (313) 359-8660 Port Sanilac			✓	✓	

	Lake fishing	River fishing	Scuba	Cruises & excursions	Handicapper accessible
Martin Marine 5095 Mohawk Drive — Surface Time - 26' Clarkston MI 48348 — Saber Six - 53' (313) 394-0449 Alpena, Mackinaw, Isle Royale				✓ ✓	
MONROE (Monroe County) Fish On II Charters 5210 Walker — Fish On II - 28' Wayne MI 48184 (313) 721-9257 Ludington	✓				H
Honey Charters 41391 Leidel Court — Scorpio's Honey - 27' Northville MI 48167 (313) 348-9825	✓				H
Kingfisher Charters 26106 San Rosa — Kingfisher - 32' St. Clair Shores MI 48081 (313) 773-8751 Frankfort	✓				H
Lindsay K Charters 34741 Michelle Drive — Lindsay K - 31' Romulus MI 48174 (313) 941-2869	✓				H
Lucy J Sportfishing Box 345 Owosso MI 48867 (517) 723-6071 Manistee	✓			✓	H

	Lake fishing	River fishing	Scuba	Cruises & excursions	Handicapper accessible
Sea Hawk Sportfishing Charters 5658 Lowe Warren MI 48092 (313) 795-3264 Frankfort Sea Hawk III - 30'	✓				H
Ice Breaker II Sport Fishing Charters 38000 Castle Drive Romulus MI 48174 (313) 941-3529 Manistee Ice Breaker Two - 27'	✓		✓		H
Waters Charter Service 26716 Osmun Madison Heights MI 48071 (313) 547-3543 Oscoda Top Kick - 27'	✓				H
MT. CLEMENS **(Macomb County)** Crew's Inn Sportfishing Charter 37865 Terra Mar Mt. Clemens MI 48045 (313) 465-4124 Lexington, Port Sanilac, Monroe, Frankfort Crew's Inn - 29'	✓				H
Sportfishing Charters 37897 Mast Mt. Clemens MI 48045 (313) 463-3474 Lexington, Port Sanilac, Detroit Predator X - 33' Predator - 30' Predator XII - 24'	✓	✓		✓	H

	Lake fishing	River fishing	Scuba	Cruises & excursions	Handicapper accessible
ST. CLAIR SHORES **(Macomb County)** Chipmunk Charter Service 41350 Garfield Chipmunk III - 30' Mt. Clemens MI 48044 Belle River	✓	✓			H
Kaptain Kristo Charter Service 6546 Lafayette Bruiser II - 33' Dearborn MI 48127 My Limit - 33' (313) 561-9857 Club Fred - 33'	✓			✓	H
T. Purdie Co. 22514 Kramer Rambl'n Boy - 42' St. Clair Shores MI 48080 (313) 773-8859				✓	H
WYANDOTTE **(Wayne County)** Tommy Bray's Charter Service 16740 Mansfield Popular Hill - 27' Detroit MI 48235 (313) 273-9183	✓	✓		✓	H

SOUTHWEST

	Lake fishing	River fishing	Scuba	Cruises & excursions	Handicapper accessible
GRAND HAVEN **(Ottawa County)** Albonac Charters 17990 N. Shore Road #59 Albonac - 30' Spring Lake MI 49456 (616) 846-6077 Muskegon, Holland, Port Sheldon	✓	✓		✓	H

	Lake fishing	River fishing	Scuba	Cruises & excursions	Handicapper accessible
Bolhouse Fishing Charters 2578 Belknap N.E. Grand Rapids MI 49505 (616) 361-0704 Garyboy IV - 35' Laker II - 33' King One - 35' Love-It - 28' Slap-Shot - 36'	✓			✓	H
Danel Charters Box 286 Grand Haven MI 49417 (616) 842-1359 Danel - 28'	✓			✓	H
Flying Frisian Charter Service 4320 Kalamazoo Ave. Grand Rapids MI 49508 (616) 455-7810 Flying Frisian - 35'	✓			✓	H
Thunderduck Sportfishing 12825 Hideaway Drive Fruitport MI 49415 (616) 847-0523 Thunder Duck - 31'	✓			✓	H
HOLLAND (Ottawa County) Bachelor One Charter Service 523 Butternut Drive #77 Holland MI 49424 (616) 399-6782 Bachelor One - 30'	✓			✓	
Melissa Anne Charters 2403 Idlewood Road Holland MI 49424 (616) 399-5219 Melissa Anne - 30'	✓			✓	H

	Lake fishing	River fishing	Scuba	Cruises & excursions	Handicapper accessible
Sowle Charters Inc. Box 3757 Springfield IL 62708 (616) 335-9329; off-season (217) 528-7533 Saugatuck, Grand Haven, South Haven Snoopy Too - 37'	✓			✓	H
NEW BUFFALO **(Berrien County)** New Buffalo Charter Service 400 S. Whittaker St. New Buffalo MI 49117 (616) 469-4510 NBC II - 31'	✓			✓	H
Striker Sportfishing Charters Box 374 New Buffalo MI 49117 (616) 469-1120 Striker - 26'	✓			✓	H
SAUGATUCK **(Allegan County)** Salmon Slammer Charters 1180 48th Ave. Hudsonville MI 49426 (616) 688-5257 Salmon Slammer - 25'	✓				H
U.S. Male A3789 64th St. Holland MI 49423 (616) 857-4156 Holland The U.S. Male - 32'	✓	✓		✓	H

195

	Lake fishing	River fishing	Scuba	Cruises & excursions	Handicapper accessible
ST. JOSEPH **(Berrien County)**					
Bills Charter Fishing 4333 S. Pipestone Sodus MI 49126 (616) 926-6461 Bills Charter - 25'	✓			✓	H
Captain Hook Fishing Safaris 4205 Hillshaven Road #58 Buchanan MI 49107 (616) 695-2123 Benton Harbor Captain Hook - 31' Captain Hook Too - 21' Kitty Hawk - 40'	✓	✓		✓	H
Caralee Charters Inc. 2801 Fir Lane South Bend IN 46615 (219) 232-0833 Benton Harbor Caralee - 28'	✓			✓	H
Climax Charter 11434 2 Mile Road Climax MI 49017 (800) 344-7443 (616) 979-2325 Climax - 25'	✓				H
Double D Charters 2091 Reggie Drive Benton Harbor MI 49022 (616) 925-5613 Double D I - 24' Double D II - 28'	✓	✓			H
Happiness Iz Charters 4583 Ridge Road Stevensville MI 49127 (800) 432-2628 Berrien Springs Happiness Iz - 30'	✓	✓	✓	✓	H

	Lake fishing	River fishing	Scuba	Cruise & excursions	Handicapper accessible
Rainbow Charters 2271 Rocky Weed Road #12 Berrien Springs MI 49103 Duck Hunter - 30' (616) 428-2009 War Eagle - 22' Benton Harbor, Kalamazoo River	✓	✓		✓	H
Reel Pleaser Charters 4124 Hollywood Road Reel Pleaser - 30' St. Joseph MI 49085 (616) 429-2395	✓			✓	H
Rouser Charters 7235 W. Johnson Road Rouser - 28 1/2' Michigan City IN 46360 (219) 879-3103	✓				H
Scorpio Charters 21320 S.R. 120 Scorpio - 28' Elkhart IN 46516 (219) 293-7179	✓				
SeaKing Sportfishing Charters 16088 Darden Road SeaKing - 30' Granger IN 46530 SeaKing II - 22' (800) 637-FISH (219) 271-9118	✓	✓			H
Sportboat Charter 1292 Seneca Sportboat - 32' Benton Harbor MI 49022 Sportboat II - 26' (616) 927-LURE Manistee	✓	✓			H

	Lake fishing	River fishing	Scuba	Cruises & excursions	Handicapper accessible
Stormin' Norman Charters 12227 Garr Road Buchanan MI 49107 (616) 695-9549 Stormin' Norman - 27'	✓	✓			H
Strong Performance 3315 Huron St. Strong Performance - 30' Kalamazoo MI 49007 (616) 342-5317 Ludington	✓				H
Sundance Sport Fishing Charters 8289 Columbia Road Sundance - 27' Eau Claire MI 49111 (616) 461-6702 Monroe	✓	✓		✓	
SOUTH HAVEN **(Van Buren County)** Catamaran Sailing Box 422 Cat Calls - 27' South Haven MI 49090 (616) 637-8951				✓	H
Margie "B" Fishing Charters 8878 W. "YZ" Ave. Margie "B" - 30' Schoolcraft MI 49087 (616) 679-4670	✓				H
Sea Wolf Fleet Box 263 Sea Wolf - 26' Bloomingdale MI 49026 Captain Chuck - 48' (616) 637-8007 off-season (616) 521-3275	✓			✓	H

	Lake fishing	River fishing	Scuba	Cruises & excursions	Handicacapper accessible
Stone Jug Charters 12070 Stone Jug Road Battle Creek MI 49017 (616) 979-9665 Stone Jug - 28'	✓				H

CENTRAL

BAY CITY (Bay County)

	Lake fishing	River fishing	Scuba	Cruises & excursions	Handicacapper accessible
S.W.A.T. Charter Service 1249 E. Munger Road Munger MI 48747 (517) 659-2288 Oscoda, Port Sanilac Battle Stations - 27'	✓				H

LANSING (Ingham County)

	Lake fishing	River fishing	Scuba	Cruises & excursions	Handicacapper accessible
J & K Steamboat Line Box C Grand Ledge MI 48837 (517) 627-2154 Spirit of Lansing - 53' Princess Laura - 77' Michigan Princess - 110' Grand Ledge, Midland, Chesaning, Cadillac,, Albion, Paw Paw				✓	H

LINWOOD (Bay County)

	Lake fishing	River fishing	Scuba	Cruises & excursions	Handicacapper accessible
Sandpiper Charter Service 1930 Windsor Lane Flint MI 48507 (313) 239-1041 Onekama Sandpiper I - 28'	✓				H
S.T. Too Charters 3543 E. Van Buren Road Alma MI 48801 (517) 681-4186 S.T. Too - 28'	✓				H

	Lake fishing	River fishing	Scuba	Cruises & excursions	Handicapper accessible
PINCONNING (Bay County) Bil-Mar Charters 3104 Grant Lane Midland MI 48642 (517) 835-2572 — Maggie-J - 30'	✓				H
NORTHEAST					
ALPENA (Alpena County) Fishin Fun Charter Service 2031 Channel Road #3 Alpena MI 49747 (517) 356-2570 — Fishin Fun - 28'	✓			✓	H
Thunder Bay Divers Inc. 160 E. Fletcher Alpena MI 49707 (517) 356-9336 — Thunder Bay Diver - 54' Ieasure Diver - 46'			✓	✓	
AU GRES (Arenac County) Bluebird Fishing Charters 1868 Oak Drive, Rte. 2 Gladwin MI 48624 (517) 876-6469 off-season (517) 426-5517 — Bluebird - 24 1/2'	✓				H
Carter's Charter 2926 Midvale Rochester Hills MI 48309 (313) 852-0141 Port Austin, Harbor Beach — Carol Ann II - 25'	✓	✓		✓	H
Grand Slam Charter 615 Hanchott St. St. Charles MI 48655 (313) 865-6915 — Grand Slam - 26'	✓			✓	

	Lake fishing	River fishing	Scuba	Cruises & excursions	Handicapper accessible
AuSABLE RIVER MOUTH **(Iosco County)** Spirit of AuSable 2230 U.S. 23 East Tawas MI 48730 (517) 739-3072 Harrisville — *Spirit of AuSable - 25'*	✓			✓	H
BLACK RIVER **(Alcona County)** Black River Charter Service 5140 Fontaine Road Black River MI 48721 (517) 471-2898 Harrisville — *Salmon Patty - 26'*	✓			✓	H
FOREST BAY COTTAGES **(Huron County)** Forest Bay Charters 2888 N. Lakeshore Port Hope MI 48468 (517) 428-4335 Harbor Beach, Port Hope — *Hot Rod II - 22'*	✓			✓	H
GRINDSTONE CITY **(Huron County)** Regal Beagle Charter 8750 Maple Valley Road Brown City MI 48416 (517) 738-5665 off-season (313) 346-3162 — *Regal Beagle - 25'*	✓				
Tenpin Sportfishing Charters 5911 Sid Drive Saginaw MI 48601 (517) 754-4437 — *Tenpin - 30'*	✓			✓	

	Lake fishing	River fishing	Scuba	Cruises & excursions	Handicapper accessible
HARBOR BEACH **(Huron County)** Blue Water Charter Service 39789 Duluth Blue Water Bandit Mt. Clemens MI 48045 - 27' (313) 463-5197 Port Sanilac, Mt. Clemens	✓				H
C. J. Hooker 3766 N. Pinnebog C. J. Hooker - 25' Elkton MI 48731 (517) 874-5270 Caseville	✓				H
Dan-D-Lou Charter Service 6348 Oak Ridge Drive Dan-D-Lou - 31' Washington MI 48094 (313) 781-6445 Port Austin	✓				H
Great Escape Charters 1933 Miles Road Great Escape - 23' Lapeer MI 48446 (313) 664-7856	✓				
Hang Loose Charter Service 2990 N. Lakeshore Hang Loose - 25' Port Hope MI 48468 (517) 428-4937 off-season (313) 651-1210 Grindstone City	✓				
Lazy Days Charters 45532 Gable Inn Lazy Days - 25' Utica MI 48317 (313) 731-3352	✓				H

	Lake fishing	River fishing	Scuba	Cruises & excursions	Handicapper accessible
Macomb Dive Center 22869 Bunert Diversion - 22' Warren MI 48093 (313) 774-0640 Grindstone City, St. Clair River			✓		
7 Cs Chartering Service 17130 Brookhurst 7 Cs - 27' Mt. Clemens MI 48044 (313) 286-4578	✓				
HARRISVILLE **(Alcona County)** Beyer's Charter Service Inc. 34910 Glover Sandy-B - 25' Wayne MI 4884 (313) 728-2514	✓	✓			H
Fish Fetcher II Charters Box 554 Fish Fetcher II - 25' Harrisville MI 48740 (517) 724-5249 Tawas	✓				
Reel-Fun Charter 771 S. US-23 Reel-Fun - 27' Harrisville MI 48723 (517) 724-5454 Oscoda, Alpena	✓				
Robin Charter 340 Hillside Drive Robin - 27' Harrisville MI 48740 (517) 724-9320 Oscoda, Alpena	✓				H

	Lake fishing	River fishing	Scuba	Cruises & excursions	Handicapper accessible
OSCODA (Iosco County) Fishworks Charters 4180 N. US-23 Oscoda MI 48750 (517) 739-5696 *Fishworks - 25'*	✓				H
Lucky Angel III Sport Fishing Chartering Service 4445 Johnson Road Oscoda MI 48750 (517) 739-9613 *Lucky Angel III - 27'*	✓				
Reel 'Em Sportfishing Charters Box 365 Oscoda MI 48750-0365 (517) 739-9454 Harrisville *Reel 'Em In - 32'*	✓	✓			H
T.M.B. Charter Service & Sales Box 301 Oscoda MI 48750 (517) 739-2301 Harrisville, Alcona *T.M.B. II - 37'*	✓			✓	H
Wendy Sue Charters 831 N. Pontiac Trail #25 Walled Lake MI 48390 (313) 669-5142 Harrisville, Tawas *Wendy Sue III - 33'*	✓		✓	✓	H
Off Shore Charters 23 E. Spring St. Port Austin MI 48467 (517) 738-5247 Harbor Beach *Shadow - 33'*	✓		✓	✓	H

		Lake fishing	River fishing	Scuba	Cruises & excursions	Handicapper accessible
Sandpiper Sport Fishing Charters 701 Hacker Road Brighton MI 48116 (313) 229-7736	Sandpiper - 24'	✓				
PORT SANILAC (Sanilac County) Bruno's Dive Shop 34740 Gratiot Mt. Clemens MI 48043 (313) 792-2040 (313) 622-9859 Mt. Clemens	Great Lakes Diver - 33'			✓	✓	H
QUANICASSEE (Tuscola County) Sea Gypsy Charter 5530 N. Garner Road Akron MI 48701 (517) 674-2437 Port Austin	Sea Gypsy - 25'	✓				H
ROCKPORT (Alpena County) A.T.'s Charter Service 17010 Dreamers Lane Alpena MI 49707 (517) 595-6267 Alpena	A.T. - 22'	✓				
Sports Page Charters 10312 Long Lake Park Road Alpena MI 49707 (517) 595-2272 Alpena, Harrisville	Sports Page - 22'	✓				

		Lake fishing	River fishing	Scuba	Cruises & excursions	Handicapper accessible
Super-Fish-All Charters 120 Glendale Alpena MI 49707 (517) 356-3734 Thunder Bay	Super-Fish-All - 21'	✓	✓			

**ROGERS CITY
(Presque Isle County)**

		Lake fishing	River fishing	Scuba	Cruises & excursions	Handicapper accessible
Bruning's Charter Service 259 N. First St. Rogers City MI 49779 (517) 734-3463	Clipped Fin	✓				

TAWAS BAY (Iosco County)

		Lake fishing	River fishing	Scuba	Cruises & excursions	Handicapper accessible
Lanski's Charter Service Box 332 Tawas City MI 48764 (517) 362-8048 Rogers City, Alpena, AuGres, Harrisville, Oscoda	Trapper - 27'	✓		✓	✓	H

NORTHWEST

**CHARLEVOIX
(Charlevoix County)**

		Lake fishing	River fishing	Scuba	Cruises & excursions	Handicapper accessible
Blue Fin Sportfishing Charters 14226 W. Garfield Rd. Charlevoix MI 49720 (616) 547-6808 Petoskey, Harbor Springs	Blue Fin II - 27'	✓			✓	
Priority Charter Services Rt. 1, Box 124 Bellaire MI 49615 (616) 377-7590 Elk Rapids	Priority - 21'	✓			✓	

		Lake fishing	River fishing	Scuba	Cruises & excursions	Handicapper acce
Ward Brothers Boats Inc. 106 E. Antrim Charlevoix MI 49720 (616) 547-2371 Petoskey, Harbor Springs	My Fran III - 31' Sandy - 31' Russell Lynn - 31'	✓			✓	H
FRANKFORT (Benzie County) Betsie Bay Charters 2520 Frankfort Hwy. Frankfort MI 49635 (616) 352-7756	Golden Girl - 30'	✓		✓	✓	H
Boon Doc's Sport Fishing 604 Lake Shore Drive Cadillac MI 49601 (616) 775-1767	Tannenbaum - 28'	✓			✓	H
Elberta Charter Basin 491 Lake St. Frankfort MI 49635 (616) 352-9934	Tadpolly - 28'	✓			✓	
Fishing Box Charters 5715 Swede Midland MI 48642 (517) 631-8157	Fishing Box II - 29'	✓			✓	H
Fish-Tale Charter Service Box 1161 Frankfort MI 49635 (616) 352-7336	Fish-Tale - 24 1/2'	✓			✓	H

	Lake fishing	River fishing	Scuba	Cruises & excursions	Handicapper accessible
Kings Charter Service 17181 Beech-Daly Road Redford MI 48240 (313) 255-7877 Grindstone City, Big Manistee River King Fish - 28' Rivermaster - 18'	✓	✓			H
Misty Blue G-3117 Corunna Rd. #269 Flint MI 48532 (313) 232-6900; off-season (313) 742-3333 Misty Blue - 33'	✓			✓	
Patina Charter Service 603 Frankfort Elberta MI 49628 (616) 352-4434 Patina VI - 34'	✓		✓	✓	H
Putney-McNeal Enterprises Inc. 531 Main St. Frankfort MI 49635 (616) 352-9493 Hussler - 28'	✓				H
Red Wing Charters Box 288 Frankfort MI 49635 (616) 352-4894 Elberta Red Wing - 33'	✓			✓	H
Slo Mo Sean Charter Fishing 4226 N. Spider Lake Road Traverse City MI (616) 352-5019; off-season (616) 947-3186 Slo-Mo Sean III - 28'	✓		✓	✓	H

		Lake fishing	River fishing	Scuba	Cruises & excursions	Handicapper accessible
West Coast Outfitters 1180 Sunset Drive Frankfort MI 49635 (616) 352-7740	West Coaster - 25'	✓				H
GLEN ARBOR **(Leelanau County)** Madison Avenue Charter Boat The Homestead Glen Arbor MI 49636 (616) 334-3872	Madison Avenue - 26'	✓		✓	✓	H
IRONTON **(Charlevoix County)** Van Dyke Sailboat Charters RR#1, 4662 Webster Bridge Road East Jordan MI 49727 (616) 536-7911	Wind Song - 30'				✓	H
LELAND (Leelanau County) Double Trouble Charters 6728 N. River Freeland MI 48623 (517) 695-9752	Double Trouble - 28'	✓				H
Fishtown Charter Service 1657 M-22 Leland MI 49654 (616) 256-9639	Carol Dee - 30' Sea Witch - 28'	✓			✓	H
Northwest Charters Ltd. 10013 Lakeview Road Traverse City MI 49684 (616) 941-4376	Far-Fetched - 28'	✓			✓	H

		Lake fishing	River fishing	Scuba	Cruises & excursions	Handicapper accessible
Schlitt's Fishing Charters 5277 Barney Road Traverse City MI 49684 (616) 947-7642 Traverse City	Beaker - 28' Beaker II - 16 1/2'	✓			✓	H
Sea Dog Charters 7427 Pinewood Court Traverse City MI 49684 (616) 946-2204	Sea Dog - 31'	✓				
LUDINGTON (Mason County) Big Jon Pro-Team Charters 2833 Neahtawanta Traverse City MI 49684 (616) 223-7790 (616) 843-3555	Pro-Team - 31'	✓			✓	H
Bob-E-Ann Charter Fishing 3845 Balsam N.E. Grand Rapids MI 49505 (616) 845-5980; off-season (616) 363-3625	Bob-E-Ann - 28'	✓				
Candyman Sportfishing Charter 4350 W. Pasadena Flint MI 48504 (616) 845-7607; off-season (313) 732-1544	Candyman - 28'	✓				H

	Lake fishing	River fishing	Scuba	Cruises & excursions	Handicapper accessible
Champagne Sportfishing Charters 5057 Dennis St. Flint MI 48506 (616) 845-1915; off-season (313) 736-9625 St. Joseph *Champagne - 31'*	✓	✓			
Court Jester Sport Fishing Charters 3741 E. Wilder #P Bay City MI 48706 (800) YOU-FISH *Court Jester - 30'*	✓				H
Dreamweaver Charters 1752 W. 98th Place Crown Point IN 46307 (616) 843-9060; off-season (219) 662-0088 *Dreamweaver III - 35'*	✓				
For Pete's Sake Sportfishing Charters 731 Collingwood Drive Davison MI 48423 (616) 843-8755; off-season (313) 653-3572 *For Pete's Sake - 26'*	✓				H
Fraden III Box 714 Ludington MI 49431 (616) 843-8254 *Fraden III - 30'*	✓				
Gnat's Charter Service 6934 W. Illinois St. Ludington MI 49431 (616) 845-1158 *Equalizer - 25'* *Popeye - 16'*	✓	✓			

	Lake fishing	?River fishing	Scuba	Cruises & excursions	Handicapper accessible
Hank's Charter Service 2697 N. Victory Corner Road Ludington MI 49431 She's Mine - 30' (616) 843-3808 Little Devil - 26'	✓				H
Lorna Jo Charters Box 474 Lorna Jo - 27' Baldwin MI 49304 (616) 745-3905	✓	✓			
Reel Rascal II Charters Box 607 Reel Rascal II - 33' Ludington MI 49431 (616) 843-7000 (616) 843-3090 Leland	✓		✓	✓	H
Therapy Too Sport Fishing Charters 261 Harbor Drive Therapy Too - 35' Ludington MI 49431 (616) 845-6095; off-season (313) 459-2033	✓			✓	H
Tiffany Too Sportfishing Charters Box 119 Tiffany Too - 26' Ludington MI 49431 (616) 845-5474	✓				H
Venture Charters 502 N. Rath Ave. Venture - 25' Ludington MI 48431 (616) 843-9253	✓				

	Lake fihsing	River fishing	Scuba	Cruises & excursions	Handicapper accessible
MANISTEE					
(Manistee County)					
Bud's Charter Service					
2380 Main St. Michelle - 31'	✓	✓			H
Manistee MI 49660					
(616) 723-9414					
Frankfort					
Dave's Charter					
345 River St. Dagati - 35'	✓	✓			H
Manistee MI 49660					
(616) 723-3569					
Dutch Treat Charters					
4334 Beckett Place Dutch Treat - 27'	✓				H
Saginaw MI 48603					
(517) 792-7983					
Ginger Brandy					
Charter Service					
30440 Balewood Ginger Brandy - 32'	✓			✓	H
Southfield MI 48076					
(313) 647-0804					
Helena Sport Fishing Charters					
5211 Georgetown Helena - 31'	✓				H
Grand Blanc MI 48439					
(313) 694-1924					
Reel Eezy Charters					
1208 Parkwood Reel Eezy - 26'	✓	✓		✓	H
Ypsilanti MI 48198					
(313) 483-6504					
River Haven Guide Service					
24 Caberfae Highway River Runt - 18'		✓		✓	H
Manistee MI 49660					
(616) 723-7479					

	Lake fishing	River fishing	Scuba	Cruises & excursions	Handicapper accessible
Sally Charter Service 312 River Bend Lane Baldwin MI 49304 (616) 745-3798 (616) 745-7601 *Sally K - 28'*	✓	✓			
Sea Ducer Charters 7945 N. Croswell Road St. Louis MI 48880 (616) 723-5350; off-season (517) 681-3353 *Sea Ducer - 28'*	✓			✓	H
Shirley Ann Charters 287 Pipers Lane Mt. Morris MI 48458 (616) 723-6238; off-season (313) 686-4175 *Shirley Ann - 35'*	✓				H
Steelhead II Charters 402 N. Deerfield Lansing MI 48917 (616) 723-3647; off-season (517) 487-3316 *Steelhead II - 26'*	✓			✓	H
Sue-Lee Charter 1331 West Lake Clio MI 48420 (616) 723-4025; off-season (313) 686-8426 Frankfort *Sue-Lee - 29'*	✓	✓	✓	✓	H
Sun Ray 515 W. Main Vernon MI 48476 (517) 288-2972 *Sun Ray II*	✓				

215

	Lake fishing	River fishing	Scuba	Cruises & excursions	Handicapper accessible
30 Pounder III 39879 Memory Lane 30 Pounder III - 31' Mt. Clemens MI 48045 (616) 723-3474; off-season (313) 463-6954	✓				H
Town Bum III Charters Box 110 Town Bum III - 27' Wellston MI 49689 (616) 848-4223	✓	✓			H
MUSKEGON **(Muskegon County)** Argo Charters 2187 Lincoln St. Argo V - 31' Muskegon MI 49441 (616) 755-6093 Pentwater	✓			✓	H
Blue Fish Charters 15263 160th Ave. Blue Fish - 32' Grand Haven MI 49417 (616) 846-4203	✓			✓	H
Celebration Charter 3274 Hanley Celebration - 30' Muskegon MI 49441 (616) 755-4234	✓			✓	
Mitzi Corp. 216 Shady Lane Mitzi - 29' Spring Lake MI 49456 (616) 842-1374; off-season (616) 744-2747 Grand Haven	✓			✓	H

	Lake fishing	River fishing	Scuba	Cruises & excursions	Handicapper accessible
NORTH MUSKEGON **(Muskegon County)** Chinook Charters 607 W. Sunset Drive N. Muskegon MI 49445 (616) 744-4493 — Chinook - 25'	✓			✓	H
Late Arrival Charters 6263 Whites Bridge Belding MI 48809 (616) 243-9721; off-season (616) 794-3356 — Late Arrival - 28'	✓			✓	
ONEKAMA **(Manistee County)** Interim Charter Service 5332 S. Nottawa Road Mt. Pleasant MI 48858 (616) 723-4536 (517) 773-7929 — Interim - 33'	✓			✓	H
Portage Lake Charters Box 337 Onekama MI 49675 (616) 889-5505 — Prime Time - 31'	✓				H
True Blue Charters Box 102 Onekama MI 49675 (616) 889-3684 — True Blue - 31'	✓				H
PENTWATER **(Oceana County)** Charlie Brown Charters Box 244 Pentwater MI 49444 (616) 869-2131 — Charlie Brown - 31'	✓			✓	H

		Lake fishing	River fishing	Scuba	Cruises & excursions	Handicapper accessible
Dew Ann Sport Fishing 2336 Darnell Walled Lake MI 48390 (313) 624-9261	Dew Ann - 27'	✓				
Teresa Ann Charter Service 345 4th Fruitport MI 49415 Grand Haven	Teresa Ann II - 24'	✓		✓	✓	H
Striker Sportfishing Charter 6851 Monroe Road Pentwater MI 49449 (616) 869-4560	Striker - 32'	✓	✓	✓	✓	H
PETOSKEY **(Emmet County)** Ruddy Duck Charters 3175 Country Club Road Petoskey MI 49770 (616) 347-3232	Ruddy Duck II - 24'	✓				H
SUTTONS BAY **(Leelanau County)** Cygnet Sailing Expeditions Box 186 Suttons Bay MI 49682 (616) 271-6637 Omena, Traverse City	Cygnet - 35'	✓			✓	H
TRAVERSE CITY **(Grand Traverse County)** Bay Breeze Yacht Charters 12935 W. Bayshore Drive Traverse City MI 49684 (616) 941-0535	30 boats ranging from 27' - 46'				✓	

	Lake fishing	River fishing	Scuba	Cruises & excursions	Handicapper accessible
Miles Charters 13692 W. Bayshore Drive Miles High - 35' Traverse City MI 49684 (616) 947-0102	✓			✓	H
Scuba North Inc. 13380 W. Bayshore Drive Solace - 26' Traverse City MI 49684 (616) 947-2520 Leland, Glen Arbor, Charlevoix,, Mackinaw City			✓	✓	
Traverse Charter Fishing 10638 Monaco Way Showtime - 31' Traverse City MI 49684 Showtime II - 20' (616) 946-4456	✓			✓	H
WHITE LAKE **(Muskegon County)** Inspiration Charters 1301 W. Riley Thompson Road Muskegon MI 49445 Inspiration - 28' (616) 766-3692	✓			✓	H
Shelley Lee 5651 Dowling St. Shelley Lee - 24' Montague MI 49437 (616) 894-2101 Muskegon, Pentwater	✓	✓	✓	✓	H
Tanbark Sailing Adventures 105 Pinecrest Road Shiloh - 46' Whitehall MI 49461 (616) 894-5084	✓			✓	H

	Lake fishing	River fishing	Scuba	Cruises & excursions	Handicapper accessible
Trans-Michigan Scuba Charters 2906 Memorial Drive Muskegon MI 49445 (616) 744-5366 Muskegon TMSC - 26'			✓		H

UPPER PENINSULA

BLACK RIVER HARBOR (Gogebic County)

	Lake fishing	River fishing	Scuba	Cruises & excursions	Handicapper accessible
LeeLinau Charter Service 128 E. Larch St. Ironwood MI 49938-2720 (906) 932-5652 LeeLinau - 34'	✓			✓	H
Sparky Charter Fishing Service U.S. Hwy. 2 - 2S235 Hurley (715) 561-2511 Sparky Rose - 31' WI 54534	✓			✓	

COPPER HARBOR (Keweenaw County)

	Lake fishing	River fishing	Scuba	Cruises & excursions	Handicapper accessible
Bergh's Fishing Charters Box 37 Copper Harbor MI 49918 (906) 289-4234 Rose of Sharon - 26'	✓			✓	H

DeTOUR VILLAGE (Chippewa County)

	Lake fishing	River fishing	Scuba	Cruises & excursions	Handicapper accessible
Island Queen Charters Box 34 DeTour Village MI 49725 (906) 297-3731 Island Queen - 24 1/2'	✓		✓	✓	H

	Lake fishing	River fishing	Sucba	Cruises & excursions	Handicapper accessible
DRUMMOND ISLAND **(Chippewa County)** Blue Boat Charters 2340 Academy Drive Blue Boat - 23' Grand Rapids MI 49503 (906) 493-5594; off-season (616) 454-0610 DeTour Village	✓				H
MACKINAC ISLAND **(Mackinac County)** Mackinac Island Charters R#2 Milligan Creek Trail Onaway MI 49765 Moonshiner - 30' (517) 733-8585 Mullet Lake	✓			✓	H
MARQUETTE **(Marquette County)** Catch-A-Finn Charters Box 397 Catch-A-Finn II - 27' Marquette MI 49855 (906) 225-6953; off-season (906) 228-3668	✓		✓		H
Double C Charters 127 Sandy Lane Double C II - 26' Marquette MI 49855 (906) 249-3258	✓		✓	✓	H
Salmon Snatcher Charter Box 513 Salmon Snatcher I Marquette MI 49855 - 30' (906) 228-8307 Salmon Snatcher II - 24'	✓				H

	Lake fishing	River fishing	Scuba	Cruises & excursions	Handicapper accessible
MENOMINEE **(Menominee County)** M & M Diving Box 74 Exception - 23' Menominee MI 49858 (906) 863-7330 Munising, Whitefish Point, Keweenaw			✓		H
ONTONAGON **(Ontonagon County)** Mary-El Sport Trolling Box 313 Mary-El - 26' White Pine MI 49971 (906) 885-5435	✓				H
Voyager Charters Box 231 Voyager - 28' Bruce Crossing MI 49912 (906) 827-3466	✓				H
SAULT STE. MARIE **(Chippewa County)** Lake Superior Charter 1931 Riverside Drive Gerald D. Neville - 50' Sault Ste. Marie MI 49783 (906) 632-6490 Brimley	✓	✓	✓	✓	H
SHELTER BAY **(Alger County)** Shelter Bay Charters H.C. Route, Box 675 Jody Lee - 30' AuTrain MI 49806 (906) 892-8230 Munising	✓			✓	H

	Lake fishing	River fishing	Scuba	Cruises & excursions	Handicapper accessible
ST. IGNACE **(Mackinac County)** Rec Diving 4424 N. Woodward Royal Oak MI 48073 (800) 999-0303 Rec Diver - 42'			✓	✓	

Chapter 12
CRUISES & TOURS

One of the best ways to enjoy Michigan waters is on an organized cruise or tour, whether for a few hours or a few days. Generally the trip includes a knowledgeable narration about scenery and attractions, natural history and local or regional history.

These trips are made on boats licensed and inspected by the U.S. Coast Guard with Coast Guard-licensed captains. The list indicates whether reservations are required; even when they're not mandatory, they're generally recommended, especially for weekend and prime summertime vacation periods. Ask in advance about parking, deposit requirements and cancellation policies, recommended attire, student and senior citizen discounts and special events. Also ask whether they accept credit cards and personal checks.

This list includes just tours and cruises offered on a regularly scheduled basis, but some of these operators also can custom-tailor longer trips or different destinations on a charter basis. If you're interested in a charter cruise, see Chapter 12. Passenger ferries are covered in Chapter 14.

		Reservations required	Overnight/ multiday trips	Food aboard	Handicapper accessible
SOUTHEAST					
WAYNE COUNTY Waterway Cruises Inc. 300 River Place, Box 39 Detroit MI 48207 (313) 567-1400	May- October 1 - 3+ hours	✓		✓	H

225

	Reservations required	Overnight/ multiday trips	Food aboard	Handicapper accessible

The cruises aboard the paddle-wheel riverboat Detroiter travel on the Detroit River, highlighting the Detroit and Windsor, Ont., shorelines, Belle Isle and Peche Isle. Overnight and weekend packages, with meals, curise and lodging are available through River Place Inn, 1000 River Place, Detroit, MI 48207, (313) 259-2500.

SOUTHWEST

ALLEGAN COUNTY

| Saugatuck Boat Cruises Box 654 716 Water St. Saugatuck MI 49453 (616) 857-4261 | May - October 1 1/2 hours | | | ✓ | H |

Cruises are conducted on the Kalamazoo River and Lake Michigan, with live narration.

OTTAWA COUNTY

| Harbor Steamer 301 N. Harbor Grand Haven MI 49417 (616) 842-8950 | Memorial Day - Labor Day 1 1/2 hours | | | ✓ | H |

Cruises follow the Grand River into Spring Lake. There also are riverboat luncheon and "harbor lights" nightime cruises.

NORTHEAST

IOSCO COUNTY

| AuSable River Queen of Oscoda 1775 W. River Road Oscoda MI 48739 (517) 739-7351 | Memorial Day Weekend - third weekend in October 2 hours | | | ✓ | H |

	Reservations required	Overnight/ multiday trips	Food aboard	Handicapper accessible

This paddlewheeler travels on the AuSable River west of Oscoda in an area known for its wildlife, Native American lore and lumbering history. Fall color tours also are offered.

NORTHWEST

CHARLEVOIX COUNTY

Bay Breeze Schooner Co.		✓		✓	H

Bay Breeze Schooner Co.
303 1/2 Bridge St.
Charlevoix MI 49720
(616) 347-0024
Off-season (616) 941-0535

Memorial Day
- Oct. 1
2 hours

The cruises are aboard an 85' schooner sailing from Charlevoix through Round Lake and Lake Charlevoix, one of the state's largest inland lakes.

Ward Brothers Cruises				✓	H

Ward Brothers Cruises
106 E. Antrim
Charlevoix MI 49720
(616) 547-2371

Mid-May -
Mid-October
1 - 2 hours

Trips on the 56' double-deck tour boat go through Lake Charlevoix into Lake Michigan. Also available are sunset cruises and fall color tours.

GRAND TRAVERSE COUNTY

Tall Ship Malibar		✓	✓	✓	H

Tall Ship Malibar
13390 S.W. Bay Shore
Traverse City MI 49684
(616) 941-2000

May -
Early October
2 - 2 1/2 hours

	Reservations required	Overnight/ multiday trips	Food aboard	Handicapper accessible

The Malabar, one of the largest sailing ships on the Great Lakes, is a traditionally rigged two-masted, top-sail schooner and is more than 100' long. It is furnished in the style of a mid-1800s windjammer. It sails from West Grand Travers Bay. In addition to regular afternoon tours, packages are available for sunset sails with bed & breakfast accommodations.

| Tall Ship Manitou 13390 S.W. Bay Shore Traverse City MI 49684 (616) 941-2000 | Mid-June - Early October 72 - 144 hours | ✓ | ✓ | ✓ | |

The Manitou offers only multiday windjammer excursions along the islands, bays and coastal villages of Lake Michigan. A 114'-long traditional two-masted, gaff rigged topsail schooner, the Manitou's itinerary varies by wind and weather conditions. Traditional destinations on the three-day and six-day cruises include Mackinac Island, Harbor Springs, Beaver Island, Sleeping Bear Dunes National Lakeshore, and activities such as kayaking, snorkeling, beachcombing and windsurfing are available.

LEELANAU COUNTY

| Bay Breeze Schooner Co. 12935 W. Bayshore Drive Traverse City MI 49684 (616) 941-0535 | May 15 - Oct. 15 24 hours | ✓ | ✓ | ✓ | |

In addition to 24-hour cruises from Traverse City, longer trips to Mackinaw are also offered.

UPPER PENINSULA

ALGER COUNTY

| Pictured Rocks Cruises Inc. Box 355, Elm Avenue Munising MI 49862 | Memorial Day Weekend - mid-October | | | | H |

	Reservations required	Overnight/ multiday trips	Food aboard	Handicapper accessible

(906) 387-2379   2 1/2 - 2 3/4 hours
Off-season (906) 387-3820

The Lake Superior route passes alongside the spectacular cliffs of Pictured Rocks National Lakeshore, where passengers see such natural landmarks as the Miners Castle, Battleship Rock, Chapel Rock and Colored Caves formations. It also passes the old lighthouse on Grand Island, which is now part of the national forest system.

CHIPPEWA COUNTY

Soo Locks Boat Tours
Box 739   May 15 - Oct. 15   ✓   H
515 E. Portage Ave.   2 - 2 3/4 hours
Sault Ste. Marie MI 49783
(906) 632-6301
(906) 632-2545

These narrated tours pass through the Soo Locks of the St. Marys River, alongside commercial freighters and the shorelines of Sault Ste. Marie, Mich., and Sault Ste. Marie, Ont. In addition to the regular sightseeing tour, the company offers a sunset dinner cruise for which reservations are recommended, and 4th of July nightime fireworks cruises.

KEWEENAW COUNTY

Fort Wilkins State Park
US 41 East   June 1 - Sept. 15   H
Copper Harbor MI 49918
(906) 289-4215

The boat leaves from Copper Harbor Marina and takes passengers to the Lighthouse Museum, where they are met by a resource person and given a tour. Hiking trails also are available.

Chapter 13

PASSENGER FERRIES

Passenger ferry service is a vital transportation link for Michigan, as a water state and as a two-peninsula state. Before the Mackinac Bridge opened in 1957, ferry service and airplanes provided the only commercially scheduled means of transportation between the Upper and Lower Peninsulas, unless you were willing to drive through Indiana and Illinois, then along the Wisconsin shore of Lake Michigan to cross into the western UP.

Today in many instances, ferries remain essential for connecting populated offshore islands with the mainland, as in Drummond, Mackinac and Beaver Island service. Elsewhere, ferries are primarily recreational, as are the ones servicing Isle Royale National Park.

Some ferry services that offer free parking do so only on a limited basis, such as for the day, while charging a fee for overnight parking. Some ferries that do not accept individual reservations will book groups in advance. Also, a ferry service is listed as handicapper-accessible only if all ships in its fleet are reported as accessible. Ask whether they accept credit cards and personal checks.

	Reservations	Motor vehicles	Bicycles	Free parking	Handicapper accessible	Ships in fleet

SOUTHEAST

**MARINE CITY, MICHIGAN
and SOMBRA, ONTARIO**
Bluewater Ferry Ltd.
451 S. Water St.
Box 122
Marine City MI 48039
(519) 892-3879 & (519) 892-3592
Year round

| | | ✓ | ✓ | ✓ | H | 2 |

**GIBRALTER and BOBLO
ISLAND, ONTARIO**
Boblo Island
440 W. Jefferson
Detroit MI 48209
(313) 843-8800
Memorial Day to Labor Day

| | | | | | H | 11 |

NORTHEAST

**CHEBOYGAN and BOIS
BLANC ISLAND**
Island Ferry Services Inc.
101 W. 2d St.
Cheboygan MI 49721
(616) 627-9445 & (616) 627-7878
May to end of November

| | ✓ | ✓ | ✓ | ✓ | H | 1 |

Plaunt Transportation Inc.
406 Water St.
Box 2
Cheboygan MI 49721
(616) 627-2354
April to December

| | ✓ | ✓ | ✓ | | | 1 |

	Reservations	Motor vehicles	Bicycles	Free parking	Handicapper accessible	Ships in fleet

NORTHWEST

BOYNE CITY and IRONTON
Charlevoix County Road Commission
1051 E. Division St.
Box 39
Boyne City MI 49712
(616) 582-7330
April to November

	✓	✓	✓	H	

CHARLEVOIX and ST. JAMES, BEAVER ISLAND
Beaver Island Boat Co.
102 Bridge St.
Charlevoix MI 49720
(616) 547-2311
Mid-April to Christmas

✓	✓	✓	✓		2

LUDINGTON, MICHIGAN and MANITOWOC, WISCONSIN
Lake Michigan Carferry Service Inc.
S. William Street
Box 31036
Ludington MI 49431
(616) 845-5555 & (616) 843-4448
Mid-May to mid-September

✓	✓	✓	✓	H	3

LELAND and MANITOU ISLANDS
Manitou Island Transit
Box 591
Leland MI 49654
(616) 256-9061
May to mid-October

✓				H	2

	Reservations	Motor vehicles	Bicycles	Free parking	Handicapper accessible	Ships in fleet

UPPER PENINSULA, /NORTHEAST

MACKINAC ISLAND and MACKINAW CITY
MACKINAC ISLAND and ST. IGNACE

Arnold Transit Co. Box 220 Mackinac Island MI 49757 (800) 542-8528 & (906) 847-3351 May to Oct. 31			✓	✓	H	
Shepler's Ferry Service 556 E. Central Box 250 Mackinaw City MI 49701 (800) 828-6157 & (616) 436-5023 May 1 - Nov. 1			✓	✓	H	6
Star Line Hydro-Jet Ferry 590 N. State St. St. Ignace MI 49781 (616) 436-5045 & (906) 643-7635 May 1 to Nov. 1			✓	✓	H	5

UPPER PENINSULA

COPPER HARBOR and ISLE ROYALE NATIONAL PARK

Isle Royale Ferry Service Inc. Box 24 Copper Harbor MI 49918 (906) 289-4437; off-season (906) 482-4950 Mid-May to end of September	✓		✓	✓	H	1

235

	Reservations	Motor vehicles	Bicycles	Free parking	Handicapper accessible	Ships in fleet
HOUGHTON and ISLE ROYALE NATIONAL PARK Ranger III Isle Royale National Park 87 N. Ripley Houghton MI 49931 (906) 482-0986 & (906) 482-0984 Memorial Day to Labor Day	✓			✓	H	1
GRAND PORTAGE, MN and ISLE ROYALE NATIONAL PARK Grand Portage-Isle Royale Transportation Line Inc. 1507 N. 1st St. Superior WI 54880 (715) 392-2100 Early May - Nov. 1	✓					2
DeTOUR VILLAGE and DRUMMOND ISLAND *Drummond Island Ferry M-134 DeTour MI 49725 (906) 297-5581 & (906) 495-5656 Year round		✓	✓		H	2
BARBEAU and NEEBISH ISLAND *Neebish Island Ferry Barbeau MI 49710 (906) 632-9404 & (906) 495-5656 April 1 - January 15		✓	✓		H	1

*Operated by Eastern Upper Peninsula Transportation Authority Building 119, Culley Road, Kincheloe MI 49788

	Reservations	Motor vehcilces	Bicycles	Free parking	Handicapper accessible	Ships in fleet
SAULT STE. MARIE and SUGAR ISLAND *Sugar Island Ferry Riverside Drive Sault Ste. Marie MI 49783 (906) 635-5421 & (906) 495-5656 Year round *Operated by Eastern Upper Peninsula Transportation Authority Building 119, Culley Road, Kincheloe MI 49788		✓	✓	✓	H	1

Chapter 14

STATE PARKS & RECREATION AREAS ON THE WATER

Given Michigan's natural, economic and recreational orientation toward water, it's not surprising that its 260,000-acre state park system shares that orientation. Nearly all its approximately 90 parks and recreation areas are on lakes or rivers of some size, ranging from the Great Lakes and the St. Clair River to small inland bodies of water and streams. Together, they front on 120 miles of all four of Michigan's Great Lakes and have 200 miles more of lake, river and stream frontage.

The majority of parks have boat launches. Many offer canoe, rowboat and pedalboat rentals. At Tahquamenon Falls State Park, you can even rent a rowboat to take you to the lower falls, then follow a scenic island trail almost a mile long. At Palms Book State Park, there's a raft ride over the state's largest natural spring. The listings indicate parks with some type of concessionaire-run boat rentals, as well as the two that offer boat tours: Fayette and Fort Wilkins in the Upper Peninsula.

Beyond boating, fishing and swimming opportunities, state parks offer other outdoor attractions, including trails for hiking, mountain biking, horseback riding, cross-country skiing, snowmobiling and snowshoeing. Many have picnic areas, playgrounds, nature centers and historic exhibits as well.

These listings name the principal body or bodies of water in or adjacent to each park. However, many have multiple lakes, streams and rivers. More details are available by contacting each park. Also, in planning your travels, remember that some of the parks' mailing addresses do not show their precise address, and some of the smaller parks share mailing addresses with larger ones nearby.

	Boat Launch	Swimming	Camping	Fishng

SOUTHEAST

JACKSON/LENAWEE
WASHTENAW COUNTIES

W.J. Hayes State Park 1220 Wampler's Lake Road Onsted, MI 49265 (517) 467-7401	Round, Wampler's Lakes	✓	✓	✓	✓

JACKSON/WASHTENAW
COUNTIES

Waterloo Recreation Area 16345 McClure Road Chelsea MI 48118 (313) 475-8307	Green, Sugarloaf Winnewana & Portage Lakes	✓	✓	✓	✓

LAPEER COUNTY

Metamora-Hadley Rec. Area 3871 Hurd Road Metamora MI 48455 (313) 797-4439	Lake Minnawanna	✓	✓	✓	✓

LENAWEE COUNTY

Lake Hudson Recreation Area 1220 Wampler's Lake Road Onsted MI 49265 (517) 467-7401	Lake Hudson	✓	✓	✓	✓

MONROE COUNTY

Sterling State Park 2800 State Park Road Monroe MI 48161 (313) 289-2715	Lake Erie	✓	✓	✓	✓

	Boat Launch	Swimming	Camping	Fishing
OAKLAND COUNTY				
Bald Mountain Recreation Area 1220 Greenshield, Route 1 Lake Orion MI 48360 (313) 693-6767 — Prince, Lower Trout, Upper Trout & Tamarack Lakes	✓	✓		✓
Dodge #4 State Park 4250 Parkway Drive Waterford MI 48328 (313) 682-0800 — Cass Lake	✓	✓		✓
Highland Recreation Area 5200 E. Highland Road (313) 887-5135 — Moore, Lower Pettibone Lakes	✓	✓	✓	✓
Holly State Recreation Area 8100 Grange Hall Road Holly MI 48442 (313) 634-8811 Boat rentals — Crystal, Heron, Wildwood, Crotched & Valley Lakes	✓	✓	✓	
Pontiac Lake Recreation Area 7800 Gale Road Waterford MI 48327 (313) 666-1020 — Pontiac Lake; Huron River	✓	✓	✓	✓
Proud Lake Recreation Area 3540 Wixom Road Milford MI 48382 (313) 685-2433 — Huron River; Proud & Moss Lakes	✓	✓	✓	✓
Seven Lakes State Park 2220 Tinsman Road Fenton MI 48430 (313) 634-7271 — Big Seven, Little Seven & Dickinson Lakes	✓	✓		✓

	Location	Boat Launch	Swimming	Camping	Fishing
OAKLAND/LAPEER COUNTIES					
Ortonville Recreation Area 5779 Hadley Road Ortonville MI 48462 (313) 627-3828	Big Fish, Tody, Davison, Algoe & Mud Lakes	✓	✓	✓	
OAKLAND/MACOMB COUNTIES					
Rochester-Utica Rec. Area 47511 Woodall Utica MI 48317 (313) 731-2110	Clinton River				✓
ST. CLAIR COUNTY					
Algonac State Park 8730 N. River Road Algonac MI 48001 (313) 765-5605	St. Clair River	✓		✓	✓
Lakeport State Park 7605 Lakeshore Road, Rte. 1 Port Huron MI 48060 (313) 327-6765	Lake Huron		✓	✓	✓
WASHTENAW/LIVINGSTON COUNTIES					
Pinckney Recreation Area 8555 Silver Hill Pinckney MI 48169 (313) 426-4913 Boat rentals	Joslin, Silver, Bruin & Halfmoon Lakes; Chain of Lakes	✓	✓	✓	✓
WAYNE COUNTY					
Maybury State Park 20145 Beck Road Northville MI 48167 (313) 349-8390	Fishing Pond				✓

	Boat Launch	Swimming	Camping	Fishing

SOUTHWEST

ALLEGAN COUNTY

Saugatuck Dunes State Park Ottawa Beach Road Holland MI 49424 (616) 399-9390	Lake Michigan		✓		

BERRIEN COUNTY

Grand Mere State Park Red Arrow Highway Sawyer MI 49125 (616) 426-4013	Lake Michigan; North & Middle Lakes				✓
Warren Dunes State Park Red Arrow Highway Sawyer MI 49125 (616) 426-4013	Lake Michigan		✓	✓	

KALAMAZOO COUNTY

Fort Custer Recreation Area 5163 W. Fort Custer Drive Augusta MI 49012 (616) 731-4200	Kalamazoo River; Jackson & Eagle Lakes	✓	✓	✓	✓

OTTAWA COUNTY

Grand Haven State Park 1001 Harbor Ave. Grand Haven MI 49417 (616) 842-6020	Lake Michigan		✓	✓	✓
Holland State Park Ottawa Beach Road Holland MI 49424 (616) 399-9390 Boat rentals	Lake Michigan; Lake Macatawa	✓	✓	✓	✓

	Boat Launch	Swimming	Camping	Fishing
VAN BUREN COUNTY				
Van Buren State Park Lake Michigan		✓	✓	
23960 Ruggles Road				
South Haven MI 49090				
(616) 637-2788				
CENTRAL				
BARRY COUNTY				
Yankee Springs Rec.Area Gun Lake	✓	✓	✓	✓
2104 Gun Lake Road				
Middleville MI 49333				
(616) 795-9081				
BAY COUNTY				
Bay City State Park Saginaw Bay		✓	✓	✓
3582 State Park Drive				
Bay City MI 48706				
(517) 684-3020				
CLINTON COUNTY				
Sleepy Hollow State Park Lake Ovid;	✓	✓	✓	✓
7835 Price Road Little Maple				
Laingsburg MI 48848 River				
(517) 651-6217				
IONIA COUNTY				
Ionia Recreation Area Sessions Lake	✓	✓	✓	✓
2880 David Highway				
Ionia MI 48846				
(616) 527-3750				
Boat rentals				

	Boat Launch	Swimming	Camping	Fishing
LIVINGSTON COUNTY Brighton Recreation Area 6360 Chilson Brighton MI 48843 (313) 229-6566 Boat rentals Shenango, Bishop, Appleton, Reed & Murray Lakes	✓	✓	✓	✓
LIVINGSTON/OAKLAND COUNTIES Island Lake Recreation Area 12950 E. Grand River Brighton MI 48116 (313) 229-7067 Boat rentals Huron River; Kent & Island Lakes	✓	✓	✓	✓

NORTHEAST

	Boat Launch	Swimming	Camping	Fishing
ALCONA COUNTY Harrisville State Park 248 State Park Road Harrisville MI 48730 (517) 724-5126 Lake Huron	✓	✓	✓	✓
CHEBOYGAN COUNTY Aloha State Park 4347 Third St. Cheboygan MI 49721 (616) 625-2522 Mullett Lake	✓	✓	✓	✓
Burt Lake State Park S. Straits Road Indian River MI 49749 (616) 238-9392 Burt Lake	✓	✓	✓	✓
Cheboygan State Park 4490 Beach Road Cheboygan MI 49721 (616) 627-2811 Lake Huron; Little Bill Elliots Creek	✓	✓	✓	✓

	Boat Launch	Swimming	Camping	Fishing
CRAWFORD COUNTY Hartwick Pines State Park R #3, Box 3840 Grayling MI 49738 (517) 348-7068 *East Branch of AuSable River*			✓	✓
North Higgins Lake State Park 11511 N. Higgins Lake Drive Roscommon MI 48653 (517) 821-6125 *Higgins Lake*	✓	✓	✓	✓
HURON COUNTY Port Crescent State Park 1775 Port Austin Road Port Austin MI 48467 (517) 738-8663 *Lake Huron; Pinnebog River*		✓	✓	✓
Albert E. Sleeper State Park 6573 State Park Road Caseville MI 48725 (517) 856-4411 *Saginaw Bay*		✓	✓	✓
IOSCO COUNTY Tawas Point State Park 686 Tawas Beach Road East Tawas MI 48730 (517) 362-5041 *Lake Huron*		✓	✓	✓
MONTMORENCY COUNTY Clear Lake State Park North M-33 Atlanta MI 49709 (517) 785-4388 *Clear Lake*	✓	✓	✓	✓
OGEMAW COUNTY Rifle River Recreation Area 2550 E. Rose City Road Lupton MI 48635 (517) 473-2258 *Rifle River; Grousehaven & Devoe Lakes*	✓	✓	✓	✓

	Boat Launch	Swimming	Camping	Fishing
PRESQUE ISLE COUNTY				
P.H. Hoeft State Park Lake Huron US 23 North Rogers City MI 49779 (517) 734-2543		✓	✓	✓
Onaway State Park Black Lake M-211 North Onaway MI 49765 (517) 733-8279	✓	✓	✓	✓
ROSCOMMON COUNTY				
South Higgins Lake State Park Higgins Lake 106 State Park Drive Roscommon MI 48653 (517) 821-6374 Boat rentals	✓	✓	✓	✓

NORTHWEST

	Boat Launch	Swimming	Camping	Fishing
CHARLEVOIX COUNTY				
Fisherman's Island State Park Lake Michigan; Box 456 McGeach Charlevoix MI 49720 & Whiskey (616) 547-6641 Creeks		✓	✓	✓
Young State Park Lake Charlevoix; 2280 Boyne City Road Chief Noonday, Boyne City MI 49712 Long, Payne & (616) 582-7523 Mirror Lakes	✓	✓	✓	✓
CLARE COUNTY				
Wilson State Park Budd Lake 910 N. First St. Harrison MI 48625 (517) 539-3021		✓	✓	✓

	Boat Launch	Swimming	Camping	Fishing
EMMET COUNTY				
Petoskey State Park 2475 Harbor-Petoskey Road Petoskey MI 49770 (616) 347-2311 — Little Traverse Bay		✓	✓	✓
Wilderness State Park Wilderness Park Drive Carp Lake MI 49718 (616) 436-5381 — Lake Michigan; Sturgeon Bay	✓	✓	✓	✓
GRAND TRAVERSE COUNTY				
Interlochen State Park South M-137 Interlochen MI 49643 (616) 276-9511 — Duck & Green Lakes	✓	✓	✓	✓
Traverse City State Park 1132 US 31 North Traverse City MI 49684 (616) 947-7193 — Grand Traverse Bay; Mitchell Creek		✓	✓	✓
LEELANAU COUNTY				
Leelanau State Park Route 1, Box 49 Northport MI 49670 (616) 386-5422 — Lake Michigan; Mud Lake		✓	✓	✓
MANISTEE COUNTY				
Orchard Beach State Park 2064 Lakeshore Road Manistee MI 49660 (616) 723-7422 — Lake Michigan		✓	✓	
MASON COUNTY				
Ludington State Park M-116, Box 709 Ludington MI 49431 (616) 843-8671 — Lake Michigan; Hamlin Lake; Sable River	✓	✓	✓	✓

	Boat Launch	Swimming	Camping	Fishing
MUSKEGON COUNTY Duck Lake State Park 3560 Memorial Drive North Muskegon MI 49445 (616) 744-3480 Lake Michigan; Duck Lake	✓	✓		✓
P.J. Hoffmaster State Park 6585 Lake Harbor Road Muskegon MI 49411 (616) 798-3711 Lake Michigan; Little Black Lake		✓	✓	✓
NEWAYGO COUNTY Newaygo State Park 2793 Beech St. Newaygo MI 49337 (616) 856-4452 Hardy Dam Pond	✓		✓	✓
OCEANA COUNTY Charles Mears State St. Park W. Lowell Street Pentwater MI 49449 (616) 869-2051 Lake Michigan		✓	✓	✓
Silver Lake State Park Route 1, Box 254 Mears MI 49436 (616) 873-3083 Lake Michigan; Silver Lake	✓		✓	✓
OTSEGO COUNTY Otsego Lake State Park 7136 Old 27 South Gaylord MI 49735 (517) 732-5485 Otsego Lake	✓	✓	✓	✓

	Boat Launch	Swimming	Camping	Fishing
WEXFORD COUNTY				
William Mitchell State Park 6093 East M-115 Cadillac MI 49601 (616) 775-7911 Boat rentals — Lakes Mitchell & Cadillac	✓	✓	✓	✓
UPPER PENINSULA				
BARAGA COUNTY				
Baraga State Park Route 1, Box 566 Baraga MI 49908 (906) 353-6558 — Keweenaw Bay; Hazel Creek	✓	✓	✓	✓
Craig Lake State Park Box 66 Champion MI 49814 (906) 339-4461 — Crag, Keewaydin, Crooked Lakes; West Branch of Peshekee River				✓
CHIPPEWA COUNTY				
Brimley State Park Route 2, Box 202 Brimley MI 49715 (906) 248-3422 — Whitefish Bay	✓	✓	✓	✓
Tahquamenon Falls State Park Star Route 48, Box 225 Paradise MI 49768 (906) 492-3415 Boat Rentals — Tahquamenon River; Sheephead, Betsy & Clark Lakes	✓		✓	✓

	Boat Launch	Swimming	Camping	Fishing
DELTA COUNTY Fayette State Park Big Bay de Noc 13700 13.25 Lane Garden MI 49835 (906) 644-2603 Boat tours	✓	✓	✓	✓
GOGEBIC COUNTY Lake Gogebic State Park Lake Gogebic H.C. 1, Box 139 Marenisco MI 49947 (906) 842-3341	✓	✓	✓	✓
HOUGHTON COUNTY F.J. McLain State Park Lake Superior; M-203 Bear Lake; Hancock MI 49930 Portage Lake (906) 482-0278 Ship Canal		✓	✓	✓
Twin Lakes State Park Lake Roland M-26 Twin Lakes Route Toivola MI 49965 (906) 288-3321	✓	✓	✓	✓
IRON COUNTY Bewabic State Park Fortune Lakes 1933 US 2 West Crystal Falls MI 49920 (906) 875-3324	✓	✓	✓	✓
KEWEENAW COUNTY Fort Wilkins State Park Copper Harbor; US 41 East Lake Fannie Copper Harbor MI 49918 Hooe (906) 289-4215 Boat tours	✓		✓	✓

	Boat Launch	Swimming	Camping	Fishing
LUCE COUNTY				
Muskallonge Lake State Park — Lake Superior; Muskallonge Lake Box 245, Route I Newberry MI 49868 (906) 658-3338	✓	✓	✓	✓
MACKINAC COUNTY				
Straits State Park — Straits of Mackinac 720 Church St. St. Ignace MI 49781 (906) 643-8620			✓	✓
MARQUETTE COUNTY				
Van Riper State Park — Lake Michigamme; Peshekee River Box 66 Champion MI 49814 (906) 339-461	✓	✓	✓	✓
MENOMINEE COUNTY				
J.W. Wells State Park — Green Bay M-35 Cedar River MI 49813 (906) 863-9747		✓	✓	✓
ONTONAGON/GOGEBIC COUNTIES				
Porcupine Mountains Wilderness State Park — Lake Superior; Carp River 599 M-107 Ontonagon MI 49953 (906) 885-5275	✓		✓	✓
SCHOOLCRAFT COUNTY				
Indian Lake State Park — Indian Lake Route 2, Box 2500 Manistique MI 49854 (906) 341-2355 Boat rentals	✓	✓	✓	✓

		Boat Launch	Swimming	Camping	Fishing
Palms Book State Park Route 2, Box 2500 Manistique MI 49854 (906) 341-2355	Big Springs	✓			

Chapter 15

NATIONAL PARKS & ARMY CORPS OF ENGINEER SITES ON THE WATER

All three of Michigan's national parks are on the water with one of them, Isle Royale National Park, surrounded by Lake Superior. Each offers a variety of water recreational opportunities in a beautiful setting. In addition, the U.S. Army Corps of Engineers has two water sites in the state, both in the Upper Peninsula.

NATIONAL PARKS

NORTHWEST

SLEEPING BEAR DUNES NATIONAL LAKESHORE
Superintendent, Sleeping Bear Dunes National Lakeshore
Box 277
Empire MI 49630
(616) 326-5134

HISTORY: Chippewa legend tells how a mother bear and her two cubs were driven by a forest fire from Wisconsin across Lake Michigan. Although the mother made it safely to the Michigan shore, the cubs drowned. A massive sand dune above the water marks the spot where the mother bear waited helplessly for her young to arrive, and it was there she died of grief. Two islands, South Manitou and North Manitou, mark the final resting place of the doomed cubs. Geologists tell a different tale about an area scoured by glaciers during the Ice Age; according to the scientists, the beach dunes were formed from beach sand, while the higher perched dunes were made by glacia sand.

In 1970, Congress authorized establishment of the national lake shore. It now includes both islands and part of the mainland along the Leelanau Peninsula. The South Manitou lighthouse still stands and is open for park service tours but has been out of service since 1958. Wilderness camping, which requires a free permit, is available on both islands and the mainland; there also are established campgrounds on the mainland and South Manitou Island.

TRANSPORTATION: The park is 25 miles west of Traverse City. Route M-22 runs through the park. Both Manitou Islands are accessible by ferry, licensed chartered boat or private boat. See Chapter 13 for more information on ferry service.

BOATING: There are boat launches along the Lake Michigan shore and inland streams and lakes. North Manitou Island, 15,000 acres large, lacks protected anchorage, meaning that boaters must anchor offshore, subject to shifts in wind and weather; boaters may use the island's dock for up to 15 minutes only to load and unload. There are no docking or fuel services available on South Manitou Island, 5,260 acres in size, although its natural harbor was crucial for Lake Michigan shipping in the 19th century.

Nearby Coast Guard stations monitor marine radio Channel 16 for emergencies.

CANOEING & KAYAKING: Canoeing and kayaking are allowed on the several creeks and rivers that pass through the park. Canoe rentals are available on the Crystal and Platte Rivers.

FISHING: Fishing is allowed in Lake Michigan and on the park's lakes and rivers, with salmon, bass, trout and pike especially popular among anglers. A state license is required.

SWIMMING: Visitors can swim in Lake Michigan and the park's inland waters.

MARITIME MUSEUM: The Sleeping Bear Point Coast Guard Station Maritime Museum is located near the Dune Climb and D.H. Day Campground. Admission is free. For more information on the museum, see Chapter 24.

DIVING: Manitou Passage Bottomland Preserve lies off the shore of Sleeping Bear Dunes National Lakeshore and encompasses the two Manitou Islands. Despite the presence of a series of lighthouses on South Manitou since 1840, many ships have run aground or sank in the area. The preserve is highly regarded for its shallow water scuba diving opportunities, while constantly shifting sands alternatively expose and cover wrecks and reefs. Among them are the steamer *Francisco Morazan* wrecked in shallow waters in 1960; the schooner

Josephine Dresden, sank alongside a dock on North Manitou in 1907; and the schooner *Supply,* lost in a 1862 storm. For more information on diving in the Manitou Passage, see Chapter 10.

UPPER PENINSULA

ISLE ROYALE NATIONAL PARK
Superintendent, Isle Royale National Park
Houghton MI 49931
(906) 482-0984.

HISTORY: For 1,000 years, Native Americans paddled to Isle Royale in the northwestern part of Lake Superior to obtain copper. In the 1830s, commercial fishing began on the 210-square-mile island, followed by settlements and farming. In the late 1800s, commercial copper mines operated with little economic success, and the island became popular as a summer vacation and excursion spot. In 1940, Congress established it as a national park, with the emphasis on wilderness; it was later designated as a United Nations biosphere reserve. It is internationally renowned for its wolf and moose population.

TRANSPORTATION: The park, an archipelago, is linked to the mainland by ferries from Houghton, Mich. (73 miles, 6 hours) and Copper Harbor, Mich. (56 miles, 4 1/2 hours), and from Grand Portage, Minn. (22 miles, 3 hours.) Expect to be charged extra for canoes, kayaks, motor boats, motors and air tanks. See Chapter 13 for more information on ferry service. The park also can be reached by float plane and private boat. No motorized vehicles are allowed on the island. Lodging is available at Rock Harbor. Camping is on a first-come first-served basis, and some sites are accessible only by kayak or canoe.

CANOEING & KAYAKING: Visitors can canoe and kayak on the island's bays and inland lakes, although landing spots on the outer shore of Lake Superior are scarce, and weather can turn windy or stormy with little advance notice. All canoeists and kayakers must use a Coast Guard-approved personal flotation device. Canoe rentals are available at Rock Harbor on the eastern end of the island and at Windigo on the western end.

Canoe routes are on the northeast half of the island. The 16 portages, ranging from .1 mile to 2 miles in length are marked with a white "P" on posts. Wheeled portage devices are prohibited.

FISHING: Visitors need a Michigan license to fish in Lake Superior. Temporary licenses are sold at Rock Harbor, Malone Bay, Windigo and Amygdaloid. No license is required for inland streams and lakes, although state possession and size limits are in effect. Only artificial bait and lures may be used on inland waters. There is a fish-cleaning facility at Rock Harbor.

SWIMMING: The National Park Service recommends against swimming because of the extremely cold temperature of Lake Superior and the presence of leeches in the warmer inland lakes.

BOATING: Before your trip or upon arrival, obtain Great Lakes Chart No. 14976, "Isle Royale." All motorized boats are required to have home state registration; boaters must present that registration at a ranger station on arrival to obtain a park permit. Overnight docking is allowed only at campgrounds and designated docks. Outboard motors are banned on inland streams and lakes.

Gasoline and oil are sold at Windigo and Rock Harbor from mid-May to late September, while pre- and post-season service is available at Mott Island and Rock Harbor; there is no diesel fuel at Windigo. Both Windigo and Rock Harbor marinas have boats and motors for rent. There are pumping stations at Rock Harbor and Windigo. The ranger stations at Mott Island and Windigo monitor marine band Channel 16, and marine weather forecast is available at all ranger stations.

DIVING: The chilly waters around Lake Superior are the graveyard for at least 10 major wrecks and dozens of their crew, and countless smaller craft. Many divers also enjoy such underwater attractions as copper veins. Collecting greenstones is allowed, although it is illegal to take artifacts. Diving is allowed only from mid-April through the end of October. Divers must obtain a free permit at a ranger station and should check on which areas are off-limits. Spear guns are prohibited.

Wrecks accessible to divers include the steamer *Algona*, run aground in 1885; the freighter *America*, sunk in 1928; the side-wheeler *Cumberland*, lost in 1877; the freighter *Emperor*, wrecked in 1947; and the freighter *Chester A. Congdon*, run aground and broken up in a 1918 storm. See Chapter 9 for more information about diving near Isle Royale.

PICTURED ROCKS NATIONAL LAKESHORE
Superintendent
Pictured Rocks National Lakeshore
Box 40
Munising MI 49862
(906) 387-2607

HISTORY: Site of the first national lakeshore, the pastel-colored cliffs of Pictured Rocks were long known to the Ojibway, who fished and hunted here and traveled past on their way to their summer fishing grounds of the St. Marys River to the east. French missionaries, trappers and explorers reached the area in the 1600s, followed in the early 19th century by settlers lured by the white pine forests. Now the cliffs and dunes along Lake Superior lure more than 500,000 visitors a year. There are visitor centers at Munising Falls and Grand Sable.

TRANSPORTATION: The national park is accessible by motor vehicle from Grand Marais to the east and from Munising to the west. For a great view of the cliffs, coupled with a narrative history of the area, take a boat tour from Munising from June through mid-October. For more information on the tour, see Chapter 12. For hikers, the North Country National Scenic Trail between New York and North Dakota runs for 42.8 miles through the park.

BOATING & CANOEING: Smalls boats and canoes are permitted on Grand Sable Lake, which has a boat launch, and on Beaver Lake and Little Beaver Lake, which don't. Canoeing on the park's rivers and streams is hampered by brush and shallowness. There also are launches at Munising and Grand Marais with access to Lake Superior, but small craft should be careful because those waters may be rough.

FISHING: Fishing is allowed in Lake Superior, on backcountry ponds and lakes, and on the park's streams and rivers. Ice fishing is popular on Munising Bay and most of the inland lakes. State regulations such as license requirements, seasons and creel limits apply and are enforced by state Department of Natural Resources conservation officers and National Park Service rangers.

MARITIME MUSEUM & LIGHTHOUSE: The Grand Marais Maritime Museum at Coast Guard Point depicts the early years of shipping, commercial fishing, lighthouses, the U.S. Life Saving Service and shipwrecks. For more information about the museum, see Chapter 24.

The Au Sable Light Station, which began operating at Au Sable Point in 1874, is a 1.5-mile walk from the Hurricane River campground in the northeast part of the park. This well-preserved lighthouse is listed on the National Register of Historic Places.

DIVING: The Alger Bottomland Preserve is located off the park shore, with shipwrecks, colorful underwater rocks and cliffs, and weedbeds for fish. Wrecks here include the steamer *Herman H. Hettler*, which struck a reef during a 1926 gale; the steamer *Manhattan*, which burned and sunk after the crew lost control in 1903; and the sidewheeler *Superior*, which ran aground against the cliffs in 1856. For more information about diving in the Alger Preserve, see Chapter 10.

ARMY CORPS OF ENGINEERS

Army Corps of Engineers District Office
Box 1027
Detroit MI 48231-1027
(313) 226-6413

Although we generally think of the Army Corps of Engineers only in terms of such activities and projects as building dams, controlling flooding and dredging harbors, the Corps also maintains hundreds of recreation areas across the country, often with boat launches, beaches and fishing.

ST. MARYS FALLS LOCKS & VISITOR CENTER

The St. Marys River, with its rapids and 21-foot-high falls, connects Lake Huron and Lake Superior, as well as marking the border between Michigan and Ontario at Sault Ste. Marie. The first lock was built by the Northwest Fur Co. in 1787 but was destroyed in the War of 1812. A replacement was built by the Fairbanks Scale Co. between 1853-1855 and turned over to the state. Then in 1881, the federal government took over the Soo Locks. Now, four locks make passage possible between Lake Huron and Lake Superior. An average of 10,000 vessels pass through the lock system each year, ranging from small passenger boats to ocean-going freighters, some more than 1,000 feet long and carrying more than 72,000 tons of cargo.

The free visitor center contains a working model of a lock, a 25-minute film called the "Great Lakes Connection" about the history and operations of the Soo Locks, artifacts, a Great Lakes relief map and photos. A public address system announces information about downbound vessels including cargo, tonnage, size and nation of registry. In addition to the visitor center, the facility is open for picnicking and day use, and there's a fountain in the park area with colored lights and synchronized music. A hydroelectric power plant is located north of the locks.

LOWER KEWEENAW ENTRY WATERWAY

Great Lakes ships use this waterway as a shortcut and for shelter from Lake Superior storms. You'll find a boat launch, marina and rest rooms here. By car, it's four miles east of Chassell on US 41.

Chapter 16

STATE FOREST
WATER ACCESS

Michigan has 3.9 million acres of state-owned forestland. They are administered through six state forests and form the largest forest system of any state. Their acreage represents 22 percent of the public and private forestland in Michigan.

For those interested in water recreation, state forests offer more than 150 primitive campgrounds with fishing, a launch -- canoe or boat -- or both. Each of the campgrounds has 5 to 50 sites, and many are also suitable for swimming.

State forests contain many non-contiguous pieces scattered across multiple counties. For example, you'll find part of the Au Sable State Forest scattered in nine mid-Michigan and northern counties in the Lower Peninsula, listings in this chapter are arranged by forest and subdivided under their principal region.

The listings indicate where there is access for boats or canoes. However, you may wish to call in advance about the type of access at a particular site. Because state forest facilities are generally more rustic than those at state parks, some of the access sites at forest campgrounds are narrow and steep carrydowns, rather than concrete or gravel ramps. The appropriate state forest management office can answer your questions.

	Boat or canoe launch	Fishing

NORTHEAST/CENTRAL/NORTHWEST

Au Sable State Forest
191 S. Mt. Tom Road
Mio MI 48647
(517)826-3211
748,458 acres

	Boat or canoe launch	Fishing
Shupac Lake: 2 mi. N of Lovells via Twin Bridge Road	✓	✓
Jones Lake: 9 mi. E of Frederic via Co. Road 612	✓	✓
Upper Manistee River: 6½ mi. W of Frederic via Co. Rd. 612	✓	✓
Manistee River Bridge: 8 mi. W of Grayling via M-72	✓	✓
Lake Margrethe: 5 mi. W of Grayling via M-72		✓
AuSable River Canoe Camp: 7 mi. E of Grayling via N. Down River & Headquarters Roads	✓	✓
Burton's Landing: 4½ mi. E of Grayling via M-72 & Burton's Landing Road	✓	✓
Keystone Landing: 6 mi. E of Grayling via M-72 & Keystone Landing Road	✓	✓
Canoe Harbor: 14 mi. SE of Grayling via M-72	✓	✓
White Pine Canoe Camp: 12 mi. E of Grayling via M-72 & McMaster's Bridge Road	✓	✓
Rainbow Bend: 15 mi. E of Grayling via M-72 & McMaster's Bridge Road	✓	✓
Parmalee Bridge: 5 mi. N of Luzerne via Co. Road 489	✓	✓
Mio Pond: 3 mi. NW of Mio via M-33 & Popps Road	✓	✓
McCollum Lake: 8.5 mi. NW of Curran via M-65 & McCollum Lake Road	✓	✓
Van Etten Lake: 4½ mi. NW of Oscoda via US 23 & F 41		✓
Hardwood Lake: 13½ mi. SE of West Branch via M-55 & Co. Road 21	✓	✓
Rifle River: 11 mi. SE of Rose City via M-33 & Peters Road	✓	✓
Ambrose Lake: 11 mi. N of West Branch via Co. Rds. 15 & 20	✓	✓
Houghton Lake: 6 mi. NW of Houghton Lake Heights via W. Shore Drive		✓
House Lake: 2½ mi. NE of Meredith via Meredith Grade		✓
Trout Lake: 3 mi NE of Meredith via Meredith Grade	✓	✓

	Boat or canoe launch	Fishing
Wildwood: 13 mi. S of West Branch via M-30 & Wildwood Shores Road		✓
Black Creek: 3 mi. NW of Sanford via Saginaw and W. River Roads		✓
Temple: 10½ mi. W of Harrison via M-61	✓	
Pike Lake: 9½ mi. NW of Farwell via M-115		
Mud Lake: 11 mi. E of Evart via US 10, M-66 & Grand & Brown Roads	✓	✓
Muskrat Lake: 12 mi. NW of Mio via M-72, Co. Road 608 & Richardson Road	✓	✓

NORTHWEST/NORTHEAST

Mackinaw State Forest
Box 667
Gaylord MI 49735
(517) 732-3541
663,843 acres

	Boat or canoe launch	Fishing
Graves Crossing: 10 mi. N of Mancelona via US 131 & M-66	✓	✓
Weber Lake: 7½ mi. NW of Wolverine via Wolverine & Prue Roads		✓
Maple Bay: 3½ mi. E of Brutus via Brutus Road	✓	✓
Haakwood: 2 mi. N of Wolverine via Old 27 & Campground Road	✓	✓
Twin Lakes: 6 mi. SE of Alverno via Black River & Twin Lakes Roads		✓
Black Lake: 11 mi. NE of Onaway via M-211, Co. Road 489, & Black Mountain & Donya Roads		✓
Ocqueoc Falls: 10 mi. NE of Onaway via M-68 & Millersburg Road		✓
Shoepac Lake: 12 mi. SE of Onaway via M-33 & Tomahawk Lake Hwy.	✓	✓
Tomahawk Lake: 11 mi. SE of Onaway via M-33 & Tomahawk Lake Hwy.	✓	✓
Tomahawk Creek Flooding: 10 mi. SE of Onaway via M-33 & Tomahawk Lake Hwy.	✓	✓
Pine Grove: 12 mi. SE of Wolverine via Wolverine & WebbL Roads		✓

	Boat or canoe launch	Fishing
Pickerel Lake: 10 mi. E of Vanderbilt via Sturgeon Valley & Pickerel Lake Roads	✓	✓
Pigeon River: 13 mi. E of Vanderbilt via Sturgeon Valley & Osmund Roads		✓
Pigeon Bridge: 11 mi. E of Vanderbilt via Sturgeon Valley Road		✓
Round Lake: 14 mi. SE of Vanderbilt via Sturgeon Valley & Round Lake Roads		✓
Lake Marjory: 1¼ mi. SE of Waters via Old US 27	✓	
Big Bear Lake: 1½ mi. SW of Vienna via Principal Meridian & Little Bear Lake Roads	✓	✓
Town Corner: 20 mi. SE of Vanderbilt via Sturgeon Valley, Tin Shanty, Chandler Dam & Meridian Line Roads	✓	✓
Little Wolf Lake: 3 mi. SE of Lewiston via Co. Road 489 & Wolf Lake Road		✓
Big Oaks: 10 mi. SW of Atlanta via Co. Rd. 487 & Avery Lake Road	✓	✓
Avery Lake: 9 mi. SW of Atlanta via Co. Rd. 487 & Avery Lake Road	✓	✓
Lake 15: 3 mi. S of Atlanta via Co. Road 489 & Lake Fifteen Road	✓	✓
Jackson Lake: 6 mi. N of Atlanta via M-33	✓	✓
Ess Lake: 16 mi. NE of Atlanta via M-33 & Co. Road 624	✓	✓
Thunder Bay River: 9 mi. SW of Alpena via M-32 & Indian Reserve Road	✓	✓
Ossineke: 1 mi. E of Ossineke via US 23		✓
Elk Hill: 13½ mi. E of Vanderbilt via Sturgeon Valley & Osmund Roads	✓	✓
Pinney Bridge: 13 mi. W of Gaylord via M-32, US 131 & Dead Alan's Hill Road		✓

NORTHWEST

Pere Marquette State Forest
8015 Mackinaw Trail
Cadillac MI 49601
(616) 775-9727
621,052 acres

	Boat or canoe launch	Fishing
Pickerel Lake: 13½ mi. NE of Kalkaska via Co. Road 612 & Sunset Trail	✓	✓
Guernsey Lake: 8 mi. W of Kalkaska via Island Lake & Campground Roads	✓	✓
Forks: 7 mi. S of Williamsburg via Williamsburg, Supply & River Roads	✓	✓
Scheck's Place: 12 mi. SW of Williamsburg via Williamsburg, Supply & Brown Bridge Roads	✓	✓
Arbutus Lake No. 4: 10 mi. SE of Traverse City via Garfield,, Potter, 4 Mile & N. Arbutus Lake Roads	✓	✓
Lake Dubonnet: 5 mi. NW of Interlochen State Park via M-137, US 31 & Wildwood Road	✓	✓
Lake Ann: 2 mi. SW of Lake Ann via Almira & Reynolds Rds.	✓	✓
Veterans Memorial: 3½ mi. E of Honor via US 31		✓
Platte River: 2½ mi. SE of Honor via US 31 & Goose Road		✓
Grass Lake: 10 mi. NE of Thompsonville via Co. Road 669 & Wallin Road	✓	✓
Healy Lake: 7½ mi. SW of Copemish via Co. Road 669 & Piagany & Entrance Roads	✓	✓
Indian Crossing: 6½ mi. NE of Sherman via Road No. 14 & Campground Road	✓	✓
Baxter Bridge: 12 mi NW of Manton via M-42 & Road No. 31	✓	✓
Old US 31: 6 mi. N of Manton on US 131	✓	✓
Spring Lake: 1½ mi. SW of Fife Lake via US 131		✓
Chase Creek: 7½ mi. NE of Manton via US 131, No. 12 Road & No. 45 1/2 Road	✓	✓
Smithville: ½ mi. NW of Smithville via M-66		✓
C.C.C. Bridge: 20 mi. SE of Kalkaska via M-72 & Sunset Trail Road	✓	✓
Reedsburg Dam: 5 mi. NW of Houghton L. via M-55 & Co. Rd. 300	✓	✓
Long Lake: 8 mi. NE of Cadillac via US 131 & Cpgd. Rd.	✓	✓
Goose Lake: 2½ mi. NW of Lake City via M-66 & Goose Lake Road	✓	✓
Long Lake: 3½ mi. NW of Lake City via M-66 & Goose Lake Road	✓	✓
Lincoln Bridge: 7 mi. N of Luther via State & 10 Mile Roads	✓	✓

	Boat or canoe launch	Fishing
Silver Creek: 5½ mi. N of Luther via State Road	✓	
Sunrise Lake: 6 mi. E of LeRoy via Sunset Lake & 15 Mile Rds	✓	✓
Carrieville: 3 mi. W of Luther via Old M-63 & Kings Hwy.		✓
Bray Creek: 1½ mi. NE of Baldwin via M-37, North St., Marysville Road & 40th St.		✓
Little Leverentz: 2 mi. NE of Baldwin via US 10 & Campground Road		✓
Big Leverentz: 2 mi. NE of Baldwin via US 10		✓
Tubbs Island: 7 mi. SW of Barryton via M-66, 17 Mile Road & 45 Ave.	✓	✓
Tubbs Lake: 6½ mi. SW of Barryton via M-66, 17 Mile Road & 45 Ave.	✓	✓

UPPER PENINSULA

Copper Country State Forest
US 41 North, Box 440
Baraga MI 49908
(906) 353-6651
430,291 acres

	Boat or canoe launch	Fishing
Emily Lake: 2½ mi. S of Twin Lake State Park via M-26 & Pike Lake Co. Road	✓	✓
Big Eric's Bridge: 6 mi. E. of Skanee via Skanee Road		✓
Big Lake: 9 mi. NW of Covington via US 141 & Plains Road	✓	✓
King Lake: 15 mi. E of Covington via M-28, US 41 & Co. Road	✓	✓
Beaufort Lake: 1½ mi. SE of Three Lakes via US 41 & Co. Road	✓	✓
Deer Lake: 17 mi. N of Crystal Falls via US 141 & Deer Lake Road	✓	✓
Lake Ellen: 4 mi. W of Channing via Campground Road	✓	✓
Glidden Lake: 6 mi. SE of Crystal Falls via M-69 & Lake Mary Road	✓	✓
West Branch: 7 mi. N of Ralph via Co. Road 581	✓	✓
Lower Dam: 11 mi. NE of Ralph via Co. Road 581	✓	✓

	Boat or canoe launch	Fishing
Gene's Pond: 6½ mi. NW of Theodore via Co. Roads 581 & 422 & Campground Road	✓	✓
Carney Lake: 16 mi. NE of Iron Mountain via M-95 & Merriman Truck Trail	✓	✓

Escanaba River State Forest
6833 Highway 2
Gladstone MI 49837
(906) 786-2351
402,696 acres

	Boat or canoe launch	Fishing
Squaw Lake: 4 mi. NW of Witch Lake via Fence River & Squaw Lake Roads	✓	✓
Horseshoe Lake North: 1¼ mi. W of Witch Lake via Fence River Road	✓	
Horseshoe Lake South: 1 mi. W of Witch Lake via Fence River Road	✓	✓
Bass Lake: 12 mi. SW of Gwinn via M-35 & Bass Lake Road	✓	✓
Pike Lake: 9 mi. SW of Gwinn via M-35 & Bass Lake Road	✓	✓
Anderson Lake West: 7 mi. SW of Gwinn via Co. Road 577	✓	✓
Witbeck Rapids: 2¼ N of Witch Lake via M-95 & Campground Road	✓	✓
Little Lake: 1 mi. SE of Little Lake via M-35	✓	✓
Laughing Whitefish: 12 mi. W of Au Train via M-28 & Campground Road		✓
Cedar River North: 6 mi. NW of Cedar River via M-35 & River Road	✓	✓

Lake Superior State Forest
309 W. McMillan Ave.
Newberry MI 49868
(906) 293-5131
1,026,058 acres

	Boat or canoe launch	Fishing
Kingston Lake: 16 mi. NE of Melstrand via Au Sable Point Road	✓	✓
North Gemini Lake: 10 mi. NE of Melstrand via Co. Road H-58 & Twin Lakes Truck Trail	✓	✓

	Boat or canoe launch	Fishing
South Gemini Lake: 12 mi. NE of Melstrand via Co. Road H-58 & Twin Lakes Truck Trail	✓	✓
Ross Lake: 14 mi. NE of Melstrand via Co. Road M-58 & Crooked Lake Road	✓	✓
Canoe Lake: 9 mi. E of Melstrand via Co. Roads H-52, 450 & Wolf Lake Road		✓
Cusino Lake: 11 mi. E of Melstrand via Co. Roads H-52 & 450	✓	✓
Stanley Lake: 15 mi. NW of Seney via Co. Road 450 & Mahoney Lake Road	✓	✓
Fox River: 5 mi. NW of Seney via Co. Road 450	✓	✓
Fox River, East Branch: 8 mi. N of Seney via M-77		✓
Portage Bay: 10 mi. S of Garden via Co. Road 483 & Portage Bay Road	✓	✓
Merwin Creek: 9 mi. NW of Gulliver via US 2 & Co. Roads 438 & 433	✓	✓
Mead Creek: 6 mi. SW of Germfask via M-77 & Co. Road 436	✓	✓
South Manistique Lake: 6 mi SW of Curtis via S. Curtis & Long Point Roads	✓	✓
Milakokia Lake: 7 mi. SW of Gould City via US 2 & Pike Lake Grade	✓	✓
Lake Superior: 15 mi. E of Grand Marais via Grand Marais Truck Trail		✓
Blind Sucker No. 1: 14 mi. E of Grand Marais via Grand Marais Truck Trail	✓	✓
Blind Sucker No. 2: 16 mi. E of Grand Marais via Grand Marais Truck Trail		✓
Pratt Lake: 28 mi. NW of Newberry via M-123 & Co. Roads 407 & 416	✓	✓
Holland Lake: 26 mi. NW of Newberry via M-123 & Co. Roads 407 & 416		✓
Pretty Lake: 27 mi. NW of Newberry via M-123, Co. Roads 407 & 416 & Campground Road	✓	✓
Perch Lake: 25 mi. N of Newberry via M-123 & Co. Road 407	✓	✓
High Bridge: 23 mi. N of Newberry via M-122 & Co. Road 407	✓	✓
Reed & Green Bridge: 31 mi. N of Newberry via M-122 & Co. Roads 401 & 410	✓	✓
Two Hearted River Canoe Camp: 28 mi. N of Newberry via M-123, Co. Road 407 & Lone Pine Camp Road	✓	✓

	Boat or canoe launch	Fishing
Mouth of Two Hearted River: 35 mi. NE of Newberry via M-123 & Co. Roads 500, 414, 412 & 423	✓	✓
Pike Lake: 29 mi. NE of Newberry via M-123 & Co. Roads 500 & 417	✓	✓
Bodi Lake: 32 mi. NW of Newberry via M-123 & Co. Roads 500 & 437	✓	✓
Culhane Lake: 30 NE of Newberry via M-123 & Co. Road 500	✓	✓
Andrus Lake: 6 mi. N of Paradise via Wire & Vermillion Road	✓	✓
Shelldrake Dam: 8 mi. N of Paradise via Wire & Vermillion Roads	✓	✓
Bass Lake: 9½ mi. N of McMillan via Co. Roads 415 & 421		✓
Sixteen Creek: 6 mi. NW of Newberry via M-123 & Charcoal Grade	✓	✓
Natalie: 4½ mi. W of Newberry via Co. Roads 405 & 43A		✓
Black River: 7 mi. NE of Naubinway via US 2 & Black River Road		✓
Garnet Lake: 1 mi SE of Garnet via H-40	✓	✓
Hog Island Point: 7 mi. E of Naubinway via US 2	✓	✓
Little Brevort Lake North: 2 mi. NE of Brevort via Carp River & Worth Roads	✓	✓
Little Brevort Lake South: 1½ mi. SE of Brevort via US 2		✓
Munuscong River: 8 mi. NE of Pickford via M-48 & Sterlingville Road	✓	✓
Maxton Bay: 4½ mi. NE of Drummond via Maxton Plains Road		✓

Chapter 17

NATIONAL FOREST WATER ACCESS

National forests sprawl across large parts of Michigan's Upper Peninsula and the northern half of the Lower Peninsula. They total more than 2.7 million acres, roughly 14 percent of the private and public forest land in Michigan.

While one major reason they were set aside under federal control is to serve the timber industry, this forestland also provides opportunities for uncrowded and often remote water-based recreation, in particular boating, canoeing, fishing and swimming.

Hiawatha National Forest covers 860,000 acres in the eastern and central Upper Peninsula. It borders on three Great Lakes -- Huron, Michigan and Superior -- as well as many inland lakes, rivers and streams, including the Au Train, Sturgeon, Whitefish and Carp Rivers. There are lighthouses at Round Island, Point Peninsula and Point Iroquois.

Ottawa National Forest is located in the western Upper Peninsula, in part along Lake Superior. Its 954,000 acres include 2,000 miles of stream, more than 700 lakes, a variety of waterfalls and picturesque Black River Harbor.

The Huron-Manistee National Forests are two geographically separate entities administered jointly by the federal government.

The Huron portion is located in the northeastern part of the Lower Peninsula, between the South Branch of the Au Sable River and Lake Huron near Oscoda. Within its 432,836 acres are a variety of waterways and a statue in memory of Michigan's pioneer lumberers.

The Manistee portion is primarily in the northwestern quadrant, reaching Lake Michigan north of Muskegon. Its 531,085 acres also encompass a wealth of rivers, streams and lakes.

Each of the following recreation sites provides fishing and/or a boat or canoe launch. All the sites offer camping except those marked with an asterisk (*).

	Boat or canoe launch	Fishing

NORTHEAST/CENTRAL/NORTHWEST

HURON-MANISTEE NATIONAL FORESTS
421 S. Mitchell
Cadillac MI 49601
(800) 821-6263, (616) 775-2421

Baldwin Ranger District (616) 745-4631

Highbanks Lake: 2 mi. W of Lilley via Forest Rte. 5396	✓	✓
Gleasons Landing: 3 mi. SW of Baldwin via M-37		✓
Old Grade: 11 mi. N of Baldwin via M-37		✓

Cadillac Ranger District (616) 775-8539

Hemlock: 5 mi. W of Cadillac via M-55	✓	✓
Peterson Bridge: 16 mi. S of Mesick via M-37	✓	✓
Seaton Creek: 7 mi. SW of Mesick via M-37	✓	✓
Olga Lake*: 16 mi SW of Cadillac via M-55	✓	
Ravine: 12 mi. W of Cadillac via M-55		✓

Manistee Ranger District (616) 723-2211

Bear Track: 6.5 mi. W of Irons via Co. Road 669	✓	✓
Dorner Lake: 2 mi. SE of Wellston via County Road	✓	✓
Driftwood Valley: 13 mi. SW of Manistee via County Road		✓
Pine Lake: 3.5 mi. SW of Wellston via County Road	✓	✓
Sand Lake: 1 mi. S of Dublin via County Road	✓	✓
Udell Rollways: 8 mi. NW of Wellston via M-55		✓
Corsair: 7 mi. NW of Tawas City via M-55		✓

White Cloud Ranger District (616) 689-6696

Benton Lake: 4 mi. W of Brohman via Pierce Drive	✓	✓
Nichols Lake: 3 mi. W of Woodland Park via M-37	✓	✓

* No camping

	Boat or canoe launch	Fishing
Pines Point: 8.5 mi. SW of Hesperia via M-82	✓	✓
Minnie Lake*: 11 mi. NW of White Cloud via 6 Mile Road	✓	
Wayside Lake*: 3 mi. SW of White Cloud via Echo Drive		✓

Mio Ranger District (517) 826-3252

Island Lake: 6 mi. N of Rose City via M-33		✓
Kneff Lakes: 8 mi. E of Grayling via M-72		✓
Mack Lake: 8.5 mi. SE of Mio via M-33		✓
Wagner Lake: 8 mi. SE of Mio via M-33		✓
Loon Lake*: 7 mi S of Mio via M-33		✓

Tawas Ranger District (517) 362-4477

Rollways: 7 mi. N of Hale via M-65		✓
Round Lake: 9 mi. NW of Tawas via M-55	✓	✓

Harrisville Ranger District (517) 724-5431

Horseshoe Lake: 4 mi. NW of Glennie via M-65	✓	✓
Jewell Lake: .5 mi. SE of Barton City via M-72	✓	✓
Pine River: 9.5 mi. E of Glennie via Co. Road 116		✓

UPPER PENINSULA

HIAWATHA NATIONAL FOREST
2727 N. Lincoln Road
Escanaba MI 48929
(906) 786-4062

Rapid River Ranger District (906) 474-6442

Flowing Well: 14 mi. E of Rapid River via Forest Hwy. 13		✓
Haymeadow Creek: 10 mi. N of Rapid River via Co. Road 509		✓
Little Bay de Noc: 9 mi. S of Rapid River via Co. Road 513	✓	

*No camping

	Boator canoe launch	Fishing
Manistique Ranger District (906) 341-5666		
Camp 7 Lake: 24 mi. NW of Manistique via Co. Road 42	✓	✓
Corner Lake: 20 mi. NW of Munising via Co. Road 440	✓	✓
Indian River: 20 mi. NW of Manistique via M-94		✓
Colwell Lake: 25 mi. NW of Manistique via M-94 & Forest Road 2246	✓	✓
Little Bass Lake: 2 mi. S of Steuben via Forest Road 2213	✓	✓
Munising Ranger District (906) 387-2512		
Widewaters: 13 mi. S of Munising via Forest Hwy. 13 & Forest Road 262	✓	✓
Pete's Lake: 12 mi. S of Munising via Forest Hwy. 13 & Forest Road 2173	✓	✓
Island Lake: 10 mi. S of Munising via Forest Hwy. 13 & Forest Road 2268		✓
Au Train Lake: 10 mi. W of Munising via Forest Roads 2276 & 2596	✓	✓
Bay Furnace: 5 mi. W of Munising via M-28		✓
Moccasin Lake*: 15 mi. S of Munising via Forest Road 13		✓
Sault Ste. Marie Ranger District (906) 635-5311		
Bay View: 27 mi. W of Sault Ste. Marie via Forest Road 3150		✓
Monocle Lake: 21 mi W of Sault Ste. Marie via Forest Road 3150	✓	✓
Soldier Lake: 30 mi. W of Sault Ste. Marie via M-28		✓
Three Lakes: 38 mi. W of Sault Ste. Marie via M-28 & Forest Road 3142		✓
St. Ignace Ranger District (906) 643-7900		
Brevoort Lake: 20 mi. W of St. Ignace via US 2 & Forest Road 3108	✓	✓

*No camping

	Boat or canoe launch	Fishing
Carp River: 8 mi. N of St. Ignace via Co. Road H-63 & Forest Road 3445		
Foley Creek: 3 mi. N of St. Ignace via Co. Road H-63		✓

OTTAWA NATIONAL FOREST
East US 2
Ironwood MI 49938
(800) 562-1201, (906) 932-1330

Bessemer Ranger District (906) 667-0261

	Boat or canoe launch	Fishing
Black River Harbor: 15 mi. N of Bessemer via Co. Road 513	✓	✓
Bobcat Lake: 3 mi. SE of Marenisco via US 2, M-64 & Forest Road 8500	✓	✓
Henry Lake: 10 mi. SW of Marenisco via US 2, M-64 & Forest Road 8100	✓	✓
Moosehead Lake: 16 mi. SE of Marenisco via M-64 & Forest Roads 8500, 730 & 6860	✓	✓
Pomeroy Lake: 15 mi. SE of Marenisco via M-64, Forest Road 7300, Co. Road 525 & Forest Road 6828	✓	✓
Langford Lake: 20 mi. SE of Marenisco via US 2, Forest Road 7300 & Co. Roads 525, 527 & 531	✓	✓

Iron River Ranger District (906) 265-5139

	Boat or canoe launch	Fishing
Golden Lake: 14 mi. NW of Iron River via US 2 & Forest Hwy. 16	✓	✓
Paint River Forks: 13 mi. NW of Iron River via US 2, Co. Road 653 & Forest Roads 2130 & 2180		✓
Blockhouse: 20 mi. N of Iron River via US 2, Co. Road 653 & Forest Roads 2130 & 2180	✓	✓
Lake Ottawa: 7 mi. W of Iron River via US 2, M-73 & Lake and Ottawa Road	✓	✓
Hagerman Lake*: 8 mi. SW of Iron River via M-73	✓	✓
State Line*: 12 mi. SW of Iron River via M-73 & Lake Ottawa & W Brule Lake Roads		✓

*No camping

	Boat or canoe launch	Fishing
Kenton Ranger District (906) 852-3501		
Tepee Lake: 7 mi. S of Kenton via Forest Hwy. 16 & Forest Road 3630	✓	✓
Sparrow Rapids: 4 mi. NW of Kenton via Forest Hwy. 16 & Forest Road 1100		✓
Sturgeon River: 15 mi. NE of Kenton via M-28 & Forest Road 2200		✓
Sparrow-Kenton Wayside: 1/8 mi. NE of Kenton via M-28 & Forest Hwy. 16		✓
Perch River*: 12 mi. NE of Kenton via M-28		✓
Lower Dam: 7 mi. SE of Kenton via Forest Hwy. 16, Lake Thirteen Road & Forest Road 3500		✓
Norway Lake: 8 mi. S of Sidnaw via M-28, Sidnaw Road & Forest Road 2400	✓	✓
Lake Sainte Kathryn: 8 mi. S of Sidnaw via M-28 & Sidnaw Road	✓	✓
Perch Lake: 11 mi. S of Sidnaw via M-28 & Sidnaw & Winslow Lake Roads	✓	✓
Ontonagon Ranger District (906) 884-2085		
Courtney Lake: 8 mi. E of Greenland via M-38 & Forest Road 1960	✓	✓
Bob Lake: 18 mi. SE of Greenland via M-38, Forest Hwy. 16 Pori Road & Forest Road 1710	✓	✓
Watersmeet Ranger District (906) 358-4551		
Marion Lake: 5 mi. E of Watersmeet via US 2 and Forest Road 3980	✓	✓
Taylor Lake: 8 mi. E of Watersmeet via US 2 and Forest Road 3960	✓	✓
Imp Lake: 6 mi. SE of Watersmeet via US 2 & Forest Road 3978	✓	✓

*No camping

	Boat or canoe launch	Fishing
Robbins Pond: 9 mi. NW of Watersmeet via US 45 & Forest Road 5230		✓
Steusser Lake*: 15 mi. NW of Watersmeet via US 45, Forest Road 5230 & Choate Road	✓	✓
Paulding Pond: 8 mi. N of Watersmeet via US 45	✓	✓
Burned Dam: 7 mi. NE of Watersmeet via Co. Road 208 & Forest Road 4500		✓
Sylvania: 8 mi. SW of Watersmeet via US 2, Co. Road 535 & Forest Road 6360	✓	✓
McCormick Wilderness: 12 mi. N of Champion via US 41 & Co. Road 607		✓

*No camping

Chapter 18

COUNTY & REGIONAL PARK WATERCRAFT RENTALS

A number of county and regional park and recreation agencies offer rentals of canoes, rowboats, pedal boats, sailboats or tubes. Because each park listed does not provide all categories of watercraft, it's a good idea to check in advance for availability. Also inquire about rental rates, operating hours and seasons, deposit requirements and minimum age rules.

SOUTHEAST

Huron-Clinton Metroparks
Box 2001
13000 High Ridge Drive
Brighton MI 48116-8001
(313) 227-2757
Canoes, pedal boats, rowboats,
 sailboats, tubes

Stony Creek Metropark
Hudson Mills Metropark
Dexter-Huron Metropark
Huron Meadows Metropark
Kensington Metropark
Delhi Metropark
Lake Erie Metropark

**Oakland County Parks
 & Recreation Commission**
2800 Watkins Lake Road
Waterford MI 48328
(313) 858-0906
Canoes, pedal boats, rowboats, tubes

Groveland Oaks Park
Independence Oaks Park
Addison Oaks Park
Red Oaks Waterpark
Waterford Oaks Waterpark

**Washtenaw County Parks
 & Recreation Commission**
Box 8645
Ann Arbor MI 48107
(313) 971-6337
Rowboats, tubes

Rolling Hills Park
Independence Lake Park

Wayne County Parks Division   Middle Rouge Parkway
33175 Ann Arbor Trail
Westland MI 48185
(313) 261-1990
Pedal boats

SOUTHWEST

St. Joseph County Parks   Rawson's King Mill Park
 & Recreation Commission
Box 427
Centreville MI 49032
(616) 467-6361
Canoes

CENTRAL

Ingham County Parks Department   Grand River Park
Box 38   Lake Lansing Park South
301 Bush St
Mason MI 48854
(517) 676-2233
Canoes, pedal boats

Eaton County Parks & Recreation   Fitzgerald Parkl
3808 Grand Ledge Hwy.
Grand Ledge MI 48837
(517) 627-7351

Isabella County Parks   Deerfield Parks
 & Recreation Commission   Meridian Park
200 N. Main Street
Mt. Pleasant MI 48858
(517) 772-0911 ext. 233

UPPER PENINSULA

Menominee County Parks Department   Shakey Lakes Park
Rte. 1, Box 183
Stephenson MI 49887
(906) 753-4582
Canoes, rowboats

SENEY NATIONAL WILDLIFE REFUGE

Chapter 19

WILDLIFE REFUGES ON THE WATER

By definition, nature preserves and wildlife refuges are places for passive recreation, places where human visitors are expected to leave few footprints and make little noise. They are meant for quiet strokes of a canoe paddle rather than the revving of an outboard motor. They welcome guests sensitive to environmental needs.

There are two major national wildlife refuges in Michigan: Seney in the Upper Peninsula and Shiawassee near Saginaw Bay. Both also oversee smaller satellite refuges. They are part of the U.S. Fish and Wildlife Service's system of about 450 refuges with more than 90 million acres of water and land dedicated to wildlife protection.

SENEY NATIONAL   (906) 586-9851
WILDLIFE REFUGE
HCR 2, Box 1
Seney MI 49883

The area now occupied by the 95,455-acre Seney preserve had been lumbered over and then unsuccessfully farmed before Congress designated it as a refuge in 1935. After the refuge was established, the Civilian Conservation Corps built dikes, ditches and water control structures that impound more than 7,000 acres of open water in 21 major pools. There are hiking and bike trails, a self-guided auto tour and visitor center. The refuge includes a 25,000-acre wilderness.

Non-motorized boating is allowed during daylight on the Manistique, Driggs and Creighton Rivers and Walsh Creek, but not on marshes or pools. Motor boats can use only the Manistique.

Fishing requires a state license. It is permitted during regular state seasons on the Ditch, Creighton, Driggs and Manistique Rivers and Walsh Creek. Fishing also is allowed on most pools from May 15 through Sept. 30, and from Labor Day through Sept. 30 on some other pools; a few pools are off-limits to fishing. Ice fishing is allowed on all pools from Jan. 1 to Feb. 28. You can fish only during daylight.

Remember: All wildlife have the right-of-way; be especially alert to geese and goslings on the dikes. The refuge has trails and an environmental study area. Motor boats, swimming and camping are not allowed.

HURON ISLANDS   (906) 586-9851
NATIONAL WILDLIFE REFUGE
c/o Seney National Wildlife Refuge
HCR 2, Box 1
Seney MI 49883

Located in Lake Superior between Marquette and the Keweenaw Peninsula, the remote Huron Islands refuge contains 147 acres on eight islands and is a wilderness area. There has been a lighthouse, now automated, on West Huron (Lighthouse) Island since 1877. West Huron is the second-largest of the islands and the only one open to the public. Register at refuge headquarters to visit for hiking or nature study; access is allowed during daylight hours only.

The other islands are closed to the public except for emergency landings by boats in distress and by scientists with special permits.

HARBOR ISLAND   (906) 586-9851
NATIONAL WILDLIFE REFUGE
c/o Seney National Wildlife Refuge
HCR 2, Box 1
Seney MI 49883

The 695-acre Harbor Island refuge is in Lake Huron's Potagannissing Bay, one mile north of Drummond Island and $3\frac{1}{2}$ miles south of the Michigan-Ontario border. It was purchased from the Nature Conservancy as a waterfowl production area under the Unique Ecosystem Program. There is a sheltered bay for boaters interested in fishing, water skiing and overnight anchorage for small craft.

There also is a sandy beach suitable for swimming.

SHIAWASSEE NATIONAL   (517) 777-5930
WILDLIFE REFUGE
6975 Mower Road
Route 1
Saginaw MI 48601

The Shiawassee refuge was created by Congress in 1953, with breeding grounds and a stopover area for migratory waterfowl. It combines wetlands, controlled pools, woods and cropland, yet is surrounded by industrial development and commercial farms. The Tittabaswasee, Shiawassee, Flint and Cass Rivers and Swan and Bullhead Creeks border, touch or cut through the refuge

Motorized and non-motorized boating are allowed, as is fishing. There are hiking trails and an environmental study area. Swimming and camping are prohibited.

MICHIGAN ISLANDS   (517) 777-5930
 NATIONAL WILDLIFE REFUGE
c/o Shiawassee National Wildlife Refuge
6975 Mower Road
Route 1
Saginaw MI 48601

The refuge was established in 1943 with three small islands, Pismire and Shoe Islands in Lake Michigan and Scarecrow Island in Lake Huron. It was later expanded to add most of Thunder Bay Island in Lake Huron and most of Gull Island in Lake Michigan. Public access is prohibited, except with a special permit for research or education.

WYANDOTTE NATIONAL   (517) 777-5930
 WILDLIFE REFUGE
c/o Shiawassee National Wildlife Refuge
6975 Mower Road
Route 1
Saginaw MI 48601

In 1961, Congress created the refuge in the Detroit River near Wyandotte to protect migratory birds and other wildlife. Its two islands, Grassy and Mammajuda, total 304 acres, and the refuge includes adjacent shallow water areas. Industrial discharges, municipal sewage, dumped dredge material and the effects of large commercial ships have damaged the lower Detroit River ecosystem, however, changing the flora and reducing use of the refuge by migratory waterfowl. The islands are off-limits to the public.

Chapter 20

BOATING, CANOEING, SCUBA, SAILING & FISHING COURSES

If you're interested in water-related fun and sports, a variety of courses are available to sharpen existing skills and develop new ones. You can select boating safety, canoeing, kayaking, boardsailing, fishing, scuba and whitewater rafting classes for credit at public and private colleges across Michigan.

While boating safety classes are optional for adults, remember that youths aged 12-16 need a Department of Natural Resources boating safety certificate to operate a motorboat unaccompanied by an adult. Such classes generally cover equipment, regulations and safe operations; boat handling; elementary seamanship; basic navigation, use of charts and other navigational aids; trailering; coastal, Great Lakes, river and inland lake boating; sailing; engine troubleshooting; and piloting.

In addition, water recreation-related classes are available at minimal cost -- and sometimes without charge -- through community education programs run by local school districts and through county and municipal park and recreation departments. Check with school districts and park departments in your area for more information. Dive shops offering certified scuba instruction are listed in the chapter on diving, Chapter 9. Also, many sporting clubs offer classes.

This chapter does not list classes in swimming, synchronized swim, water safety instructor certification, board diving, lifeguarding or water aerobics.

STATEWIDE

U.S. Power Squadrons

Boating Safety
(800) 336-2628

The Raleigh, N.C.-based United States Power Squadrons maintains 21 Squadrons, or local chapters, in Michigan, including 11 in the Detroit-Port Huron-Ann Arbor area. Those local Squadrons offer boating safety courses for the public every spring and fall. Call its toll-free number weekdays between 8 a.m. and 4:30 p.m. to receive the name and phone number of the Squadron nearest you and for information on the time and location of courses in your area.

SOUTHEAST

HILLSDALE COUNTY
Hillsdale College Physical Education & Health Dept. Hillsdale MI 49242 (517) 437-7341	Scuba

JACKSON COUNTY
Jackson YMCA Center 127 W. Wesley Jackson MI 49201 (517) 782-0537	Scuba

MACOMB COUNTY
Macomb County Community College Physical Education Dept. 14500 Twelve Mile Road Warren MI 48093-3896 (313) 445-7999	Windsurfing; Scuba

MONROE COUNTY
Monroe Family YMCA 1111 W. Elm Ave. Monroe MI 48161 (313) 241-2606	Scuba

OAKLAND COUNTY
American Youth Hostels 3024 Coolidge Berkley MI 48072	Kayaking; Sailing
Oakland Community College Physical Education & Recreation Dept. 2480 Opdyke Road Bloomfield Hills MI 48304-2266 (313) 540-1500	Kayaking; Scuba; Boardsailing

South Oakland YMCA 1016 W. Eleven Mile Road Royal Oak MI 48067 (313) 547-0030	Scuba

ST. CLAIR COUNTY

Blue Water YMCA 700 Fort St. Port Huron MI 48060 (313) 987-6400	Scuba
St. Clair Community College Physical Education Dept. 323 Erie St. Port Huron MI 48060 (313) 984-3881	Scuba

WASHTENAW COUNTY

Ann Arbor Parks & Recreation Dept. Argo Canoe Livery 1055 Longshore Drive Ann Arbor MI 48105 (313) 668-7411	Canoeing
Eastern Michigan University Health, Physical Education & Recreation Dept. Ypsilanti MI 48197 (313) 487-4636	Sailing; Canoeing

WAYNE COUNTY

Livonia Family YMCA 14255 Stark Road Livonia MI 48154 (313) 261-2161	Canoeing Safety; Kayaking
Schoolcraft College Physical Education, Health & Recreation Dept. 18600 Haggerty Road Livonia MI 48152-2696 (313) 462-4400	Sailing; Canoeing; Scuba
Wayne State University Physical Education Activity Dept. 5050 Cass Ave. Detroit MI 48202 (313) 577-2424	Scuba

Western Branch YMCA 1601 Clark St. Detroit MI 48209 (313) 554-2136	Boating Safety; Canoeing; Boating

SOUTHWEST

BERRIEN COUNTY

Lake Michigan College Physical Education Dept. 2755 E. Napier Ave. Benton Harbor MI 49022 616) 927-3571	Canoeing; Scuba
Niles-Buchanan Family YMCA 315 W. Main St. Niles MI 49120 (616) 683-1552	Scuba

CALHOUN COUNTY

Albion College Physical Education Dept. Albion MI 49224 (517) 629-1000	Canoeing
Calhoun County Facilities & Services Dept. 315 W. Green St. Marshall MI 49068 (616) 781-0815	Boating Safety
Kellogg Community College Physical Education Activity Dept. 450 North Ave. Battle Creek MI 49017-3397 (616) 965-3932	Sailing; Canoeing; Whitewater Rafting; Scuba

KENT COUNTY

Calvin College Physical Education & Recreation Dept. Grand Rapids MI 49546 (616) 957-6000	Scuba
Downtown YMCA 33 Library St. N.E. Grand Rapids MI 49503 (616) 458-1141	Scuba; Canoeing; Kayaking; Sailing; Windsurfing

Grand Rapids Junior College   Canoeing
Physical Education Dept.
143 Bostwick Ave., N.E.
Grand Rapids MI 49503-3295
(616) 771-4000

Southeast Family Branch YMCA   Scuba
730 Forest Hills S.E.
Grand Rapids MI 49546
(616) 285-9077

CENTRAL

BAY COUNTY
Bay Area Family YMCA   Scuba
111 N. Madison Ave.
Bay City MI 48708
(517) 895-8596

Bay County Parks & Recreation Dept.   Boating Safety;
800 John F. Kennedy Drive   Fishing
Bay City MI 48706
(517) 893-5531

GENESEE COUNTY
Flint YMCA   Canoeing
411 E. Third St.
Flint MI 48503
(313) 232-9622

Mott Community College   Canoeing; Fishing
Physical Education Dept.
1401 E. Court St.
Flint MI 48503
(313) 762-0200

INGHAM COUNTY
Central Branch YMCA   Canoeing; Scuba;
301 W. Lenawee   Kayaking
Lansing MI 48933
(517) 484-4000

Lansing Community College   Canoeing; Sailing;
Physical Education and Athletics Dept.   Windsurfing; Scuba;
Box 40010   Sailing; Cruising;
Lansing MI 48901-7210   Fishing
(517) 483-1957

Parkwood Branch YMCA   Scuba
2306 Haslett Road
East Lansing MI 48823
(517) 332-8657

IONIA COUNTY
Ionia YMCA Program Center   Scuba
250 E. Tuttle Road
Ionia MI 48846
(616) 527-5760

ISABELLA COUNTY
Central Michigan University   Canoeing; Scuba
Physical Education & Sport Dept.
Mt. Pleasant MI 48859
(517) 774-4000

MECOSTA COUNTY
Mecosta County Park Commission   Boating Safety
22250 Northland Drive
Paris MI 49338
(616) 832-3246

Ferris State University   Sailing; Canoeing
Physical Education Dept.
Big Rapids MI 49307-2295
(616) 592-2000

MONTCALM COUNTY
Montcalm Community College   Scuba
Physical Education Dept.
2800 College Drive S.W.
Sidney MI 48885-9746
(517) 328-2111

SAGINAW COUNTY
Saginaw Valley State University   Sailing
Physical & Health Education Dept.
University Center, MI 48710-0001
(517) 749-4000

Boating, Canoeing, Scuba, Sailing & Fishing Courses

HOUGHTON COUNTY
Michigan Technological University
Physical Education Dept.
1400 Townsend Drive
Houghton MI 49931-1295
(906) 487-1885

Bait & Fly Casting

MARQUETTE COUNTY
Northern Michigan University
Health, Physical Education
 & Recreation Dept.
Marquette MI 49855
(906) 227-1000

Canoeing; Scuba

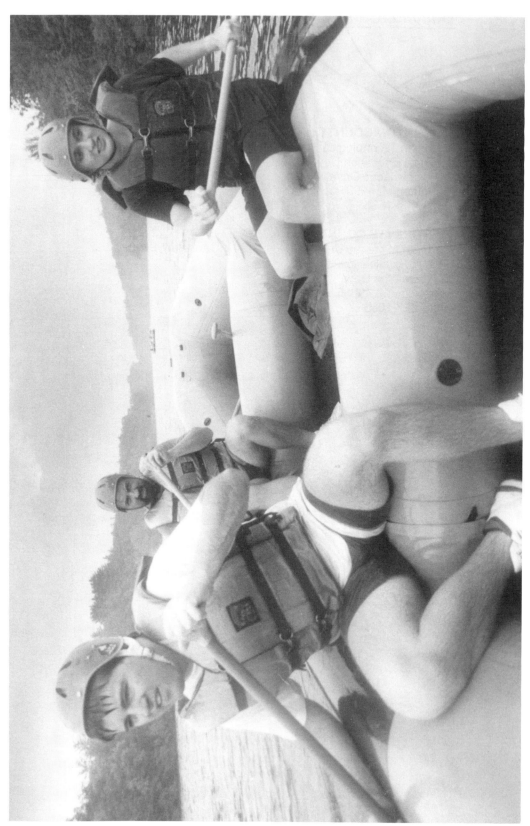

Chapter 21

WHITEWATER RAFTING

Whitewater rafting in Michigan? Sure thing.

True, you won't find the frequent, cascading rapids of West Virginia's New and Gauley Rivers, or of New York's Hudson River during the Adirondack Mountains spring melt. And admittedly the cliffs don't soar as spectacularly above you as they do while rafting along the Green River through Dinosaur National Monument in Colorado and Utah.

Even so, your adrenaline will pump and the scenery will please while whitewater rafting along the Menominee River.

The river forms the border between the western Upper Peninsula and neighboring Wisconsin. Here you'll confront rapids with names such as Sand Portage Falls, the Tongue, Hell Hole, Misicot Falls and Volkswagen Rock. An upstream dam ensures satisfactory water levels throughout most of the summer.

Detroit News reporter Tom BeVier wrote this about his run through Piers Gorge on the Menominee: "We beached the rafts and climbed to the top of a sheer, granite bluff perhaps 50 feet high. It was a chaos of rocks and currents. The first drop into the rapids was fully six feet -- perhaps eight -- into a confusion of white water and noise.... In an instant, we were racing toward the edge and then over it. Water poured into the raft and over us. People gasped for breath. We fought it. Paddle! paddle! The currents tipped us and spun us. We banged off rocks. Once we almost went over. And then we were through."

Outfitters provide life jackets, paddles, helmets and experienced guides. They recommend you bring a swim suit, wool shirt or sweater, wool socks, unlined windproof jacket, tennis shoes and a strap for your glasses, plus a set of dry clothes. Trips take place rain or shine. Check in advance about reservation and deposit requirements, costs, group discounts and nearby camping and lodging facilities, and cancellation policies.

If you're looking for formal instruction in whitewater rafting, Kellogg Community College offers a one-credit course. According to the college, the class is designed to give students experience in applying whitewater rafting concepts and practices, including trip

preparation, paddling techniques, river evaluation, safety, rescue and elementary survival. For more information, write to the Physical Education Department at Kellogg Community College, 450 North Ave., Battle Creek MI 49017-3397 or call (616) 965-3931.

These outfitters offer whitewater rafting trips along the Menominee through Piers Gorge:

Argosy Adventures   April - September

Box 22

Niagara WI 54151

(715) 251-3886

Kosir's Rapid Rafts   Memorial Day weekend
- Labor Day weekend

HCR, Box 172A

Athelstane WI 54104

(715) 757-3431

Chapter 22

KAYAKING & ROWING

SEA KAYAKING

Sea kayaking has grown in popularity, in Michigan and elsewhere. The boats are sleek, stable and easily paddled, what outfitter Uncommon Adventures describes as "very gentle-mannered cousins to whitewater kayaks -- Eskimo rolls are not a requirement." Paddlers will discover that they are better designed for tracking a straight line than for turning quickly. They're used for tours, recreation and racing.

An annual Great Lakes Sea Kayak Symposium is held in Grand Marais, on the southern shore of Lake Superior near Pictured Rocks National Lakeshore. It is principally an educational event with seminars and lectures, guided trips, workshops, night paddling, boat trials, displays by manufacturers and water paddling clinics. Guided tours explore the spectacular cliffs, sea caves, waterfalls, shipwrecks, lighthouses, Grand Sable Dunes and other coastline features. Sponsors include Great River Outfitters of Bloomfield Hills, Inland Seas Kayak Co. of Petoskey, the city of Grand Marais and the American Canoe Association. For more information, write to the Great Lakes Sea Kayak Club, 3721 Shallow Brook, Bloomfield Hills MI 48013, or call (313) 644-6909 or (313) 683-4770.

Several times each year, the club sponsors a sea kayaking rendezvous at different spots on the Great Lakes. The rendezvous include trips of various lengths and skill levels. Club members are involved in such policy issues as water access and proposals to require registration of canoes and kayaks. The club newsletter, "Great Lakes Sea Kayaker," includes articles about the sport and classified ads for guided trips, equipment and instruction.

For more information on sea kayaking in Michigan, you also can contact:

• British Canoe Union, 5135 Resort Pike, Petoskey MI 49770. The phone number is (616) 347-1114.
• Great Lakes Sea Kayak Safety Network, 2033 Milford, Grand Rapids MI 49504. The phone number is (616) 791-9313.
• International Klepper Society, Box 973, Good Hart, MI 49737.

• West Michigan Coastal Kayakers Association, 1205 E. Giles Road, N. Muskegon MI 49445.

Uncommon Adventures, an East Lansing outfitter, offers escorted sea kayak tours in Michigan. A typical season includes basic instructional classes, day tours within a two-hour radius of Lansing, multi-day tours in the Les Cheneaux Islands area of northern Lake Huron and Isle Royale National Park, and a bed-and-breakfast kayak workshop in Portage Lake and Lake Michigan. The company also offers day and multi-day canoe trips in Michigan, as well as windsurfing clinics.

For more information, write to Uncommon Adventures, Box 6066, East Lansing MI 48826, or call (517) 882-6114.

You'll also find kayaking courses listed in Chapter 20.

ROWING

Rowing, or crew, competitions and regattas are not limited to Oxford and Cambridge vying in England or Harvard and Yale vying in this country. The sport has long had Michigan ties; the Detroit Boat Club, established in 1839, is the oldest active club in the United States. By 1873, there were 14 rowing clubs in the state. Michigan now boasts a number of public or university crew clubs affiliated with the U.S. Rowing Association, a nonprofit organization that serves as the country's Olympic governing body for rowing in the United States.

SOUTHEAST

OAKLAND COUNTY
Detroit Boat Club
c/o Richard Bell
27551 Rackham
Lathrup Village MI 48076

Friends of Detroit Rowing   (313) 882-4420
c/o Chris Costello
2757 Windemere
Birmingham MI 48009

WASHTENAW COUNTY
Ann Arbor Community Rowing   (313) 769-9086

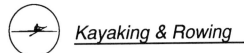

Box 3128
Ann Arbor MI 48106

University of Michigan Crew   (517) 684-0009
North Campus Recreation Building
2376 Hubbard Road
Ann Arbor MI 48109

WAYNE COUNTY
Ecorse Rowing Club   (313) 671-2042
Box 29055
Ecorse MI 48299

Grosse Ile Rowing Club
Grosse Ile Recreation Department
8841 Macomb
Grosse Ile MI 48138

Wyandotte Boat Club   (313) 282-6596
Box 341
Wyandotte MI 48192

CENTRAL

BAY COUNTY
Bay City Rowing Club   (517) 684-1919
400 W. Lafayette
Bay City MI 48708

INGHAM COUNTY
Lansing Oar & Paddle Club   (517) 337-2521
311 S. Jenison
Lansing MI 48915

Michigan State University Crew   (517) 351-2594
231 IM West
East Lansing MI 48824

DAVID COATES, THE DETROIT NEWS

Chapter 23

WATERSKIING & SURFING

Waterskiing continues to grow in popularity with competitions, clinics, an annual convention, other organized events and even a Michigan Water Skiers Hall of Fame. About 20 official tournaments are held around Michigan each summer. The state association also places special emphasis on waterskiing opportunities for people with disabilities, and Michigan has hosted national and international competitions for the physically challenged.

There also are water skiing teams at the University of Michigan, Michigan State University and Western Michigan University.

For more information, contact the Michigan Water Ski Association, Box 507, Fenton MI 48430. Here are its affiliated clubs:

SOUTHEAST

OAKLAND COUNTY
Tivoli Gardens
c/o John Beith
3534 Ramada Drive
Highland MI 48031

WASHTENAW COUNTY
Ford Lake Water Ski Club
c/o Dan Mrowczynski
1113 Pearl St.
Ypsilanti MI 49197

Whitmore Lake Ski Club
Box 139
Whitmore Lake MI 48189

WAYNE COUNTY
Belleville Water Ski Club
13256 Lake Pointe Pass
Belleville MI 48111

Homecare
c/o Chet Kuskowski
15201 Century Drive, Suite 604
Dearborn MI 48120

SOUTHWEST

CALHOUN COUNTY
Riverside Ski Club
3481 Country Club Way
Albion MI 49224

KENT COUNTY
West Michigan Water Ski Association
Box 1401
Grand Rapids MI 49501

CENTRAL

GENESEE COUNTY
Silver Lake Ski Club
Box 171
Fenton MI 48430

Spray Masters Water Ski Club
11460 Orchardview Drive
Fenton MI 48430

SURFING

Well, Michigan is a long way from the famed surfing beaches of Hawaii, California and Australia, but plenty of surfers catch the waves on Lake Michigan. Heavy surf is less common here than on the Pacific Coast, and freshwater waves are less buoyant than salty ocean water, so Michigan surfers use larger, less maneuverable boards than their West Coast counterparts. There are even surfing competitions and tournaments at Grand Haven. Other popular surfing spots include Muskegon, Charlevoix and St. Joseph.

For more information, contact the Great Lakes Surfing Association, Box 7281, Bloomfield Hills MI 48302-7281. The phone number is (313) 334-3147.

Chapter 24
MARITIME MUSEUMS

Given that lakes and rivers have shaped Michigan geographically, culturally, economically and recreationally, it should be no surprise that maritime museums are found throughout the state. They display, illuminate and interpret Michigan's nautical heritage from the earliest days of Native American settlement to the present. Many provide research facilities with books, maps and other documents for the casual reader and serious scholar.

In addition to these museums specializing in maritime themes, others include nautical artifacts, programs and activities on a regular or special basis. For example, the Empire Area Museum collection on the Leelanau Peninsula highlights that area's 1888-1917 shipping enterprises; the Michigan Historical Museum in Lansing has Great Lakes and Native American artifacts; and the Les Cheneaux Historical Museum in Cedarville has a collection of scale models of boats.

Also, the Mackinac State Historic Parks Commission operates parks on Mackinac Island and in Mackinaw City that are intimately connected with the state's maritime heritage. Their collections include drawings and photos of Great Lakes steam-powered and sailing ships and the bell and gyrocompass from the ferry *Chief Wawatam*, which, in 1913, began to carry railroad cars across the Straits of Mackinac between the Upper and Lower Peninsulas. The Old Mackinac Point Lighthouse at Colonial Michilimackinac State Park was built in 1892 and served until 1957. The park's 55-foot *Welcome*, a wooden-hulled replica of a 1775 sailing vessel, is moored in Mackinaw City. For more information, write to Mackinac State Historic Parks, Box 370, Mackinac Island MI 49757, or phone (906) 847-3328 from mid-May to mid-October, or (517) 373-4296 off-season.

SOUTHEAST

ST. CLAIR COUNTY

Huron Lightship Museum   (313) 982-0891
Pine Grove Park   Admission
Port Huron MI 48060   Mid-May - Sept.
The 97-foot-long *Huron* was built in 1920 and was the last Great

Lakes lightship -- the equivalent of a floating lighthouse -- when it withdrew from active service in 1971. Now a national historic landmark refurbished by the Lake Huron Lore Marine Society, it is open for tours. It is moored on the St. Clair River.

The nearby Museum of Arts & History operates the *Huron* and is open year round. It features a gallery of marine lore, including artifacts, ship models and a reconstructed Great Lakes freighter pilothouse. Other exhibits include mammoth bones, archeological remains of a Woodlands Culture fishing village, scenes of the 17th-century French-built Fort St. Joseph and the 19th-century American-built Fort Gratiot, railroad models and memorabilia of inventor Thomas Alva Edison's local boyhood home. The Museum of Arts and History is at 115 6th St. in Port Huron. Admission is free.

WAYNE COUNTY

Dossin Great Lakes Museum	(313) 267-6440
100 Strand	Donation
Belle Isle	Year round
Detroit MI 48207	

This internationally renowned museum on the Detroit River focuses on history of the Great Lakes and boats that sailed them. Exhibits include a restored pilothouse from the freighter *William Clay Ford*, the restored 40-foot hydroplane *Miss Pepsi* and the Gothic Room lounge from the 1912 D&C passenger steamer *City of Detroit III*. There also is a special exhibition about the Storm of Nov. 8, 1913, the most destructive storm to hit the Great Lakes since commercial navigation began; eight freighters were lost without survivors on Lake Huron alone.

It is operated by the city of Detroit's Historical Department.

SOUTHWEST

ALLEGAN COUNTY

S.S. Keewatin	(616) 857-2464
Blue Star Highway & Union Street	Memorial Day
Box 638	- Labor Day
Douglas MI 49406	Admission

The 350-foot *S.S. Keewatin*, once a Canadian Pacific Railway passenger steamer plying the upper Great Lakes, first sailed in 1907 and was retired in 1965. It boasted 108 staterooms, a mahogany-paneled Edwardian dining salon and a galley that prepared 1,000 meals a day. Billed as the "last of the classic steamships," it is now moored just south of the Saugatuck-Douglas Bridge and is open for guided tours.

VAN BUREN COUNTY

Lake Michigan Maritime Museum   (616) 637-8078
Dyckman Avenue at Bridge   Admission
Box 534   Year round
South Haven MI 49090

The museum features permanent and temporary exhibits about Michigan's maritime trades and the people who worked in them, as well as shipbuilding and Native American boats. Among the vessels on display are a commercial fishing tug and restored Coast Guard ships. It is the state's only institution able to conserve long-submerged artifacts such as two dugout canoes in its collection. The museum houses the Marialyce Canonie Great Lakes Research Library. Other features include oral histories from lighthouse keepers, a waterfront park, underwater archeological research facilities and a watercraft collection. Public programs are offered, and there is municipal marina transient boat mooring at the museum dock.

Although the Legislature has authorized the museum to join the Michigan Bureau of History's state-run musuem system, the transfer had not occurred as of publication due to budget problems.

NORTHEAST

HURON COUNTY

Lighthouse Park Museum   (517) 428-4749
7320 Lighthouse Road   May 30 - Oct. 1
Port Hope MI 48468   Free

The museum features shipwreck artifacts and photographs.

PRESQUE ISLE COUNTY

Old Presque Isle Lighthouse & Museum   (517) 595-2787
5295 Grand Lake Road   May 15 - Oct. 15

Presque Isle MI 49777   Admission

Visitors can climb the hand-chisled circular stone staircase of this 35-foot tower with its 4-foot-thick walls overlooking the harbor. If you forget to count on your way up, there are 140 steps. The lighthouse tower was formally lit in September 1840 and stayed in service until 1870, when a taller replacement was finished a mile away. There is a hands-on museum in the English-style whitewashed brick lighthouse keeper's cottage. Among the cottage furnishings are Currier and Ives prints and a pump organ. Displays include foghorns, ship models, shipwreck artifacts, pewter and copper kitchenware, binnacles, Fresnel lenses and compasses. There also is a 3,425-pound bronze bell, one of the largest in Michigan and bigger than the Liberty Bell; it was moved here from Lansing City Hall.

NORTHWEST

CHARLEVOIX COUNTY
Marine & Harbor Museum   (616) 448-2254
Beaver Island   Mid-June
Box 263   - Labor Day
St. James MI 49782   Admission

Housed in a 1906 net shed at St. James Harbor on Lake Michigan, the museum's exhibits include material about lighthouses, life saving, shipbuilding, shipwrecks, commercial fishing and local ships, as well as exhibits about local geology and other islands in the Beaver archipelago. It is run by the Beaver Island Historical Society.

The group also operates the Old Mormon Print Shop and log Protar Home, both on the National Register of Historic Places. The print shop was used by followers of James Jesse Strang, the self-styled Mormon "king" of the island, to publish religious tracts and the first newspaper in northern Michigan. The Protar home was occupied by an Estonian immigrant who served as a lay physician.

GRAND TRAVERSE COUNTY
Schooner *Madeline*   (616) 946-2647
Clinch Park Marina   May 15
Box 1108   - Sept. 30
Traverse City MI 49685   Donations

This 56-foot replica of the 1845 Great Lakes working schooner *Madeline* is docked at the marina in Traverse City. Volunteers spent 40,000 hours and $400,000 over a five-year period to build the ship. As a floating museum, it offers exhibits about the ship's history, and also sets sail for training crews.

LEELANAU COUNTY

Sleeping Bear Point Coast Guard Station	(616) 326-5134
Sleeping Bear Dunes National Lakeshore	Spring - Fall
Box 277	Free
Empire MI 49630	

A restored former Coast Guard station, the museum featuresship-wrecks, Great Lakes shipping, history of the U.S. Life Saving Service -- forerunner of today's U.S. Coast Guard -- and the Coast Guard itself. As author George Weeks wrote in Sleeping Bear, Yesterday and Today: "Long before the modern Coast Guard, with its highly visible helicopters and rescue boats that patrol by air and sea, the Great Lakes' Heroes of the Storm were surfmen who stood watch on remote shorelines and risked their lives rowing on raging seas in open boats."

This station, typical of about five dozen along the Great Lakes, was built in 1901 about $\frac{1}{2}$ mile northwest of its present location; it was moved here in 1931 because drifting sand threatened the buildings, while the heavy surf made it hard to launch rescue boats. The museum has a restored surfmen's bunkroom and lake steamer pilot house exhibit. The boathouse has been restored to represent the Life Saving era of 1901-1915 with lifeboat, surfboat, line-throwing gun, beach car, safety gear and apparatus. The museum, run by the National Park Service, is located along Sleeping Bear Bay north of the Sleeping Bear Dunes National Lakeshore visitor center.

UPPER PENINSULA

ALGER COUNTY

Grand Marais Maritime Museum	(906) 494-2669
Coast Guard Point	July 1
Box 395	-Labor Day
Grand Marais MI 49839	Free

The museum is run by the National Park Service as part of Pictured Rocks National Lakeshore on the Lake Superior coast. Its collection includes Grand Marais fishing industry artifacts from around 1900 and a Fresnel lens from the Au Sable Light Station. In addition, there are exhibits about shipwrecks, the U.S. Life Saving Service, lighthouses and the early years of commercial shipping in the region.

CHIPPEWA COUNTY

Great Lakes Shipwreck Memorial Museum	(906) 492-3436
Whitefish Point	Memorial Day
Paradise MI 49768	- Oct. 15
	Admission

Located on the site of the first Lake Superior light station, the museum includes a diorama about the ill-fated *Edmund Fitzgerald*, which sank off Whitefish Point in November 1975. Also, there are film and video presentations about Great Lakes shipwrecks, a huge lens from the White Shoal Lighthouse, a carved wooden eagle from the steamer *Vienna*, which sank in an 1892 collision, and other exhibits. It is housed at the Whitefish Point Light Station, whose light still guides passing ships. The light station appears on the National Register of Historic Places.

It is located 10 miles north of Paradise and operated by the non-profit Great Lakes Shipwreck Historical Society, headquartered at 111 Ashmun, Sault Ste. Marie, MI 49783. The society has developed award-winning documentary films and established a program for historic renovation in the area it calls the "Graveyard of the Great Lakes."

Museum Ship *Valley Camp*	(906) 632-3658
501 E. Water St.	May 15 - Oct. 15
Sault Ste. Marie MI 49783	Admission

This 1917 steam-powered Great Lakes freighter, *Valley Camp*, was an ore carrier before it was converted to museum status near the Soo Locks. Visitors explore its engine room, crew quarters, pilot house, dining rooms, captain's quarters and other facilities. On board is a museum that bills itself as the world's Great Lakes maritime museum. It features exhibits, models, videos and photos on shipwrecks and shipbuilding, including lifeboats recovered from the *Edmund Fitzgerald*. The ship is on the National Register of Historic Places.

Le Sault de Ste. Marie Historical Sites, which owns the *Valley Camp*, is a non-profit group that conserves and interprets the history of the St. Marys River and Great Lakes. It also operates the nearby Tower of History and the 19th-century homes of Bishop Frederic Baraga, the noted Austrian-born Roman Catholic missionary, and Indian agent-writer-politician Henry Rowe Schoolcraft.

Point Iroquois Light Station	(906) 437-5272
c/o Hiawatha National Forest	Memorial Day
Route 1, Lakeshore Drive	- Labor Day
Brimley MI 49783	Free

The Point Iroquois Light Station, which is on the National Register of Historic Places, includes an interpretive museum covering lighthouse history, technology and the daily life of lightkeepers, their families and their staffs. The location does seem remote, but a museum brochure notes, "Despite hard work and long hours, life at Point Iroquois had its advantages. Compared with more isolated stations, Point Iroquois offered space and a home-like atmosphere. With increased water traffic, it was necessary to expand personnel. By 1908, the light station housed a head keeper, two assistants and their families. They formed their own self-sustaining community complete with a schoolhouse and a teacher for their children."

The light is no longer in use, having been replaced by a nearby automatic signal beacon across Whitefish Bay in 1962. Visitors can also climb 72 steps to the top of the 65-foot brick tower for a view of Lake Superior, and can walk the wildflower-lined paths leading from the lighthouse to the beach.

The lighthouse is in Hiawatha National Forest at the headwaters of the St. Marys River, 20 miles west of Sault Ste. Marie and 51 miles east of Tahquamenon Falls. It is operated for the U.S. Forest Service by the Bay Mills-Brimley Historical Research Society.

MACKINAC COUNTY

Sunken Treasures Maritime Museum	(906) 643-7635
Star Line Museum & Mall	May 15 - Oct. 15
St. Ignace MI 49781	Admission

This museum at the Star Line ferry dock includes a scale reproduction of 1855 steamboat wreckage with a full-sized diver coming down the anchor line to view scattered artifacts. There also is a reproduction of a steamer purser's office with original artifacts and a cabin view of an early schooner with its original cabin wall.

PACIFIC SALMON

Since 1870 several unsuccessful attempts have been made to establish Pacific salmon in the Great Lakes. In 1966 at this site the Department of Conservation released coho fingerlings, hatchery-reared from eggs given by the state of Oregon. They migrated to Lake Michigan and fed on its enormous alewife population. Augmented by subsequent annual plantings, the coho became firmly established. By 1970 the sport fishery catch reached ten million pounds. Other species of Pacific salmon-the chinook and kokanee -were also successfully introduced to the Great Lakes area in the late 1960s. To complete their life cycle the salmon return to their home stream to spawn and then die. Millions of salmon are now planted each year. In 1973 the world's largest recorded coho, weighing over thirty-nine pounds, was taken at a state weir.

Chapter 25

HISTORICAL MARKERS

Given the critical role that lakes, rivers and their natural resources have played in Michigan's economic and recreational development, it is fortunate that this maritime heritage is honored by historical markers across the state. They commemorate waterways and light-houses, shipwrecks and ship builders, fisheries and boats, shipping and recreation, and a variety of other reminders of this heritage.

These markers are more than metal plaques, however, because they help us appreciate our own past, our own legacies and our own experiences in the Great Lake State. We should recall the events and impact that makes each of these sites worth public attention. Laura Ashlee of the state Bureau of History, editor of Traveling Through Time, recalled her reaction to reading a marker at an historic light-house in the Thumb: "I wondered if Presque Isle lighthouse keeper Patrick Garrity ever felt isolated and suffered from cabin fever."

The text of one of the most unusual -- in location -- markers is not included because it had been authorized but not installed as of this writing. Intended as Michigan's first underwater state historic plaque, it's planned for a spot about three miles from Lexington in Lake Huron, the final resting place of the *Sport*, a steel-hulled harbor tug that sank in 49 feet of water during a Dec. 13, 1920, storm. The crew escaped by lifeboat, but the *Sport* wasn't found until 1987. Before the drama of its demise, the tug operated in the Ludington area from 1873 until 1913, then was brought to Port Huron. Its last voyage was an ill-fated mission to pick up a barge at Harbor Beach. The wreck is located in the state's Sanilac Shores Bottomland Preserve.

Most of these markers were erected by the Michigan Historical Commission at sites designated on the State Register of Historic Places. Others were dedicated by local historical commissions, the Michigan Outdoor Writers Association and State Bar of Michigan.

SOUTHEAST

MACOMB COUNTY
Lake Saint Clair (Lac Sainte Claire)
Lac Ste. Clair Park, St. Clair Shores

French explorers discovered and named Lake Saint Clair on August 12, 1679. Among the party of thirty-four men were voyageur Rene-Robert Cavalier, Sieur de la Salle and Roman Catholic friar Father Louis Hennepin. Aboard the *Griffin*, the first sailing vessel on the Upper Lakes, the group sailed from the Niagara Falls area on August 7, 1679, and entered the Detroit River on August 11. They reached Lake Saint Clair the following day and named it Lac Sainte Claire in honor of Sainte Claire of Assisi whose feast day fell at that time. It was Sainte Claire who established the order of Franciscan nuns, the Order of the Poor Claires. Government officials and map makers later changed the spelling to the present form of Saint Clair. This led to some confusion as to the true original of the name of the lake.

Michigan Historical Commission

MONROE COUNTY
Famous Waterfront
Sterling State Park, Monroe

First land for Sterling State Park was acquired in 1935 as a gift from Monroe Piers Land Company and was named in honor of Wm. C. Sterling, prominent statesman and first Commodore of the Monroe Yacht Club organized in 1887. Monroe County's waterfront on Lake Erie has been famous since pioneer days for its great flights of waterfowl, spring and fall. The French shot the winged game, trapped muskrat and speared sturgeon for livelihood. In later years the marshes have attracted sportsmen from far and wide. Water sports flourished at an early date. In 1878 a Monroe four-man rowing crew swept American competition and went to Henley, England, for an international rowing regatta. Muskrat dinners featured by the old Yacht Club in 1900s became a community tradition and are continued by present day groups.

Monroe County Historical Commission

Lake Erie
Sterling State Park, Monroe

Named for the Erie Indians, this was the last of the Great Lakes discovered by white men. The French were exploring the upper lakes as early as 1615, but they avoided the region to the south, which was the realm of hostile Iroquois Indians. Then in 1669, Adrien Jolliet entered Lake Erie from the Detroit River and followed the north shore eastward. The final link was added to the mighty inland waterway so vital in Michigan history.

Michigan Historical Commission

Port of Monroe

Winchester at E. Front Street, Monroe

The port of Monroe one mile east of here is one of the oldest on the Great Lakes. Only port in Michigan on Lake Erie, and located strategically on its most westerly shore, it was a major point of entry for Michigan settlement and for passage of Chicago bound settlers from 1800 to 1860. During the period of sail-borne commerce, and until 1835, the harbor development centered at the old mouth of the River Raisin two miles south. The Monroe port has been officially recognized by the Federal Government since 1826. The turning basin was dug and the channel deepened beginning in 1932. The port terminal building was completed in 1939.

Monroe County Historical Commission

ST. CLAIR COUNTY

Fort Gratiot Light

Omar and Garfield Streets, Port Huron

This lighthouse, the oldest in Michigan, was built in 1829 to replace a tower destroyed by a storm. Lucius Lyon, the builder, was deputy surveyor general of the Northwest Territory and later a United States senator from Michigan. In the 1860s workers extended the tower to its present height of eighty-six feet. The light, automated in 1933, continues to guide shipping on Lake Huron into the narrow and swift-flowing St. Clair River.

Michigan Historical Commission

Huron Lightship

Pine Grove Park, Port Huron

Commissioned in 1921, the *Huron* began service as a relief vessel for other Great Lakes lightships. She is ninety-seven feet long, twenty-four feet in beam and carried a crew of eleven. On clear nights her beacon could be seen for fourteen miles. After serving in northern Lake Michigan the *Huron* was assigned to the Corsica Shoals in 1935, These shallow waters, six miles north of Port Huron, were the scene of frequent groundings by lake freighters in the late nineteenth century. A lightship station had been estab-

lished there in 1893, since the manned ships were more reliable than lighted buoys. After 1940 the *Huron* was the only lightship on the Great Lakes. Retired from Coast Guard service in 1970, she was presented to the city of Port Huron in 1971.
Michigan Historical Commission

St. Clair River
M-29, Clay Township
   Linking the upper and lower Great Lakes, this river has become one of the world's great marine highways. In the 1700s canoes passed by here with furs destined to adorn Europe's royalty. Ships built in Marine City by Sam and Eber Brock Ward during the mid-1800s carried many immigrants up this river on their way to new homes in the West. By the 1900s mighty freighters returned from the north with iron ore, copper, grain -- products of these settlers' labor.
Michigan Historical Commission

Water Speed Capital
City of Algonac Park, Algonac
   For more than a century, Algonac has played a leading role in ship building, from sailing cargo ships to large pleasure craft, racing boats and World War II landing craft. Between 1921 and 1931, Christopher Smith and Gar Wood built ten *Miss Americas* in Algonac. Smith and Wood worked together on the first; however, Wood was responsible for the rest. The *Miss Americas* held the Harmsworth trophy, symbol of the world's water speed supremacy, from 1921 to 1933. In 1932, Wood's *Miss America* X raced over a measured mile to establish the world's water speed record at 124.91 miles per hour. During the 1930s, Smith adopted the name Chris Craft Corporation. The firm became one of the world's largest builders of power pleasure boats. Headquartered in Algonac for many years, it had other manufacturing plants in Michigan, Ohio, Missouri, Tennessee, Florida and Italy.
Michigan Historical Commission

WAYNE COUNTY
Angus Keith House
9510 Horse Mill Road, Grosse Ile
   Angus Keith (1819-1899), a Great Lakes steamship captain, was

born on Grosse Ile. In 1850 he purchased this property and later built this house. In 1858, Keith married Isabella Norvell, the daughter of John Norvell, who was one of Michigan's original U.S. senators. Keith's father, William Keith, commanded both naval and merchant ships. Angus Keith sailed the lakes for forty years and operated commercial vessels including lumber carriers for the Peshtigo Lumber Company.

Michigan Historical Commission

SOUTHWEST

OTTAWA COUNTY
Holland Harbor Lighthouse
Holland Harbor, Holland State Park, Park Township

The first lighthouse built at this location was a small, square wooden structure erected in 1872. In 1880 the lighthouse service installed a new light atop a metal pole in a protective cage. The oil lantern was lowered by pulleys for service. At the turn of the century a steel tower was built for the light, and in 1907 the present structure was erected. Named the Holland Harbor South Pierhead Lighthouse, it has a gabled roof that reflects the Dutch influence in the area. The lighthouse, popularly referred to as "Big Red," was automated in 1932. When the U.S. Coast Guard recommended that it be abandoned in 1970, citizens circulated petitions to rescue it. The Holland Harbor Lighthouse Historical Commission was then organized to preserve and restore this landmark.

Michigan Historical Commission

Holland Harbor
Holland Harbor, Holland State Park, Park Township

When seeking a location for his Netherlands emigrant followers in 1847, the Reverend A.C. Van Raalte was attracted by the potential of using Black Lake (Lake Macatawa) as a harbor. However, the lake's outlet to Lake Michigan was blocked by sandbars and silt. Van Raalte appealed to Congress for help. The channel was surveyed in 1849, but was not successfully opened due to inadequate appropriations. Frustrated, the Dutch settlers dug the channel themselves. On July 1, 1859, the small steamboat *Huron* put into port. Here, in 1886, the government established the harbor's first life-saving station. By 1899 the channel had been relocated and harbor work completed. This spurred business and resort expansion. In 1900 over 1,095 schooners, steamers and barges used the harbor.

Michigan Historical Commission

CENTRAL

BAY COUNTY
Saginaw Bay
Bay City State Park, Bangor Township

This bay derives its name from the Sauk Indians who once dwelt by its shores. Adrien Jolliet, on his voyage down Lake Huron's western shore in 1669, first made it known to the white man. In the late 1800s an immense lumber industry flourished in the region. Schooners by the scores daily passed through the bay bringing to the sawmills more logs and hauling off cut lumber. The bay's waters for years also made fishing good business.

Michigan Historical Commission

EATON COUNTY
Second Island
Second Island, Grand River, Grand Ledge

Graced by the natural beauty of these soaring sandstone ledges, Grand Ledge was once famous for its Seven Islands Resort, a recreation area centered on this island from 1870 to 1910. At the turn of the century the ledges made this city one of the most popular resort areas in lower Michigan. Excursion trains brought thousands to enjoy this area which featured steamboat rides, a boat livery, a hotel and vaudeville theater, mineral wells, a roller coaster and fishing. In 1976 the Grand Ledge Area Bicentennial Commission erected the band pavilion.

Michigan Historical Commission

INGHAM COUNTY
Grand River
Riverfront Park, Lansing

The Grand River and its valley were formed by the melting of the continental glacier that retreated from this area some twelve thousand years ago. Known by Chippewa Indians as Washtanong (further country) and by the French as le Riviere Grand, the Grand is Michigan's longest river. From its headwaters in northern Hillsdale and southern Jackson counties, it flows 270 river miles and drops 460 feet in elevation before entering Lake Michigan at Grand Haven. Together with its tributaries, it drains a 5,570-square-mile watershed, including all or part of eighteen counties. Lansing is located in the upper portion of the river basin where the Grand changes direction from northward to westward. The Red Cedar River, one of seven major tributaries, enters one mile upstream from here.

Michigan Historical Commission

Grand River History
Riverfront Park, Lansing

The Grand River has been an important resource and travel route throughout Michigan's past. To the Indians, the Grand River provided a route for travel and trade and a valley for hunting and agriculture. Seventeenth-century French explorers were the first Europeans to see the river. In the eighteenth century French, British and American fur traders canoed the Grand and its tributaries. The journal of Detroit fur trader Hugh Heward, who passed by this site in 1790, is thought to be the first written record of travel near present-day Lansing. In the mid-nineteenth century the Grand became an important means of transportation for logs and lumber. In the twentieth century the waters of the Grand have been used for industrial and agricultural production, as well as recreation.

Michigan Historical Commission

28,000-mile Canoe Voyage
Riverfront Park, Lansing:

Commemorating a 28,000-mile continent-circling canoe voyage by two Lansing adventurers, Verlen Kruger and Steve Landick. They completed their world record odyssey in 3½ years, landing at this site on the Grand River Dec. 15, 1983.

Michigan Outdoor Writers Association

NORTHEAST

CHEBOYGAN COUNTY
Inland Waterway
Burt Lake State Park, Tuscarora Township

The glaciers of the last Ice Age retreated to the north some 25,000 years ago, leaving behind the lakes that rank as Michigan's most notable geographic feature. Among the state's largest inland lakes is Burt Lake, named after William A. Burt, who, together with Henry Mullett, made a federal survey of the area from 1840 to 1843. By following the Cheboygan River, Mullett Lake and Indian River to Burt Lake, then up Crooked River to Crooked Lake, Indians and fur traders had only a short portage to Little Traverse Bay. Thus they avoided the trip through the Straits. Completion of a lock on the Cheboygan in 1869 opened this inland waterway to the Cheboygan Slack Water Navigation Company, whose vessels carried passengers and freight until railroads put it out of business. Day-long excursions over these waters became popular with tourists.

Michigan Historical Commission

CRAWFORD COUNTY
Au Sable River Boat
Grayling Fish Hatchery, Grayling

Commemorating the origination of the Au Sable Riverboat at Grayling about 1872 by Reuben S. Babbitt Sr., an early settler, guide and operator of fishing camps on the AuSable and Manistee rivers. Unique to the AuSable, the boat fitted a special need for fishing and recreation, and has been faithfully reproduced to this day by subsequent builders.

Michigan Outdoor Writers Association

Michigan Grayling
Grayling Fish Hatchery, Grayling

Although fishermen had been catching this fish in such rivers as the Manistee, Pere Marquette and Au Sable for some years, its classification as true grayling came only in 1864. The thrill of landing this fish drew sportsmen from the country over as railroads entered northern Michigan in the 1870s. The town of Grayling was the center for fishing trips on the Au Sable. Habitat changes following deforestation were making Michigan grayling rare by about 1900, and by about 1930 they were extinct.

While now extinct in Michigan, members of the grayling family are found in Montana, Europe and the Arctic. The grayling are related to the trout and salmon and are distinguished by a thyme-like odor and a long wavy dorsal fin, a superb mark of beauty. Measuring from twelve to fifteen inches, the Michigan grayling lived in cold, swift streams and were a gamy fish and delicious as food.

Michigan Historical Commission

HURON COUNTY
Bay Port Fishing District
Promenade Street, Bay Port, Fairhaven Township

The Gillingham Fish Company was established in 1886; the Bay Port Fish Company, in 1895. At their peak in the 1920s and 1930s, they shipped tons of perch, walleye, herring, whitefish and carp to New York and Chicago in refrigerated railroad cars. Once known as one of the largest fresh water commercial fishing ports in the world, Bay Port retains a commercial fishery that operates much as it did in the past. Bay Port also offers sport fishing, water skiing, ice fishing and hunting.

Michigan Historical Commission

PRESQUE ISLE COUNTY
Lake Huron
US 23 Roadside Park, Huron Beach
Lake Huron

This, the fifth largest lake in the world, was the first of the Great Lakes seen by white men. By following the Ottawa River route, Samuel de Champlain in 1615 came to the "Freshwater Sea." It was half a century before the French fully understood the lake's size. Lake shipping has swelled immensely since the *Griffin's* solitary voyage in 1679. Much of the shore is still as wild as when the Huron Indians were the only travelers on the lake.

Michigan Historical Commission

Old Presque Isle Lighthouse
Presque Isle Harbor, Presque Isle Township

Presque Isle Harbor is one of Lake Huron's safest harbors of refuge. Its name comes from this peninsula which, translating from the French, is "almost an island." Indians and Frenchmen portaged across the peninsula to avoid several miles of open lake. When vessels came to the harbor in increasing numbers, Congress in 1838 appropriated $5,000 for a lighthouse. Jeremiah Moors of

Detroit in 1840 completed this lighthouse, which today is one of the oldest surviving lighthouses on the Great Lakes. Pat Garrity, the last keeper of this lighthouse, was appointed by President Lincoln. Four of Garrity's children, raised in the keeper's house, became lighthouse keepers. In 1870 a new lighthouse to the north was completed along with two range lights for the entrance to the harbor.

Michigan Historical Commission

Presque Isle Light Station
4500 E. Grand Lake Road, Presque Isle Township

This lighthouse, built in 1870 by Orlando M. Poe, is one of three Great Lakes towers built from the same plans. It replaced the smaller 1840 harbor light. The conical brick tower rises 113 feet from a limestone foundation. The Third Order Fresnel lens was made by Henri LePaute of Paris. Patrick Garrity, the keeper of the harbor light, lit the lamp for the first time at the opening of the 1871 navigation season. Garrity served here until 1885 when he became keeper of the Harbor Range Lights. His wife, Mary, sons Thomas, Patrick and John, and daughter Anna all served as light keepers in this area. In 1890 a steam-operated fog signal manufactured by Variety Iron Works of Cleveland, Ohio, was installed. The light was automated in 1970 by the U.S. Coast Guard.

Michigan Historical Commission

NORTHWEST

BENZIE COUNTY
Pacific Salmon
Platte River Hatchery, Beulah

Since 1870 several unsuccessful attempts have been made to establish Pacific salmon in the Great Lakes. In 1966 at this site the Department of Conservation released coho fingerlings, hatchery-reared from eggs given by the state of Oregon. They migrated to Lake Michigan and fed on its enormous alewife population. Augmented by subsequent annual plantings, the coho became firmly established. By 1970 the sport fishery catch reached ten million pounds. Other species of Pacific salmon -- the chinook and kokanee -- were also successfully introduced to the Great Lakes area in the late 1960s. To complete their life cycle the salmon return to their home stream to spawn and then die. Millions of salmon are now planted each year. In 1973 the world's largest recorded coho, weighing over thirty-nine pounds, was taken at a state weir.

Michigan Historical Commission

LAKE COUNTY
Brown Trout
M-37, Pleasant Plains Township

On April 11, 1884, the first recorded planting of brown trout (Salmo pariole) in the United States was made into the Pere Marquette River system by the Northville, Michigan, Federal Fish Hatchery. The trout eggs from which the planting of forty-nine hundred fry was made had been obtained from Baron Friedrich Von Behr of Berlin, Germany, by Fred Mather, superintendent of the Cold Spring Harbor Federal Fish Hatchery at Long Island, New York. Some brown trout eggs had been shipped to the United States and distributed to various fisheries in the country for observation in 1883, but the Northville station was the first to stock American waters with this fish. From this beginning, the species (known in Germany as Bachforelle) has become widely established throughout the United States.

Michigan Historical Commission

Public Access to Public Water
Peterson's Landing, Banks of the Pine River, Luther

Public Access to Public Water. On a pleasant May morning in 1925, Gideon Gerhardt stepped into the Pine River near here to do a little trout fishing. That act triggered one of the most important public water rights cases in United States history, Collins v. Gerhardt. The resulting decision affirmed the rights of the public to the use of public waters. The land surrounding Mr. Gerhardt's chosen fishing spot was owned by Frank Collins, who brought a civil action for trespass. After a local court ruled in favor of Mr. Collins, the case reached the Michigan Supreme Court, which reversed the decision. Speaking for the majority in April 1926, Justice John S. McDonald wrote, "So long as water flows and fish swim in Pine River, the people may fish at their pleasure in any part of the stream subject only to the restraints and regulations imposed by the state.

Federal appeals kept the issue alive until 1936, but the legal principle set forth by the Michigan Supreme Court remained unshaken, and guarantees to future generations the right to the recreational use of Michigan's rivers and streams.

State Bar of Michigan & Mason-Lake Counties Bar Association

LEELANAU COUNTY
Early State Parks
Sleeping Bear Dunes National Lakeshore, Glen Arbor

By the end of World War I, with the rapid growth of the recreation industry in Michigan, a need for a state-wide parks system had arisen. In 1919 the State Park Commission was established. D.H. Day State Park, honoring the commission's chairman, was the first park that it set up. When state parks were transferred to the Conservation Department in 1921 over twenty other sites had been acquired, most of them, like D.H. Day State Park, beautifully located on lake shores.

Michigan Historical Commission

Great Lakes Sport Fishery
Village Marina, Northport

Great Lakes sport trolling was pioneered off Northport in the early 1920s. Traverse City native George Raff was the first to discover that lake trout could be caught by trolling in Traverse Bay's protected waters. Prior to this, trout fishing was mainly a commercial enterprise, in which large quantities of the species were caught by net. Traverse City restaurant owners eagerly bought Raff's catches. Starting with one small boat, about sixteen feet long, Raff later began the areas's first sports charter service. He charged each angler one dollar an hour, and guaranteed success. Methods he and his wife, Nell, developed for catching trout and other game fish species have spread throughout the Great Lakes.

Sport trolling for lake trout almost vanished in the 1940s due to over-fishing by commercial netters and sea lamprey attacks on the trout. Chemicals finally controlled the lampreys, while state laws outlawed gill nets. In the 1960s, the Michigan Fishery Commission planted coho and Chinook salmon for a new sport fishery. Using the methods developed near Northport in the 1920s, plus other techniques -- such as using piano wire, wooden and metal reels and lures made from tin cans and bicycle spokes -- trollers again began catching salmon, brown and lake trout and steelheads throughout most of the Great Lakes. In 1981 sport fishing brought Michigan over $3 billion in tourist revenues and attracted 700,000 licensed anglers in the Great Lakes.

Michigan Historical Commission

MASON COUNTY
Armistice Day Storm
Stearns Park, Ludington

On November 11, 1940, a severe storm swept the Great Lakes area. As it crossed Lake Michigan, ships and seamen fought to reach safety away from its blinding winds and towering seas. Between Big and Little Points Sable the freighters *William B. Davock* and *Anna C. Minch* foundered with the loss of all hands. The crew of the *Novadoc*, driven aground south of Pentwater, battled icy winds and water for two days before being rescued by local fishermen. At Ludington the car-ferry *City of Flint 32* was driven ashore, her holds flooded to prevent further damage. Elsewhere lives were lost and ships damaged in one of Lake Michigan's greatest storms.

Michigan Historical Commission

S.S. Pere Marquette 18
Stearns Park, Ludington

At least twenty-nine persons died when this vessel sank in Lake Michigan twenty miles off the Wisconsin coast on September 9, 1910. One of the Ludington carferry fleet, the 350-foot *S.S. Pere Marquette 18* was traveling from this port to Wisconsin. About midlake a crewman discovered that the ship was taking on vast amounts of water. The captain set a direct course for Wisconsin and sent a distress signal by wireless. He and the crew battled for four hours to save the boat but she sank suddenly. All of the officers and many of the crew and passengers perished, among them the first wireless operator to die in active service on the Great Lakes. The *S.S. Pere Marquette 17*, aided by other ships who also heeded the wireless message for help, rescued more than thirty survivors but lost two of her own crew. The exact cause of this disaster remains a mystery.

Michigan Historical Commission

OCEANA COUNTY
Veterans' Day Storm
Village of Pentwater Memorial Marina, Pentwater

The most disastrous day in the history of Lake Michigan shipping was Armistice (now Veterans') Day, November 11, 1940. With seventy-five-mile-per-hour winds and twenty-foot waves, a raging storm destroyed three ships and claimed the lives of fifty-nine seamen. Two freighters sank with all hands lost, and a third, the *Novadoc*, ran aground with the loss of two crew members. Bodies washed ashore throughout the day. As night fell, a heavy snow storm arrived. Rescue efforts by the Coast Guard and local citizens continued for three days after the storm. Three Pentwater fishermen were later recognized by the local community and the Canadian government for their bravery in rescuing seventeen sailors from the *Novadoc*.

Michigan Historical Commission

Graveyard of Ships
Village of Pentwater Memorial Marina, Pentwater

The twenty-mile span of Lake Michigan between Little Point Sable, at Silver Lake, and Big Point Sable, north of Ludington, has earned a reputation as the "Graveyard of Ships." Beginning with the loss of the *Neptune* in 1848 through the Armistice (now Veterans') Day Storm of 1940, nearly seventy vessels have gone down in these treacherous waters. Gales and November snow storms have made navigation of this part of the lake a sailor's nightmare. Significant among the losses near Pentwater Harbor were the schooner *Wright* in 1854, the *Minnie Corlett* and the *Souvenior* in 1875, the *Lamont* in 1879 and the tug *Two Brothers* in 1912. The freighters *William B. Davock*, *Anna C. Minch* and *Novadoc* were all lost on November 11, 1940.

Michigan Historical Commission

UPPER PENINSULA

ALGER COUNTY
Lake Superior
Scott Falls Roadside Park, Au Train Township

Le lac superieur the French called it, meaning only that geographically it lay above Lake Huron. In size, however, Lake

Superior stands above all other freshwater lakes in the world. The intrepid Frenchman Brule discovered it around 1622. During the 1650s and 1660s French fur traders, such as Radisson and Groseilliers, and Jesuits such as Fathers Allouez and Menard, explored this great inland sea. Within 250 years fur-laden canoes had given way to huge boats carrying ore and grain to the world.
Michigan Historical Commission

CHIPPEWA COUNTY
Whitefish Point Lighthouse
Intersection of M-123 and Whitefish Point Road, Whitefish Township

This light, the oldest active on Lake Superior, began operating in 1849, though the present tower was constructed later. Early a stopping place for Indians, voyageurs and Jesuit missionaries, the point marks a course change for ore boats and other ships navigating this treacherous coastline to and from St. Mary's Canal. Since 1971 the light, fog signal and radio beacon have been automated and controlled from Sault Ste. Marie.
Michigan Historical Commission

DELTA COUNTY
Escanaba River: The Legend
Opposite Pioneer Trail Park, Wells Township

This is the land of the Chippewa Indians and the legendary Hiawatha. Indian villages existed along the banks of the river, and Indians were living here when the first white men came to this region in the 1600s. The Indians named the river for the flat rocks over which it runs. In The Song of Hiawatha, Longfellow described how Hiawatha "crossed the rushing Escanaba" in pursuit of Mudjekeewis, whom he slew to avenge the death of his mother. The last Indian lands in the Upper Peninsula were ceded to the United States in 1842. This closed an era that began about ten thousand years ago.
Michigan Historical Commission

MACKINAC COUNTY
Round Island Lighthouse
Municipal Park, Mackinac Island

The Round Island Lighthouse, seen south of this site, was com-

pleted in 1895. Operating under the auspices of the United States government, this facility was in continuous use for fifty-two years. It was manned by a crew of three until its beacon was replaced by an automatic light in 1924. A sole caretaker occupied and operated the station from 1924 to 1947. Following the construction of a new automatic beacon near the breakwater off the south shore of Mackinac Island, the lighthouse was abandoned. The United States Forest Service now supervises the structure, which is located in the Hiawatha National Forest. The lighthouse serves as a sentinel for the past, reminding visitors of the often precarious sailing and rich history of the Straits of Mackinac.
Michigan Historical Commission.

Lake Michigan
US 2, Moran Township
This lake, the sixth largest in the world, was discovered in 1634 by Jean Nicolet, who explored this northern shore to Green Bay but found no Orientals as the French in Quebec had hoped he would. The general size and outline of the lake was established in the 1670s by Marquette and Jolliet. They named it Lake Michigan. Its elongated shape was an obstacle to transcontinental expansion, but its waters soon proved a real boon to commerce.
Michigan Historical Commission

Mackinac Straits
I-75 Rest Area and Visitors Center, St. Ignace
Nicolet passed through the straits in 1634 seeking a route to the Orient. Soon it became a crossroads where Indian, missionary, trapper and soldier met. From the 1600s through the War of 1812 first Frenchmen and Englishmen, then Briton and American fought to control this strategic waterway. In 1679 the *Griffin* was the first sailing vessel to ply these waters. The railroad reached the straits in 1862. Until the Mackinac Bridge was opened in 1957, ferries linked the north and south.
Michigan Historical Commission

MARQUETTE COUNTY
First American Flag Over Lake Superior
Sunset Point, Presque Isle Park, Marquette
Hereabouts along the shores of Presque Isle the first American

flag to float over Lake Superior was brought by Governor Lewis Cass, governor of Michigan Territory, on the 22nd day of June 1820
  Marquette County Historical Society

Chapter 26

LIGHTHOUSES

With a legacy dating back to 1818, Michigan lighthouses symbolize the state's Great Lakes heritage. Even in an age of high-tech boating, shipping and navigation, many are still in operation, albeit automatically. All together, there are now 104 lighthouses along the Michigan coasts. Some are accessible to the public by land or water, including the automated Thunder Bay Island Lighthouse on Lake Huron and Big Bay Point Light, which is also a bed-and-breakfast, on Lake Superior. Several are museums devoted to Great Lakes and local history.

As these descriptions by the Michigan Department of Transportation show, the surviving lighthouses have architectural, cultural and historic significance beyond their original nautical roots:

• **Mackinac Point:** "Old Mackinac Point built in 1892 on the Straits of Mackinac was visible for 16 miles. The round brick tower, 6 feet in diameter and 40 feet tall, is attached to a two-story rectangular keeper's dwelling. With the opening of the Mackinac Bridge in 1957, the ships used the lights on the bridge to guide them, making the lighthouse obsolete."

• **Eagle Harbor:** "Eagle Harbor was authorized by Congress in March 1849 at a cost of $4,000 and rebuilt in 1871 at a cost of $14,000. The octagonal brick light tower is 10 feet in diameter with walls 12 inches thick. It supports a 10-sided cast iron lantern and is 44 feet high. In addition to the keepers dwelling, the Eagle Harbor complex includes a brick oil house, fog signal building and two frame houses."

• **South Manitou Island:** "South Manitou Island Light was built in 1839 and rebuilt in 1871 as a conical brick structure 18 feet in diameter at the base and 104 feet tall. A large steam fog horn was added in 1875, replacing the fog bell that had been in service for many years. In 1958, the Coast Guard abandoned the station and it is now an historical museum which is part of the Sleeping Bear Dunes National Lakeshore."

- **Point Betsie Light:** "Point Betsie was built in 1858 at a cost of $3,000 at the southern end of the Manitou Passage. The original name was Pointe Aux Becs Scies. This was such an important light that the original 37-foot tower was replaced with a 100-foot structure. The Coast Guard automated Point Betsie in 1983, when it was the last staffed light station on the east shore of Lake Michigan. The crystal lamp originally burned coal oil, then kerosene. Now it is automated and electric."

- **Fort Gratiot Light:** "The first lighthouse on Lake Huron, built in 1825 and raised 20 feet in 1861, is made of white brick and stands 86 feet high. It has a lightkeeper's dwelling adjacent to it and is the oldest surviving lighthouse in Michigan."

The following list is arranged from the southeast corner of the state at the Detroit River to the southwest, by way of the Straits of Mackinac, to St. Joseph on Lake Michigan. It then runs from Menominee Point on Lake Michigan eastward around the Upper Peninsula, ending at Ontonagon near the Wisconsin border.

1. Detroit River Light

2. Grosse Ile North Channel Front Range Light

3. Detroit Lighthouse Depot

4. William Livingstone Memorial Light

5. Windmill Point Light

6. Lake St. Clair Light

7. St. Clair Flats Old Channel Range Light

8. Peche Island Rear Range Light

9. Lightship Huron

10. Fort Gratiot Light

11. Port Sanilac Light

12. Harbor Beach (Sand Beach) Light

13. Pointe Aux Barques Light

14. Port Austin Reef Light

15. Charity Island Light

16. Gravelly Shoal Light

17. Saginaw River Rear Range Light

18. Tawas Point Light

19. Sturgeon Point Light

20. Alpena Light

21. Thunder Bay Island Light

22. Middle Island Light

23. Old Presque Isle Light

24. Forty Mile Point Light

25. Cheboygan River Range Front Light

26. Fourteen Foot Shoal Light

27. Poe Reef Light

28. Bois Blanc Island Light

29. Spectacle Reef Light

30. Round Island Light

31. Martin Reef Light

32. DeTour Point Light

33. Old Mackinac Point Light

34. McGulpin's Point Light

35. Waugoschance Light

36. Skillagalee (Ile Aux Galets) Light

37. White Shoal Light

38. Gray's Reef Light

39. St. Helena Island Light

40. Lansing Shoal Light

41. Seul Choix Point Light

42. Squaw Island Light

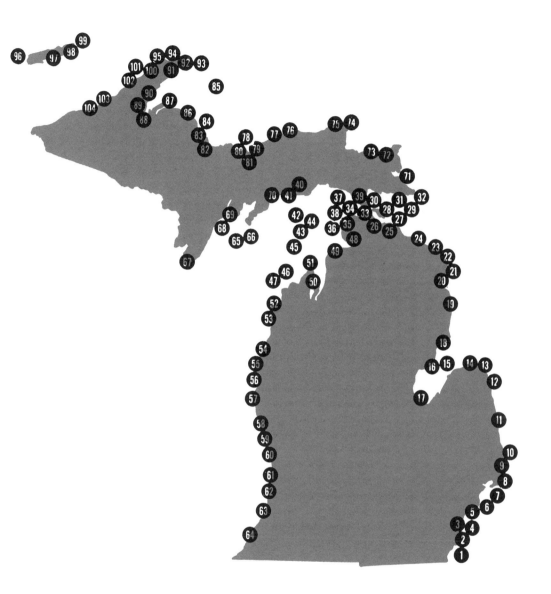

MICHIGAN DEPARTMENT OF TRANSPORTATION

43. Beaver Island (Beaver Head)

44. Beaver Island Harbor Light

45. South Fox Island Light

46. North Manitou Shoal Light

47. South Manitou Shoal Light

48. Little Traverse (Harbor Point) Light

49. Charlevoix South Pier Light

50. Mission Point (Old Mission Point) Light

51. Grand Traverse (Vat's Head Point) Light

52. Point Betsie Light

53. Frankfort North Breakwater Light

54. Manistee North Pierhead Light

55. Big Sable Point (Grand Point Au Sable) Light

56. Ludington North Pierhead Light

57. Little Sable Point (Petite Pointe Au Sable) Light

58. White River Light

59. Muskegon South Pier Light

60. Grand Haven South Pier Inner Light

61. Holland Harbor (Black Lake) Light

62. Saugatuck (Kalamazoo River) Light

63. South Haven South Pier Light

64. St. Joseph North Pier Outer Light

65. St. Martin Island Light

66. Poverty Island Light

67. Menominee North Pier Light

68. Minneapolis Shoal Light

69. Peninsula Point Light

70. Manistique East Breakwater Light

71. Round Island Light

72. Cedar Point (Round Island Point) Rear Range Light

73. Point Iroquois Light

74. Whitefish Point Light

75. Crisp's Point Light

76. Grand Marais Harbor Range Light

77. Au Sable Point Light

78. Grand Island North Light

79. Grand Island East Channel Light

80. Grand Island West Channel Light

81. Munising Range Light

82. Marquette Harbor Light

83. Presque Isle Harbor Breakwater Light

84. Granite Island Light

85. Stannard Rock Light

86. Big Bay Point Light

87. Huron Island Light

88. Sand Point Light

89. Portage Lake Lower Entrance Light

90. Portage River (Jacobsville) Light

91. Mendota (Bete Grise) Light

92. Gull Rock Light

93. Manitou Island Light

94. Copper Harbor Light

95. Eagle Harbor Light

96. Rock of Ages Light

97. Isle Royale (Menagerie Island) Light

98. Rock Harbor Light

99. Passage Island Light

100. Eagle River Light

101. Sand Hills Light

102. Keweenaw Waterway Upper Entrance Light

103. Fourteen Mile Point Light

104. Ontonagon Light

TOM BUCHKOE

Chapter 27

SPECIAL DELIGHTS ON THE WATER

Expected the unexpected on and near the water. Sometimes it's bad news, such as the storm that suddenly materializes from clear skies. Sometimes it's good news, calm weather instead of the anticipated squalls.

And sometimes it's a special delight, something extraordinary and pleasurable and memorable. Here are some you can encounter on the waters of Michigan:

SAILING RACES

The two best-known summer sailing events in Michigan are the annual yacht races to Mackinac Island, one from Port Huron and the other from Chicago. Both attract world-class competitors and generate celebrations at departure and arrival.

Detroit's Bayview Yacht Club sponsors the Port Huron-Mackinac race, which bills itself as the largest and best-publicized sailing event in the Midwest. There are more than 250 entrants and 2,500 crew members from about 60 yacht clubs. Crews range in number from five to more than 25, and their boats from 30 to 78 feet long. Covering the course takes two to three days, depending on wind strength and direction.

For more information, write to Bayview Yacht Club, 100 Clairpointe, Detroit MI 48215 or call (313) 822-1853.

The Chicago Yacht Club sponsors the Chicago-Mackinac race. It's the oldest regularly scheduled long distance race in the world, a tradition for well over 80 years. At 330 statute miles, it's also the world's longest fresh water yachting competition; the record speed is about 26 hours, though most participants take two to three days. About 265-270 yachts of 27 to 70 feet in length compete.

For more information, write to the Chicago Yacht Club, Foot of Monroe Street, Chicago IL 60603 or call (312) 861-7777.

For more information on other Great Lakes sail racing events,

contact these affiliates of the U.S. Sailing Association:
- Lake Huron Yacht Racing Association, 304 Edison Blvd., Port Huron MI 48060. Phone (313) 987-2220.
- Lake Michigan Sail Racing Federation, Box 40, Williams Bay WI 53191. Phone (414) 245-5146 or (414) 245-6242.
- Lake Superior Yachting Association, 605 Lake Ave. N., Duluth MN 55806. Phone (218) 726-0561 or (218) 726-1393.
-

FLOATING RESTAURANT

The Boat   (313) 249-9745
3649 Pte. Tremble Road
Algonac MI 48001

Dine on the water, literally. This restaurant, owned by Joyce Bryson and her son Artie, is located on a 135-foot boat moored on the North Channel of the St. Clair River next to the Harsens Island Ferry. Before its arrival in Michigan, the M.V. Port Welcome carried passengers between Baltimore and Annapolis, Md. The decor, appropriately, is nautical blue, with mahogany and thousands of feet of wrapped ropes.

SPECIAL BRIDGES

A boater's or canoeist's view of a bridge is far different from a motorist's perspective, or that of a pedestrian or bicyclist. Although Michigan has more than 11,000 bridges, here are a few that stand out from the vantage point below:
- The Mackinac Bridge stretches for five miles across the Straits of Mackinac, linking the Upper and Lower Peninsulas.
- The Blue Water Bridge, 1.4 miles long, crosses the St. Clair River between Port Huron and Sarnia, Ont.
- The Fallasburg Covered Bridge, built of white pine in 1871, crosses the Flat River in Kent County.
- The Siphon Bridge in Manistique is supported in part by the Manistique River; water is atmospherically forced under it.
- The Houghton-Hancock Bridge is a double deck lift span across the Portage Lake waterway on the Keweenaw Peninsula.
- The Ambassador Bridge above the Detroit River is privately owned and connects Detroit with Windsor, Ont.

• The International Bridge, two miles long, crosses the Soo Locks and St. Marys River between the two Sault Ste. Maries, Michigan's and Ontario's.

GHOST SHIP

Countless ships, from rowboats and canoes to huge tankers and freighters, have disappeared in the Great Lakes, sometimes taking crew and cargo to the depths. A few such ships, sunk long ago, are still seen from time to time, or so some mariners claim.

One is the *Bannockburn*, a 245-foot steamer of the Montreal Transportation Co., which vanished in Lake Superior in a November 1902 storm. Built in England only nine years earlier, the *Bannockburn* under Capt. George R. Wood's command was carrying a load of 85,000 bushels of wheat from Port Arthur, northwest of Isle Royale, to Georgian Bay when it disappeared. The only debris found was a life preserver and an oar, and no signs of the 21 crew were ever discovered.

As author Dwight Boyer wrote in Ghost Ships of the Great Lakes:

> "Superstitious sailors, and there were still many around in the early years of the century, likened the *Bannockburn* to the legendary *Flying Dutchman* of salt water, a vessel that vanished off the Cape of Good Hope in a gale, only to reappear on the seas as a mysterious phantom ship, most frequently sighted during the night watches as she beats to windward on her endless voyage. On stormy nights, several sailors claimed to have seen the *Bannockburn*, buffeting her way down Lake Superior, her lamps blinking in the storm scud, while in the darkened pilothouse her master looked vainly for the welcoming flash of Caribou Island Light."

So if, on some stormy night, you should spot a mysterious three-masted, 1,620-ton steel-hulled steamer fighting its forlorn way across Lake Superior, if you should hear screams almost drowned out by the wind, salute the memory of Capt. Wood and his crew, and tell their hapless tale to others.

LIGHTHOUSE BED-&-BREAKFAST

Big Bay Point Lighthouse   (906) 345-9957
3 Lighthouse Road

351

Big Bay MI 49808

You'll find the reputedly haunted Big Bay Point Lighthouse bed-and-breakfast on a rocky cliff overlooking Lake Superior and the Huron Mountains. It's the Great Lakes' only privately owned and privately operated lighthouse. Built of brick in 1896, it was purchased a century later for use as an inn. The 60-foot lighthouse stands on 52 acres, with 4,500 feet of shoreline. It's a registered historic landmark with original doors and stairways.

As legend tells, the structure is haunted by the ghost of the first lighthouse keeper, William Pryor, who hanged himself in the early 1900s. One guest reported seeing Pryor, garbed in his blue uniform, at the foot of her bed, and others have spotted his spectral form roaming the cliffs.

The lighthouse has six guest rooms, a huge first-floor living room fireplace and a second-floor library. From the top of the tower, guests can watch the sun set behind the mountains. Nearby are lake and fly fishing, snowshoeing, ice fishing, canoeing, mountain biking, skiing, rock collecting, off-road bicycling and wilderness hiking. It's 26 miles from Marquette.

PUTTING THE GREAT LAKES INTO MUSIC

When singer-songwriter Mark Mitchell heads out from Marquette in his 23-foot wooden double-ender, his mind is on Lake Superior's past and present. As a boater and musician, he finds inspiration in the struggles between the Great Lakes and the ships that sail them.

One of his true tales involves the Duluth-bound *D.M. Clemson*, which sank off Crisp Point in Lake Superior in 1908, having barely survived storms on two previous voyages. In "Say Goodbye to the *Clemson*," Mitchell sings:

> Say goodbye to your *Clemson* and be ye forewarned
> That the fates always have the last word.
> A ship may fight through a great storm or two
> But she never sails back from the third.
> The ship owners scoff at the legends and tales
> There's no room in their busy minds.
> The season is short, there's cargo to haul
> And it damn better be hauled on time.

Another song, "Black Sunday," recounts the fate of the *Henry B. Smith*, a 7-year-old steel-hulled freighter that sank on Lake Superior in the Great Storm of November 1913. The 545-foot *Smith* was regarded as unsinkable -- until the storm that sank or grounded dozens of Great Lakes ships, causing more than 240 deaths. The doomed ship left Marquette at the onset of the storm, and some witnesses reported that the crew was still battening down the hatches when it left port, and Mitchell says the only debris ever found was a bottle with a note from the captain recounting the final few moments of the doomed ship's fate.

For information on tapes, records and school performances, write to Mark Mitchell at 342 W. Crescent, Marquette MI 49855 or call (906) 228-8897.

ENTERTAINMENT ON THE SHORE

It was 1937, the middle of the Depression, when the first Chesaning Showboat was launched on the Shiawassee River with local performers aboard. In the decades since then, internationally known performers have come to Chesaning to entertain during a week-long festival each July. The audience sits in the outdoor Showboat Amphitheatre while the boat cruises down the river, docks at the stage and serves as the backdrop for evening performances.

During the day, the festival features a free entertainment tent, an arts and crafts show, downtown sidewalk sales, exhibits and crafts demonstrations.

For more information, write to the Chesaning Showboat, 123 W. Broad St., Chesaning MI 48616 or call (517) 845-3056.

ISLAND EXPLORER WATER TRAIL

The Discover Michigan Trail System is expanding nautically with the 140-mile Island Explorer Water Trail. Linking a chain of small islands between Sault Ste. Marie and DeTour Village, there will be boating and fishing docks, hiking trails, rustic campgrounds, swimming beaches and possible restoration of explorer settlements and historic Native American encampments, according to the Department of Natural Resources forest recreation program, which designed the concept. The route includes access to various public launch sites, parks, marinas, lodging and state forest campgrounds, as well as scenic vistas.

Anchoring the trail would be 900-acre Lime Island in the St. Marys River at the eastern tip of the Upper Peninsula. The island, which includes archeologically significant sites, is two miles across the water from the village of Raber in Chippewa County.

SHIVER ON THE RIVER

There are plenty of fishing tournaments throughout Michigan, but one of the most challenging weatherwise is Saginaw's annual winter Shiver on the River walleye fishing competition. Participants aren't limited to the Saginaw River and also can seek prize-winning fish on Saginaw Bay, the Shiawassee River and the Tittabawassee River. There's a special bonus if an angler catches a state record-breaking walleye. The tournament is sponsored by the city of Saginaw, Saginaw News and Huron Fish Co.

For more information, call (800) 444-9979 or (517) 790-0330.

CANOE MARATHON

The annual Au Sable River Canoe Marathon has been a premier competition for more than 45 years. Each July, 25 to 30 crews from the United States and Canada take the Grayling-to-Oscoda challenge, leaving Saturday evening and arriving about 15 hours and 50,000 paddle strokes later. The event is sponsored by Au Sable River International Canoe Marathon Inc., a nonprofit group. The marathon and related weekend events draw about 40,000 spectators. It's also part of a triple crown of North American canoe racing, with the General Clinton race in upstate New York and Le Classique marathon in Quebec.

For more information, write to the Greenbush-Oscoda Lodging Association, Box 397, Oscoda MI 48730 or call (800) 235-GOAL; or write to the Grayling Area Visitors Council, 213 James St., Grayling MI 49738 or call (800) YES-8837.

GREAT LAKES MARITIME ACADEMY

Considering a maritime career? If so, the only degree-granting program in the state is at Northwestern Michigan College in Traverse

City. There you can earn an associate's degree at its Great Lakes Maritime Academy. The three-year program includes 270 days aboard ship. The curriculum includes courses in navigation; maritime discipline; communications; shipboard damage control; electrical theory; steam and diesel engineering; shiphandling; electronic aids to navigation; ship construction and stability; maritime labor relations; refrigeration. marine electrical engineering; Great Lakes meteorology; cargo storage; maritime law; license preparation; and naval science. There are scholarships and grants available for academy cadets.

For more information, write to Northwestern Michigan College Maritime Academy, 1701 E. Front St., Traverse City MI 49684 or call (616) 922-0650.

STUDENTS ON THE WATER

The Inland Seas Education Association in Traverse City offers a "Schoolship" program in which middle school classes have an opportunity to learn about Great Lakes ecology, history and culture and to develop an interest in active stewardship of the lakes. Most half-day sessions are held aboard the 106-foot schooner *Malabar*, with some aboard the 114-foot schooner *Manitou*; shipboard activities are intended to complement traditional classroom studies. The program covers lake biology, meteorology, geology, chemistry, physics, navigation, the arts and culture. Students take part in such activities as trawling for fish, collecting and testing water samples, and examining plants.

Programs for adults, families and non-school groups are available during the summer. The association also sponsors multi-day college-level adventure courses aboard the *Manitou*, combining education with sailing and navigation skills, as well as daylong and overnight programs for small groups aboard the 35-foot ketch *Cygnet*.

The Schoolship welcomes volunteers to serve as instructors to work in teams for at least four days each summer. Volunteer schedules are flexible to accommodate job and child care needs. Prior knowledge of sailing or marine science is not required, and some volunteers have backgrounds as writers, teachers or artists. They undergo orientation and training sessions and will be prepared for the American Sail Training Association's level 1 deckhand and aquatic sciences certificates.

For more information, write to the Inland Seas Education Association, Box 4223, Traverse City MI 49685-4223 or call (616) 941-5577.

FESTIVALS

The Great Lakes and inland waters provide a perfect backdrop for community-oriented summer festivals and events. Here are some popular events:

•U.S. Coast Guard Festival in Grand Haven. It all began with a picnic in 1924 and grew to festival status in 1932, when the Coast Guard cutter *Escanaba* was first assigned to the city. Cosponsored by the neighboring communities of Spring Lake and Ferrysburg, the festival includes a parade, maritime museum and ship tours, fireworks, the world's largest musical fountain, drum and bugle corps performances, a reunion of Coast Guard veterans and a Coast Guard memorial ceremony. Incidentally, each summer Grand Haven also hosts a classic boat rendezvous and a sand sculpture contest.

For more information, write to the Coast Guard Festival Committee, Box 694, Grand Haven MI 49417 or call (616) 842-4910.

•Maritime Days Summer Festival in Marine City. Overlooking Canada where the Belle River joins the St. Clair River, this picturesque city offers riverfront parks, ferry service to Sombra, Ont., and vistas for watching freighters, fishing boats and pleasure craft pass by. The festival includes an antique and classic boat show, parade, arts and craft show, music, fireworks and dancing.

For more information, write to the Marine City Chamber of Commerce, Box 521, Marine City MI 48039 or call (313) 765-4501.

•Canoe the Kazoo Day. Sponsored by the nonprofit Kalamazoo River Protection Association and Friends of the River, the annual event starts at Merrill Park in Comstock with a presentation about progress in ridding the river of hazardous wastes, followed by a race and scavenger hunt. It ends in Kalamazoo's Verburg Park.

For more information, write to the Kalamazoo County Convention & Visitors Bureau, 128 N. Kalamazoo Mall, Kalamazoo MI 49007 or call (616) 381-4003.

• Water Festival in Three Rivers. What more appropriate place for a festival than a city crossed by three rivers -- the Portage, Rocky and St. Joseph? That's what this community has hosted for close to four decades. Events include a "water spectacle" float parade, fireworks, canoe rides, a canoe swamp, carnival and entertainment.

For more information write to the Three Rivers Area Chamber of Commerce, 140 W. Michigan Ave., Three Rivers MI 49093 or call (616) 278-8193.

Chapter 28

MANUFACTURERS & BOAT SHOWS

Given Michigan's status as a prime boating, fishing and water recreation state, it's logical that many companies manufacture marine-related products here, ranging from components and accessories such as paddles, trailers, tackle, anchors and docks to boats, canoes and kayaks. Many of these companies have national and international markets and reputations for their products.

American Anchor Inc.   Anchors
8696 S. Mason Drive
Newaygo MI 49337
(616) 652-3100

Armstrong Marine   Boat accessories
Box 381
Three Rivers MI 49093
(616) 273-1415

Associated Metals Inc.   Downriggers & weights
48586 Downing
Wixom MI 48393
(313) 344-4688

Attwood Corp.   Hydrofoils & trim tabs
1916 N. Monroe St.
Lowell MI 49331
(616) 897-9241

Bargman Co.   Lights & switches
129 Industrial Ave.
Coldwater MI 49036
(517) 279-7594

Bay de Noc Lure Co.   Lures
Box 71
Gladstone MI 49837
(906) 428-1133

Bear Paw Tackle Co.   Rods, reels, fishing line,

Box 355
Bellaire MI 49615
(616) 533-8604

boating & fishing accessories

Betsie Bay Kayak
Box 1706
Frankfort MI 49635
(616) 352-7774

Kayaks & paddles

Big Jon Inc.
14393 Peninsula Drive
Traverse City MI 49684
(800) 637-7590; (616) 223-4286

Downriggers, lures, rod holders
& trolling accessories

Carlisle Paddles
Box 488
Grayling MI 49738
(517) 348-9886

Paddles & oars

C & C Marketing
2415 Porter St. S.W.
Wyoming MI 49509
(616) 530-9012

Lures

Cipa Mirrors
3350 Griswald
Port Huron MI 48060
(800) USA-CIPA

Water ski & boat accessories

C-Loc Retention Systems Inc
Box 180283
Utica MI 48318
(313) 731-9516

Erosion control walls

Convenience Marine Products Inc.
Box 152
Grand Rapids MI 49501-0152
(616) 454-8337

Fire protection systems

DetMar Corp.
2001 W. Alexandrine
Detroit MI 48208
(313) 831-1155

Marine hardware
& instrumentation

Dick Scott & Co. 1993 Ottawa Beach Road Holland MI 49424 (616) 399-9420	No-icer
Douglas Marine Corp. Box 819 Douglas MI 49406 (616) 857-4308	Power boats
Dymex Inc. Box 343 Algonac MI 48001 (313) 794-4340	Propellers
Eppinger Manufacturing Co. 6340 Schaefer Dearborn MI 48126 (313) 582-3205	Fishing lures
4Sea Corp. 4624 13th St. Wyandotte MI 48192 (313) 284-2310	Boat trailers
Four Winns 4 Winn Way Cadillac MI 49601 (616) 775-1351	Power boats
Gougeon Brothers Inc. Box 908 Bay City MI 48707 (517) 684-7286	Epoxy products
Grand Craft Corp. 430 W. 21st St. Holland MI 49423 (616) 396-5450	Power boats
Hadley Products 2851 Prairie S.W. Grandville MI 49418 (616) 530-3283	Air horns

Handy Marketing Co.
4394 Airwest S.E.
Grand Rapids MI 49512
(616) 698-8335

Electric worm getters & water weed control

High Seas Inc.
4861 24th Ave.
Port Huron MI 48060
(313) 385-4411

Sea steps, rails, pulpits stanchions & fittings

Hoefgen Canoes
N1927 Highway M-35
Menominee MI 49858
(906) 863-3991

Canoes, kayaks & duck skiffs

Holiday Distributing Co.
3903 Francis St.
Jackson MI 49203
(517) 782-6619

Docks

Instant Marine
2222 Hilton Road
Ferndale MI 48220
(313) 398-1011

Docks

Invader Downriggers
315 Garden Ave.
Holland MI 49423
(616) 396-3564

Downriggers & accessories

I.T.C.
401 W. Washington
Zeeland MI 49464
(616) 772-9411

Boat accessories

Jackson Canvas Co.
1227 Francis St.
Jackson MI 49203
(517) 787-1330

Chart cases, awnings, floatable sea anchors & stow-aways

Kool Kards
2365 Ridge Road
White Lake MI 48383
(800) 252-2SKI

Boat accessories

Kysor/Medallion
17150 Hickory
Spring Lake MI 49456
(616) 847-3700

Marine instrumentation

L & M Manufacturing Inc.
6016 N. M-30
Hope MI 48628
(517) 689-4010

Boat hoists

Lakeshore Products
855 W. Chicago
Quincy MI 49082
(517) 639-3815

Docks & pier hardware

Land & Sea Products Inc.
3106 Three Mile Road N.W.
Grand Rapids MI 49504
(800) 321-1548; (616) 791-0331

Holding tank chemicals

Logic Control Systems
1900 S. Livernois
Rochester Hills MI 48307
(313) 656-5868

Boat accessories

Mason Tackle Co.
Box 56
Otisville MI 48463
(800) 356-3640; (313) 631-4571

Fishing line and leaders

Michi-Craft Inc.
701 W. Front Street
Burr Oak MI 49030
(616) 489-5012

Canoes, rowboats, kayaks &
paddles

Michigan Wheel Corp.
1501 Buchanan Ave. S.W.
Grand Rapids MI 49507
(616) 452-6941

Propellers

Nautical Engineering
Box 5380
Northville MI 48167
(313) 349-7077

Radar mounts, sailboard holders,
cleats & hardware

Performance Line Co
Box 427
Drayton Plains MI 48330
(313) 674-4500

Ropes, handles & water ski accessories

Phase Four Coatings & Accessories
33700 Groesbeck
Fraser MI 48026
(313) 296-9595

Boat alarms

Playbouy Pontoon Manufacturing Inc.
903 Michigan Ave.
Alma MI 48801
(517) 463-2112

Pontoon boats & trailers

Power Plus Products Inc.
3236 Pine Lake Road
West Bloomfield MI 48324
(313) 535-7508

Waterski accessories

Powerquest Boats
2385 112th Ave.
Holland MI 49424
(616) 772-9474

Power boats

Proos Manufacturing Co.
1037 Michigan St. N.E.
Grand Rapids MI 49503
(616) 454-5622

Downriggers, rod holders & accessories

Sawyer Canoe
234 S. State
Oscoda MI 48750
(517) 739-9181

Canoes & paddles

Saxmayer
320 W. Adrian
Blissfield MI 49228
(517) 486-2164

Boat lifts & dock supports

Sherwood
6331 E. Jefferson Ave.
Detroit MI 48207
(313) 259-2095

Marine engine cooling pumps

Signaltone Inc.   Horns
946 Frisbie St.
Cadillac MI 49601-9261
(616) 775-4402

Spartan International Inc.   Adhesive trim products
1845 Cedar
Holt MI 48842
(517) 694-3911

T & L Products   Mounts
7856 Reinbold
Reese MI 48757
(517) 868-4428

Thetford Corp.   Marine heads & chemicals
Box 1285
Ann Arbor MI 48106
(313) 769-3032

Thompson Boat Co.   Power boats
7335 Martin Road
St. Charles MI 48655
(517) 865-8281

Tiara Yachts   Power boats
725 E. 40th St.
Holland MI 49423-5392
(616) 392-7163

Tops-in-Quality Inc.   Hoists, stern rails, pulpits,
Box 148   ladders & fittings
Marysville MI 48040
(313) 364-7150

Triton Industries Inc.   Pontoon boats
3001 N. Logan St.
Lansing MI 48906
(517) 323-0808

Tru-Trac Industries Inc.   Anchors, rod holders &
Box 713   accessories
Ludington MI 49431
(616) 845-7844

Walker Downriggers 8100 Neptune Drive Kalamazoo MI 49009 (616) 385-2727	Downriggers & accessories
Walker International 1901 W. Lafayette Blvd. Detroit MI 48216 (313) 496-1171	Rods, reels & tackle
Yar-Craft 1213 20th Ave. Menominee MI 49858 (906) 863-4497	Power boats

BOAT SHOWS

Boat shows serve as forums for manufacturers, on-the-water and off-the-water marinas, boat financing institutions and other vendors to display their products and services, with all the latest bells and whistles. For the public, shows provide a convenient opportunity to become informed consumers, with the ability to see and compare a wide array of products and to talk with knowledgeable staff. Industry statistics indicate that 85 percent of the boats sold in this country are sold either at shows or as a direct result of first being seen at a show. In addition, customers can sometimes negotiate better prices in such a competitive environment than at individual dealerships.

This chapter lists major annual boat and boat-and-fishing shows across Michigan, with the names and addresses of their organizers. Shopping malls often host small shows, and other shows may be held on a periodic basis at local arenas. Shows dedicated to fishing are listed in Chapter 8.

SOUTHEAST

MACOMB COUNTY

Boat Show USA Metropolitan Beach Metro Park Mt. Clemens	Recreational Promotions Inc. 1177 Cadieux Road Grosse Pointe Park MI 48230 (800) 521-8802; (313) 886-7887

OAKLAND COUNTY
Pontiac Silverdome Boat, Sport
& Fishing Show
Pontiac Silverdome
Pontiac

ShowSpan Inc.
1400 28th St. S.W.
Grand Rapids MI 49509
(616) 530-1919

WAYNE COUNTY
Detroit Boat & Fishing Show
Cobo Convention & Exhibition Ctr.
Detroit

Mich. Boating Industries Assn.
41740 W. Six Mile Rd., Ste. 100
Northville MI 48167
(800) 932-2628; (313) 344-1330

CENTRAL

INGHAM COUNTY
Central Mich. Boat Show
Lansing Center
Lansing

Convention Management Serv.
2920 W. St. Joseph
Lansing MI 48917
(517) 485-2309

SAGINAW COUNTY
Saginaw Boat & Fishing Show
Saginaw Civic Center
Saginaw

Shockley Inc.
1490 Delta Drive
Saginaw MI 48603
(517) 790-2217

NORTHWEST

GRAND TRAVERSE COUNTY
Grand Traverse Marine Dealers
Association Boat Show & Sale
Traverse City
Grand Traverse Resort

Traverse City Area Chamber
of Commerce
Box 387
Traverse City MI 49685
(616) 947-5075

KENT COUNTY
Grand Center Boat Show
Grand Center
Grand Rapids

ShowSpan Inc.
1400 28th St. S.W.
Grand Rapids MI 49509
(616) 530-1919

Chapter 29

U.S. COAST GUARD STATIONS

The U.S. Coast Guard provides several vital services for boaters and other recreational water users. They include safety inspections, search-and-rescue missions, licensing of charter boats carrying more than six passengers, licensing of ferries and, through the Coast Guard Auxiliary, boating safety courses.

Michigan is part of the 9th Coast Guard District, headquartered at 1240 E. Ninth St., Cleveland OH 44199-2060. The district telephone number is (216) 522-3950. There are three group offices in Michigan, each serving as regional headquarters for several of the state's 16 search and rescue stations. In addition, the Coast Guard maintains two air stations and two marine safety inspection offices in Michigan.

According to essential safety recommendations from the Coast Guard, things to "know before you go" include:

- Weather conditions.

- Stability and handling of the boat you will use.

- Your personal responsibilities and limitations.

- Waters you plan to use, including currents, tides, sandbars and other hazards.

- How to use your equipment.

- Emergency equipment and safety devices, including properly fitted life jackets.

- Navigation rules and safe boating courtesy.

- Boating doesn't mix well with alcohol or drugs.

AIR STATIONS

SOUTHEAST

U.S. Coast Guard Air Station
 Selfridge Air National Guard Base
 Mt. Clemens MI 48045-5011
    (313) 465-1331

NORTHWEST

U.S. Coast Guard Air Station
 Traverse City MI 49684-3586
    (616) 922-8210

MARINE SAFETY OFFICES

SOUTHEAST

U.S. Coast Guard Marine Safety Office
 Foot of Mt. Elliot Ave.
 Detroit MI 48207-4380
    (313) 568-9580

UPPER PENINSULA

U.S. Coast Guard Marine Inspection Office
 Municipal Building
 St. Ignace MI 49781-1425
    (906) 643-8080

GROUP OFFICES

SOUTHEAST

U.S. Coast Guard Group   (313) 568-9500
Foot of Mt. Elliot Ave.
Detroit MI 48207-4380

SOUTHWEST

U.S. Coast Guard Group   (616) 847-4517
650 Harbor Ave.
Grand Haven MI 49417-1752

UPPER PENINSULA

U.S. Coast Guard Group   (906) 635-3217
Sault Ste. Marie MI 49783-9501

SEARCH AND RESCUE STATIONS

SOUTHEAST

MACOMB COUNTY
U.S. Coast Guard Station   (313) 778-0590
24802 Jefferson Ave.
St. Clair Shores MI 48080-1391

ST. CLAIR COUNTY
U.S. Coast Guard Station   (313) 984-2602
Port Huron MI 48060-2998

WAYNE COUNTY
  U.S. Coast Guard Station   (313) 331-3110
  Belle Isle
  Detroit MI 48207-4376

SOUTHWEST

BERRIEN COUNTY
  U.S. Coast Guard Station   (616) 983-1371
  127 N. Pier St.
  St. Joseph MI 49085-1042

OTTAWA COUNTY
  U.S. Coast Guard Station   (616) 842-2510
  601 Harbor Drive
  Grand Haven MI 49417-1741

CENTRAL

BAY COUNTY
  U.S. Coast Guard Station   (517) 892-0555
  2405 Weadock Road
  Essexville MI 48732-9602

NORTHEAST

HURON COUNTY
  U.S. Coast Guard   (517) 479-3285
  104 Richie Drive
  Harbor Beach MI 48441-1042

IOSCO COUNTY
  U.S. Coast Guard Station   (517) 362-4428
  East Tawas MI 48730-9506

NORTHWEST

BENZIE COUNTY
U.S. Coast Guard Station   (616) 352-4242
Box 192
Frankfort MI 49635-0192

CHARLEVOIX COUNTY
U.S. Coast Guard Station   (616) 547-2541
Box 258
Charlevoix MI 49720-0258

MANISTEE COUNTY
U.S. Coast Guard Station   (616) 732-7412
523 Fifth Ave.
Manistee MI 49660-1315

MASON COUNTY
U.S. Coast Guard Station   (616) 843-9088
Ludington MI 49431-2089

UPPER PENINSULA

CHIPPEWA COUNTY
U.S. Coast Guard Station   (906) 635-3217
Sault Ste. Marie MI 49783-950   (906) 635-3230

MACKINAC COUNTY
U.S. Coast Guard Station   (906) 643-9191
St. Ignace MI 49781-1899

MARQUETTE COUNTY
U.S. Coast Guard Station   (906) 226-3312
400 Coast Guard Road
Marquette MI 49855-3864

WAYNE COUNTY SHERIFF'S DEPARTMENT

Chapter 30

SHERIFF'S MARINE DIVISIONS

In 78 of Michigan's 83 counties, sheriffs departments have established Marine Divisions to enforce provisions of the Marine Safety Act. Their principal area of operations is on inland waters, though they may also patrol coastal and harbor areas in conjunction with the U.S. Coast Guard and state Department of Natural Resources.

Although the make-up and size of a Marine Division varies from county to county, generally they are a combination of full-time deputies and reserve officers. There is usually at least one certified diver in each division.

Their duties include safety inspections of watercraft and equipment, free boating safety classes. They issue civil citations for minor infractions such as wake violations and make arrests for criminal conduct on the water, such as drunken boating or negligent homicide.

In addition, the Marine Divisions investigate boating accidents and conduct search, rescue and recovery missions.

SOUTHEAST

Hillsdale
165 W. Fayette, Hillsdale MI 49242
(517) 437-7317

Jackson
212 W. Wesley St., Jackson MI 49201
(517) 788-4208

Lapeer
2408 Genesee St., Lapeer MI 48446
(313) 667-0443

Lenawee
405 N. Winter St., Adrian MI 49221
(517) 263-0524

Macomb
43565 Elizabeth Rd., Mt. Clemens MI 48043
(313) 469-5151

Monroe
100 E. Second, Monroe MI 48161
(313) 243-7070

Oakland
1201 N. Telegraph, Pontiac MI 48053
(313) 858-5001

St. Clair
204 Bard St., Port Huron MI 48060
(313) 987-1700

Washtenaw
2201 Hogback Rd., Ann Arbor, MI 48107
(313) 971-4978

Wayne
1231 St. Antoine, Detroit MI 48226
(313) 224-2222

SOUTHWEST

Allegan
112 Walnut St., Allegan MI 49010
(616) 673-5441

Berrien
919 Port St., St. Joseph, MI 49805
(616) 983-7141

Branch
23 E. Pearl St., Coldwater MI 49036
(517) 278-2325

Calhoun
212 S. Grand, Marshall MI 49068
(616) 781-9806

Cass
101 N. Rowland, Cassopolis MI 49031
(616) 445-2481
Kalamazoo
1500 Lamont, Kalamazoo MI 49001
(616) 385-6174

Kent
701 Ball Ave. NE, Grand Rapids MI 49503
(616) 774-3111

Ottawa
3100 Port Sheldon Rd., Hudsonville MI 49426
(616) 669-2800

St. Joseph
Box 339, Centreville MI 49302
(616) 467-9045

Van Buren
205 S. Kalamazoo, Paw Paw MI 49079
(616) 657-4247

CENTRAL

Barry
1212 W. State St., Hastings MI 49058
(616) 948-4800

Bay
503 Third St., Bay City MI 48708
(517) 892-9551

Clinton
100 W. Cass, St. Johns MI 48879
(517) 224-6791

Eaton
117 W. Harris, Charlotte MI 4881
(517) 543-3510

Genesee
917 Beach St., Flint MI 48502
(313) 257-3406
Huron
120 S. Heisterman, Bad Axe, MI 48413
(517) 269-6421

Ingham
Box 70, Mason MI 48854
(517) 676-2431

Ionia
100 Library, Ionia MI 48846
(616) 527-0400

Isabella
207 Court St., Mt. Pleasant MI 48858
(517) 772-5911

Livingston
150 Highlander Way, Howell MI 48843
(517) 546-2440

Mecosta
225 S. Stewart, Big Rapids MI 49307
(616) 592-0150

Midland
301 W. Main, Midland MI 48640
(517) 832-6600

Montcalm
659 N. State St., Stanton MI 48888
(517) 831-5253

Saginaw
208 S. Harrison, Saginaw MI 48602
(517) 790-5400

Sanilac
65 N. Elk, Sandusky MI 48471
(313) 648-2000

Tuscola
420 Court St., Caro MI 48723
(517) 673-8161

NORTHEAST

Alcona
214 W. Main, Harrisville MI 48704
(517) 724-6271

Alpena
320 Johnson St., Alpena MI 49707
(517) 354-4128

Arenac
126 N. Grove St., Standish MI 48658
(517) 846-4561

Cheboygan
Box 70, Cheboygan MI 49720
(616) 627-3155

Crawford
200 W. Michigan, Grayling MI 49738
(616) 348-6341

Gladwin
501 W. Cedar, Gladwin MI 48624
(517) 426-9284

Iosco
428 Lake St., Tawas City MI 48763
(517) 362-6164

Montmorency
M-32 West (Box 280), Atlanta MI 49709
(517) 785-4238

Ogemaw
806 W. Wright, West Branch MI 48661
(517) 345-3111

Oscoda
Box 147, Mio MI 48647
(517) 826-3214

Otsego
124 S. Court, Gaylord MI 49735
(517) 732-6484

Presque Isle
467 N. Second St., Rogers City MI 49779
(517) 734-2156

Roscommon
109 George St., Roscommon MI 48653
(517) 275-5101

NORTHWEST

Antrim
207 Cayuga (Box 568) Bellaire MI 49615
(616) 533-8627

Benzie
Box 116, Beulah MI 49617
(616) 882-4484

Charlevoix
1000 Grant, Charlevoix MI 49720
(616) 547-4461

Clare
225 W. Main St., Harrison MI 48625
(517) 539-7166

Emmet
450 Bay St., Petoskey MI 49770
(616) 347-2032

Grand Traverse
320 Washington, Traverse City MI 49684
(616) 922-4504

Kalkaska
605 N. Birch, Kalkaska MI 49646
(616) 258-8686

Lake
1153 Michigan Ave., Baldwin MI 49304
(616) 745-2711

Leelanau
201 Chandler, Leland MI 49654
(616) 256-9829

Manistee
1525 Parkdale, Manistee MI 49660
(616) 723-3585

Mason
302 N. Delia St., Ludington MI 49431
(616) 843-3475

Missaukee
120 Pine St., Lake City, MI 48651
(616) 839-4338

Muskegon
25 W. Walton, Muskegon MI 49440
(616) 724-6351

Newaygo
300 Williams, White Cloud MI 49349
(616) 689-6623

Oceana
216 Lincoln, Hart MI 49420
(616) 873-2121

Osceola
325 W. Upton, Reed City MI 49677
(616) 832-2288

Wexford
820 Carmel St., Cadillac MI 49601
(616) 779-9211

UPPER PENINSULA

Baraga
12 N. Third St., L'Anse MI 49946
(906) 524-6177

Chippewa
331 Court St., Sault Ste. Marie MI 49783
(906) 635-6355

Delta
111 N. Third St., Escanaba MI 49829
(906) 786-3633

Dickinson
300 E. "D" St., Iron Mountain, MI 49801
(906) 774-6262

Gogebic
Iron Street, Bessemer MI 49911
(906) 667-0203

Houghton
403 E. Houghton Ave., Houghton MI 49931
(906) 482-4411

Iron
2 S. 6th St., Crystal Falls MI 49920
(906) 875-6669

Luce
411 W. Harrie, Newberry MI 49868
(906) 293-8431

Mackinac
470 N. Marley, St. Ignace MI 49781
(906) 643-7325

Marquette
236 Baraga Ave., Marquette MI 49855
(906) 228-6980

Menominee
831 Tenth Ave., Menominee MI 49858
(906) 863-4441

Ontonagon
620 Conglomerate St., Ontonagon MI 49953
(906) 884-4901

Appendix A

Travel & Recreation Information Sources

Regional and local tourist and convention bureaus and chambers of commerce are valuable sources of free information as you plan your travel and recreational activities. From them you can learn about motels and hotels, campgrounds, restaurants, bed-and-breakfasts, performing arts events, festivals, road conditions, parks, cultural and historic sites, nature preserves and other attractions. Many have toll-free telephone numbers.

STATEWIDE

Michigan Travel Bureau
Box 30226
Lansing MI 48909   (800) 543-2YES

REGIONAL

East Michigan Tourist Association
One Wenonah Park
Bay City MI 48708   (517) 895-8823

Eastern Upper Peninsula Tourist Association
100 Marley
County Courthouse
St. Ignace MI 49781   (906) 643-7343

Metropolitan Detroit Convention & Visitors Bureau
100 Renaissance Center, Suite 1950
Detroit MI 48234   (313) 259-4333

Greater Detroit Chamber of Commerce
600 W. Lafayette Blvd.
Detroit MI 48826
                                                     (313) 964-4000
Southwestern Michigan Tourist Council
c/o Howard Johnson's
2699 M-139
Benton Harbor MI 49022   (616) 925-6301

Upper Peninsula Travel & Recreation Association
Box 400
Iron Mountain MI 49801

(800) 562-7134
(906) 774-5480

West Michigan Tourist Association
136 E. Fulton St.
Grand Rapids MI 49503

(616) 456-8557

LOCAL

Greater Albion Chamber of Commerce
300 N. Eaton St.
Albion MI 49224

(517) 629-5533

Alger County Chamber of Commerce
Box 405
Munising MI 49862

(906) 387-2138

Greater Algonac Chamber of Commerce
Box 363
Algonac MI 48001

313) 794-5511

Allegan Area Chamber of Commerce
Box 338
Allegan MI 49010

(616) 673-2479

Allen Park Chamber of Commerce
6601 Park Ave.
Allen Park MI 48101

(313) 382-7303

Alma Chamber of Commerce
1110 W. Superior
Alma MI 48801

(517) 463-5525

Alpena Area Chamber of Commerce
133 Johnson St.
Alpena MI 49707

(800) 582-1906
(517) 354-4181

Anchor Bay Chamber of Commerce
Box 22
New Baltimore MI 48047

(313) 949-4120

Ann Arbor Convention & Visitors Bureau
211 E. Huron, Suite 6
Ann Arbor MI 48104

(313) 995-7281

Atlanta Area Chamber of Commerce
Box 410
Atlanta MI 49709

(517) 785-3400

Auburn Area Chamber of Commerce
Box 215
Auburn MI 48611

(517) 662-4408

Auburn Hills Chamber of Commerce
64 N. Saginaw St., Suite 101B
Pontiac MI 48342

(313) 335-9695

AuGres Chamber of Commerce
Box 455
AuGres MI 48703   (517) 876-6688

Bad Axe Chamber of Commerce
Box 87
Bad Axe MI 48413   (517) 269-7661

Baraga County Tourist & Recreation Association
Box 556
Baraga MI 49908   (906) 524-7444

Battle Creek Area Visitors & Convention Bureau
34 W. Jackson St., Suite 4-B
Battle Creek MI 49017   (616) 962-2240

Bay County Convention & Visitors Bureau
Box 2129
Bay City MI 48706   (517) 893-1222

Belding Area Chamber of Commerce
120 Covered Village
Belding MI 48809   (616) 794-2210

Bellaire Chamber of Commerce
Box 205
Bellaire MI 49615   (616) 533-6023

Belleville Area Chamber of Commerce
116 Fourth St.
Belleville MI 48111   (313) 697-7151

Bellevue Chamber of Commerce
218 S. Main St.
Bellevue MI 49021   (616) 763-9403

Benzie County Chamber of Commerce
Box 505
Beulah MI 49617   (616) 882-5801

Greater Berkley Chamber of Commerce
Box 1253
Berkley MI 48072   (313) 544-9464

Berrien Springs/Eau Claire Chamber of Commerce
Box 222
Berrien Springs MI 49103   (616) 471-2351

Bessemer Chamber of Commerce
Rte. 1, Box 25
Bessemer MI 49911   (906) 663-4542

Birmingham/Bloomfield Chamber of Commerce
240 Martin St.
Birmingham MI 48009   (313) 644-1700

Blissfield Chamber of Commerce
Box 25
Blissfield MI 49228   (517) 486-3836

Blue Water Area Tourist Bureau
520 Thomas Edison Parkway
Port Huron MI 48060

(800) 852-4242
(313) 987-8687

Boyne City Chamber of Commerce
28 S. Lake
Boyne City MI 49712

(616) 582-6222

Boyne Country Convention & Visitors Bureau
Box 694
Petoskey MI 49770

(616) 348-2755

Bridgeport Area Chamber of Commerce
Box 387
Bridgeport MI 48722

(517) 777-9180

Greater Brighton Area Chamber of Commerce
131 Hyne St.
Brighton MI 48116

(313) 227-5086

Bronson Chamber of Commerce
Box 152
Bronson MI 49028

(517) 369-1110

Brooklyn/Irish Hills Chamber of Commerce
106 Main St.
Brooklyn MI 49230

(517) 592-8907

Buchanan Area Chamber of Commerce
119 Main St.
Buchanan MI 49107

(616) 695-3291

Burr Oak Chamber of Commerce
Box 308
Burr Oak MI 49030

(616) 489-5075

Cadillac Area Visitors Bureau
222 Lake St.
Cadillac MI 49601

(800) 225-2537
(616) 775-9776

Canton Chamber of Commerce
44968 Ford Road, Suite K
Canton MI 48187

(313) 453-4040

Capac Area Chamber of Commerce
Box 386
Capac MI 48014

(313) 395-2243

Caro Area Chamber of Commerce
121 N. State, Suite 2
Caro MI 48723

(517) 673-5211

Carson City Area Chamber of Commerce
Box 18
Carson City MI 48811

(517) 584-6543

Cassopolis Area Chamber of Commerce
Box 154
Cassopolis MI 49031

(616) 445-2891

Cedar Springs Area Chamber of Commerce
Box 415
Cedar Springs MI 49319   (616) 696-3260

Central Lake Chamber of Commerce
Box 428
Central Lake MI 49622   (616) 544-3322

Central Macomb County Chamber of Commerce
58 North Ave.
Mt. Clemens MI 48043   (313) 463-1528

Charlevoix Area Convention & Visitors Bureau
408 Bridge St.   (800) 367-8557
Charlevoix MI 49720   (616) 547-2101

Charlotte Chamber of Commerce
207 S. Cochran Ave.
Charlotte MI 48813   (517) 543-0400

Cheboygan Area Tourist Bureau
Box 69
Cheboygan MI 49721-0069   (616) 627-7183

Chelsea Area Chamber of Commerce
Box 94
Chelsea MI 48118   (313) 475-1145

Chesaning Chamber of Commerce
220 E. Broad St.
Chesaning MI 48616   (517) 845-3055

Clare Area Chamber of Commerce
609 McEwan
Clare MI 48617   (517) 386-2442

Clarkston Chamber of Commerce
Box 938
Clarkston MI 48347   (313) 625-8055

Clawson Chamber of Commerce
615 N. Main St.
Clawson MI 48017   (313) 435-2450

Coldwater/Branch County Chamber of Commerce
20 Division St.
Coldwater MI 49036   (517) 278-5985

Coloma Area Chamber of Commerce
Box 418
Coloma MI 49038   (616) 468-3377

Coopersville Area Chamber of Commerce
289 Danforth St.
Coopersville MI 49404   (616) 837-9731

Davison Area Chamber of Commerce
102 E. 2d St.
Davison MI 48423   (313) 653-6266

Dearborn Chamber of Commerce
15544 Michigan Ave.
Dearborn MI 48126   (313) 584-6100

Dearborn Heights Chamber of Commerce
24624 W. Warren
Dearborn Heights MI 48127   (313) 274-7480

Delta County Tourist & Recreation
230 Ludington St.
Escanaba MI 49829-4098   (906) 786-2192

Dickinson County Tourism Association
Box 672
Iron Mountain MI 49801   (906) 774-2002

Greater Dowagiac Chamber of Commerce
107 Beeson St.
Dowagiac MI 49047   (616) 782-8212

Greater Durand Area Chamber of Commerce
100 W. Clinton St.
Durand MI 48429   (517) 288-3715

East Detroit Chamber of Commerce
Box 24
East Detroit MI 48021-2389   (313) 776-5520

East Jordan Chamber of Commerce
Box 137
East Jordan MI 49727   (616) 536-7351

Edmore Area Chamber of Commerce
Box 103
Edmore MI 48829   (313) 427-5821

Edwardsburg Chamber of Commerce
Box 575
Edwardsburg MI 49112   (616) 663-2756

Elberta Chamber of Commerce
Box 337
Elberta MI 49628   (616) 352-9264

Elk Rapids Area Chamber of Commerce
Box 854
Elk Rapids MI 49629   (616) 264-8202

Evart Area Chamber of Commerce
129 N. Main St.
Evart MI 49631   (616) 734-5594

Farmington/Farmington Hills Chamber of Commerce
33411 Grand River Ave.
Farmington MI 48335-3521   (313) 474-3440

Fennville Area Chamber of Commerce
Box 484
Fennville MI 49408   616) 561-5013

Fenton Area Chamber of Commerce
207 Silver Lake Road
Fenton MI 48430   (313) 629-5447

Ferndale Chamber of Commerce
400 E. Nine Mile Road
Ferndale MI 48220   (313) 542-2160

Fife Lake Chamber of Commerce
Box 117
Fife Lake MI 48633   (616) 879-4471

Flint Area Convention & Visitors Bureau
400 N. Saginaw St., Suite 101A   (800) 288-8040
Flint MI 48502   (313) 232-8900

Flushing Area Chamber of Commerce
Box 44
Flushing MI 48433   (313) 659-4141

Four Flags Area Council on Tourism
321 E. Main St.
Box 10
Niles MI 49120-3720   (616) 683-3720

Frankenmuth Convention & Visitors Bureau
635 S. Main St.
Frankenmuth MI 48734   (517) 652-6106

Freeland Area Chamber of Commerce
Box 484
Freeland MI 48623   (517) 695-6620

Fremont Chamber of Commerce
33 W. Main St.
Fremont MI 49412   (616) 924-0770

Garden City Chamber of Commerce
30120 Ford Road, Suite D
Garden City MI 48135   (313) 422-4448

Gaylord/Otsego County Convention & Tourist Bureau
125 S. Otsego
Gaylord MI 49735   (517) 732-4000

Gladwin County Chamber of Commerce
608 W. Cedar
Gladwin MI 48624   (517) 426-5451

Gogebic Area Convention & Visitors Bureau
Box 706
Ironwood MI 49938
                                                     (906) 932-4850
Grand Blanc Chamber of Commerce
131 E. Grand Blanc Road
Grand Blanc MI 48439   (313) 695-4222

Grand Haven/Spring Lake Area Visitors Bureau
1 South Harbor Dr.
Grand Haven MI 49417   (616) 842-4499

Grand Ledge Area Chamber of Commerce
Box 105
Grand Ledge MI 48837-0105   (517) 627-2383

Grand Rapids Area Convention & Visitor Bureau
245 Monroe NW   (800) 678-9859
Grand Rapids MI 49503   (616) 459-8287

Greater Grandville Chamber of Commerce
2905 Wilson Ave., Suite 101A
Grandville MI 49468-0175   (616) 531-8890

Grand Traverse Convention & Visitors Bureau
415 Munson Ave., Suite 200   (800) 872-8377
Traverse City MI 49684   (616) 947-1120

Grayling Area Visitors Council
213 James St.   (800) 937-8837
Grayling MI 49738   (517) 348-2921

Greenbush Chamber of Commerce
4115 S. US 23
Greenbush MI 48838   (517) 739-7635

Greenville Area Chamber of Commerce
202 S. Lafayette St.
Greenville MI 48838   (616) 754-5697

Gun Lake Area Chamber of Commerce
77 124th Ave.
Shelbyville MI 49344   (616) 672-7822

Hale Area Chamber of Commerce
Box 68
Hale MI 48739   (800) 722-8229

Hamtramck Chamber of Commerce
9435 Joseph Campau
Hamtramck MI 48212   (313) 875-7877

Harbor Beach Chamber of Commerce
149 N. Fourth St.
Harbor Beach MI 48441   (517) 479-6450

Harbor Country Chamber of Commerce
3 W. Buffalo
New Buffalo MI 49117-0497   (616) 469-5409

Harbor Springs Chamber of Commerce
Box 37
Harbor Springs MI 49740   (616) 347-4150

Harrison Area Chamber of Commerce
809 N. First
Harrison MI 48625   (517) 539-6011

Hart-Silver Lake Chamber of Commerce
Box 69
Hart MI 49420   (616) 873-2247

Hastings Area Chamber of Commerce
Box 236
Hastings MI 49058   (616) 945-2454

Hazel Park Chamber of Commerce
Box 85
Hazel Mark MI 48030   (313) 543-8556

Hesperia Area Chamber of Commerce
Box 32
Hesperia MI 49421-0032   (616) 854-1080

Highland Park Chamber of Commerce
12541 Second Ave.
Highland Park MI 48203   (313) 868-6420

Hillman Area Chamber of Commerce
Box 506
Hillman MI 49746   (517) 742-3739

Greater Hillsdale Chamber of Commerce
49 S. Howell St.
Hillsdale MI 49242   (517) 439-4341

Holland Area Convention & Visitors Bureau
171 Lincoln Ave.
Holland MI 49423   (616) 396-4221

Holly Area Chamber of Commerce
102 Civic Drive
Holly MI 48442   (313) 634-1900

Houghton Lake Chamber of Commerce
1625 W. Houghton Lake Drive
Houghton Lake MI 48269   (517) 366-5644

Howell Area Chamber of Commerce
404 E. Grand River Ave.
Howell MI 48843   (517) 546-3920

Hudson Area Chamber of Commerce
Box 45
Hudson MI 49247   (517) 448-8983

Hudsonville Chamber of Commerce
Box 216
Hudsonville MI 49426   (616) 896-9020

Huron County Tourist Association
Huron County Building
Bad Axe MI 48413   (517) 269-8463

Huron Shores Chamber of Commerce
Box 151
Harrisville MI 48740   (517) 724-5107

Huron Township Chamber of Commerce
19132 Huron River Drive
New Boston MI 48164   (313) 753-4220

Huron Valley Area Chamber of Commerce
371 N. Main
Milford MI 48381   (313) 685-7129

Imlay City Area Chamber of Commerce
Box 206
Imlay City MI 48444   (313) 724-1361

Indian River Resort Region Chamber of Commerce
Box 57
Indian River MI 49749   (616) 238-9325

Inkster Chamber of Commerce
26700 Princeton
Inkster MI 48141   (313) 225-0450

Interlochen Chamber of Commerce
Box 13
Interlochen MI 49643   (616) 276-7141

Ionia Area Chamber of Commerce
428 W. Washington St.
Ionia MI 48846   (616) 527-2560

Iron County Tourism Council
1 E. Genesee
Iron River MI 49935   (906) 265-3822

Ironwood Tourism Council
100 E. Aurora St.
Ironwood MI 49938   906) 932-1122

Isabella County Convention & Visitors Bureau   (800) 772-4433
210 E. Broadway   (517) 772-4433
Mt. Pleasant MI 48858

Greater Ishpeming Chamber of Commerce
661 Palms Ave.
Ishpeming MI 49849   (906) 486-4841

Ithaca Chamber of Commerce
Box 44
Ithaca MI 48847   (517) 875-3640

Jackson Convention & Tourist Bureau   (800) 245-5282
109 W. Washington   (517) 783-3330
Jackson MI 49201

Jennison Chamber of Commerce
Box 405
Jennison MI 49428

Kalamazoo County Convention & Visitors Bureau
128 N. Kalamazoo Mall
Kalamazoo MI 49005   (616) 381-4003

Greater Kalkaska Area Chamber of Commerce
350 S. Cedar St.
Kalkaska MI 49646-0291   (616) 258-9103

Keeweenaw Tourism Council
Box 336
Houghton MI 49931

800) 338-7982
(906) 482-2388

Lake City Area Chamber of Commerce
229 S. Main
Lake City MI 49651

(616) 745-4331

Lake County Chamber of Commerce
Box 130
Baldwin MI 49304

(616) 745-4331

Lake Gogebic Area Chamber of Commerce
Box 114-B
Bergland MI 49910

(906) 575-3265

Lakes Area Chamber of Commerce
8585 PGA Drive, Suite 102
Walled Lake MI 48390

(313) 624-2826

Lakeshore Convention & Visitors Bureau
567 Dyckman
Box 28
South Haven MI 49090

(616) 637-5252

Greater Lansing Convention & Visitors Bureau
119 Pere Marquette
Box 15066
Lansing MI 48901-5066

(517) 487-6800

Lapeer Area Chamber of Commerce
446 Pine St.
Lapeer MI 48446

(313) 664-6641

Leelanau County Chamber of Commerce
Box 212
Lake Leelanau MI 49653

(616) 256-9895

Lenawee County Chamber of Commerce
216 N. Main St.
Adrian MI 49221

(517) 265-5141

LeRoy Chamber of Commerce
104 Underwood
LeRoy MI 49655

(616) 768-4443

Les Cheneaux Chamber of Commerce
Box 10
Cedarville MI 49719

(906) 484-3935

Lewiston Area Chamber of Commerce
Box 656
Lewiston MI 49756

(517) 786-2293

Lexington Chamber of Commerce
Box 142
Lexington MI 48450

(313) 359-2262

Lincoln Park Chamber of Commerce
3014 Fort St.
Lincoln Park MI 48146   (313) 386-0140

Linden/Argentine Chamber of Commerce
Box 565
Linden MI 48451   (313) 750-8794

Litchfield Chamber of Commerce
Box 343
Litchfield MI 49252   (517) 542-2351

Livonia Chamber of Commerce
15401 Farmington Road
Livonia MI 48154-2892   (313) 427-2122

Lowell Area Chamber of Commerce
Box 224
Lowell MI 49331   (616) 897-9161

Ludington Area Convention & Visitors Bureau
5827 W. US 10
Box 160   (800) 542-4600
Ludington MI 49431   (616) 845-0324

Mackinaw Area Tourist Bureau
Box 658   (800) 666-0160
Mackinaw City MI 49701   (616) 436-5664

Mackinac Island Chamber of Commerce
Box 451
Mackinac Island MI 49757   (906) 847-3783

Madison Heights Chamber of Commerce
26385 John R
Madison Heights MI 48701   (313) 542-5010

Manchester Chamber of Commerce
Box 433
Manchester MI 48158   (313) 428-7722

Manistee County Chamber of Commerce
11 Cyprus St.
Manistee MI 49660   (616) 723-2575

Manistique Area Chamber of Commerce
Box 72
Manistique MI 49854   (906) 341-8433

Marine City Chamber of Commerce
515 S. Parker, Suite G
Marine City MI 48039
                                                               (313) 765-4501
Marion Chamber of Commerce
Box 279
Marion MI 49665   (616) 743-2461

Marlette Area Chamber of Commerce
Box 222
Marlette MI 48453   (517) 635-2429

Marquette County Tourism Council
501 S. Front St.
Marquette MI 49855

(800) 544-4321
(906) 228-7740

Marshall Area Chamber of Commerce
109 E. Michigan Ave.
Marshall MI 49068

(616) 781-5163

Marysville Area Chamber of Commerce
2827 Gratiot Blvd., Suite 3
Marysville MI 48040

(313) 364-6180

Mason Area Chamber of Commerce
148 E. Ash St.
Mason MI 48854

(517) 676-1046

McBain Area Chamber of Commerce
Box 53
McBain MI 49657

(616) 825-2416

Mecosta County Convention & Visitors Bureau
246 N. State St.
Big Rapids MI 49307

(800) 833-6697
(616) 796-7640

Menominee Area Chamber of Commerce
1005 Tenth Ave.
Menominee MI 49858

(906) 863-2679

Metro East Chamber of Commerce
27601 Jefferson Ave.
St. Clair Shores MI 48081-2053

(313) 777-2741

Midland County Convention & Visitors Bureau
300 Rodd St.
Midland MI 48640

(800) 678-1961
(517) 839-9901

Monroe County Convention & Tourist Bureau
Box 1094
Monroe MI 48161

(800) 252-3011
(313) 242-3366

Montrose Area Chamber of Commerce
Box 628
Montrose MI 48457

(313) 639-3475

Mt. Pleasant Area Chamber of Commerce
210 E. Broadway
Mt. Pleasant MI 48858

(517) 772-2396

Munising Visitors Bureau
Box 310
Munising MI 49862

(906) 387-4864

Muskegon County Convention & Visitors Bureau
349 W. Webster Ave
Muskegon MI 49440

(800) 235-3866
(616) 722-3751

Nashville Chamber of Commerce
311 N. State St.
Nashville MI 49073

(517) 852-9593

Newaygo Chamber of Commerce
330 Adams St.
Newaygo MI 49337   (616) 652-3068

Newberry Chamber of Commerce
Box 308
Newberry MI 49868   (906) 293-5562

Northville Community Chamber of Commerce
195 S. Main St.
Northville MI 48167   (313) 349-7640

Novi Chamber of Commerce
25974 Novi Road
Novi MI 48375   (313) 349-3743

Oakland County Chamber of Commerce
1052 W. Huron St.
Waterford MI 48328   (313) 688-4747

Onaway Chamber of Commerce
310 W. State St.
Onaway MI 49765   (517) 733-6620

Ontonagon Tourism Council
Box 266
Ontonagon MI 49953   (906) 884-4735

Orion Area Chamber of Commerce
Box 236
Lake Orion MI 48361-0236   (313) 693-9300

Greater Ortonville Chamber of Commerce
Box 152
Ortonville MI 48462   (313) 627-2811

Oscoda/AuSable Chamber of Commerce
100 W. Michigan
Oscoda MI 48750   (517) 739-7322

Oscoda Lodging Association
Box 165
Oscoda MI 48750   (517) 739-5156

Otsego Chamber of Commerce
100 W. Allegan St.
Otsego MI 49078   (616) 694-6880

Ottawa County Association of Commerce & Industry
1 South Harbor Drive
Grand Haven MI 49417   (616) 842-4910

Owosso-Corunna Area Chamber of Commerce
215 N. Water St.
Owosso MI 48867   (517) 723-5149

Oxford Area Chamber of Commerce
Box 142
Oxford MI 48051   (313) 628-4691

Paradise Area Tourism Council
Box 64
Paradise MI 49768   (906) 492-3927

Greater Paw Paw Chamber of Commerce
Box 105
Paw Paw MI 49079   (616) 657-5395

Pentwater Area Chamber of Commerce
Box 614
Pentwater MI 49449   (616) 869-4150

Petoskey Regional Chamber of Commerce
401 E. Mitchell
Petoskey MI 49770   (616) 347-4150

Pigeon Chamber of Commerce
Box 618
Pigeon MI 48755   (517) 453-2506

Pinconning Area Chamber of Commerce
Box 856
Pinconning MI 48650   (517) 879-2816

Plainwell Chamber of Commerce
Box 95
Plainwell MI 49080   (616) 685-8877

Plymouth Community Chamber of Commerce
386 S. Main St.
Plymouth MI 48170   (313) 453-1540

Pontiac Chamber of Commerce
64 N. Saginaw St., Suite 101B
Pontiac MI 48342   (313) 335-9600

Greater Port Huron/Marysville Chamber of Commerce
920 Pine Grove Ave.
Port Huron MI 48060   (313) 985-7101

Greater Port Sanilac Business Association
Box 402
Port Sanilac MI 48469

Portland Area Chamber of Commerce
1327 Grand River Ave.
Portland MI 48875   (517) 647-2100

Quincy Chamber of Commerce
Box 4
Quincy MI 49082   (517) 639-3115

Ravenna Chamber of Commerce
Box 177
Ravenna MI 49451   (616) 853-2190

Redford Township Chamber of Commerce
26050 Five Mile
Redford MI 48239   (313) 535-0960

Reed City Area Chamber of Commerce
Box 27
Reed City MI 49677   (616) 832-5431

Reese Chamber of Commerce
12880 Washington
Reese MI 48757   (517) 776-7525

Richmond Chamber of Commerce
Security Bank Building
Richmond MI 48062   (313) 727-7581

River Country Tourism Council
150 N. Main St.
Box 70
Centreville MI 49032   (616) 467-4505

Greater Rochester Area Chamber of Commerce
71 Walnut, Suite 110
Rochester MI 48307   (313) 651-6700

Rockford Area Chamber of Commerce
Box 520
Rockford MI 49341   (616) 866-2000

Rogers City Chamber of Commerce
Box 55
Rogers City MI 49779   (517) 734-2535

Romeo-Washington Chamber of Commerce
Box 175
Romeo MI 48065   (313) 752-4436

Greater Romulus Chamber of Commerce
31200 Detroit Industrial Expressway
Romulus MI 48174   (313) 326-4290

Greater Royal Oak Chamber of Commerce
411 S. Lafayette
Royal Oak MI 48067   (313) 547-4000

Saginaw County Convention & Visitors Bureau   (800) 444-9979
901 S. Washington   (517) 752-7164
Saginaw MI 48601

Saline Area Chamber of Commerce
107 1/2 E. Michigan Ave.
Saline MI 48176   (313) 429-4494

Greater Sandusky Area Chamber of Commerce
26 W. Speaker
Sandusky MI 48471   (313) 648-4445

Sanford Area Chamber of Commerce
Box 98
Sanford MI 48657   (517) 687-2800

Saugatuck/Douglas Convention & Visitors Bureau
Box 28

Saugatuck MI 49453   (616) 857-5801

Sault Ste. Marie Tourism Bureau
2581 I-75 Business Spur   (800) 647-2858
Sault Ste. Marie MI 49783   (906) 632-3301

Schoolcraft County Chamber of Commerce
Box 72
Manistique MI 49854   (906) 341-5010

Scottville Chamber of Commerce
133 S. Main
Scottville MI 49454   (616) 757-3301

Sebewaing Chamber of Commerce
108 W. Main St.
Sebewaing MI 48759   (517) 883-2150

Shelby Chamber of Commerce
Box 193
Shelby MI 49455   (616) 861-4054

Shepherd Area Chamber of Commerce
Box 111
Shepherd MI 48883-0111   (517) 828-6683

Skidway Lake Area Chamber of Commerce
2777 Greenwood Road
Prescott MI 48756-4041   (517) 873-4150

Greater South Haven Area Chamber of Commerce
535 Quaker St.
South Haven MI 49090   (616) 637-5171

South Lyon Area Chamber of Commerce
214 S. Lafayette
South Lyon MI 48178   (313) 437-3257

Southern Wayne County Chamber of Commerce
20600 Eureka, Suite 315   (313) 284-6000

Southfield Chamber of Commerce
16250 Northland Drive, Suite 130
Southfield MI 48075   (313) 557-6400

St. Charles Area Chamber of Commerce
110 W. Spruce
St. Charles MI 48655   (517) 865-8287

St. Helen Chamber of Commerce
Box 642
St. Helen MI 48656   (517) 389-3725

St. Ignace Area Tourism Association
11 S. State St.
St. Ignace MI 49781   (906) 643-6950

St. Johns Area Chamber of Commerce
Box 61
St. Johns MI 48879   (517) 224-7248

St. Louis Area Chamber of Commerce
Box 161
St. Louis MI 48880   (517) 681-3825

Standish Chamber of Commerce
Box 458
Standish MI 48658   (517) 846-7867

Sterling Heights Area Chamber of Commerce
12900 Hall Road, Suite 110
Sterling Heights MI 48313   (313) 731-5400

Sturgis Area Chamber of Commerce
200 W. Main
Sturgis MI 49091   (616) 651-5758

Suttons Bay Chamber of Commerce
Box 212
Lake Leelanau MI 49653   (616) 256-9895

Swartz Creek Area Chamber of Commerce
Box 267
Swartz Creek MI 48473   (313) 635-9643

Tawas Bay Tourist Bureau
Box 10
Tawas City MI 48764   (517) 362-8643

Tecumseh Chamber of Commerce
101 W. Chicago Blvd.
Tecumseh MI 49286   (517) 423-3740

Three Rivers Area Chamber of Commerce
140 W. Michigan Ave.
Three Rivers MI 49093   (616) 278-8193

Thunder Bay Regional Convention & Visitors Bureau   (800) 582-1906
Box 65   (517) 354-4181
Alpena MI 49707

Traverse City Area Chamber of Commerce
202 E. Grandview Parkway
Traverse City MI 49685-0387   (616) 947-5075

Troy Chamber of Commerce
4555 Corporate Drive, Suite 300
Troy MI 48098   (313) 641-8151

Trufant Area Chamber of Commerce
Box 2
Trufant MI 49347   (616) 984-2153

Twin Cities Area Chamber of Commerce
Box 1208
Benton Harbor MI 49023-1208   (616) 925-0044

Vassar Chamber of Commerce
Box 126
Vassar MI 48768   (517) 823-2601

Warren/Center Line/Sterling Heights Chamber
of Commerce
30500 Van Dyke, Suite 118
Warren MI 48093   (313) 751-3939

Wayland Chamber of Commerce
160 W. Superior
Wayland MI 49348   (616) 792-2265

Wayne Chamber of Commerce
35816 W. Michigan Ave.
Wayne MI 48184   (313) 721-0359

West Bloomfield Chamber of Commerce
6668 Orchard Lake, Suite 209
West Bloomfield MI 48322   (313) 626-3636

West Branch/Ogemaw County Travel & Visitors Bureau
422 W. Houghton Ave.
West Branch MI 48661   (517) 345-2821

Westland Chamber of Commerce
36900 Ford Road
Westland MI 48185   (313) 326-7222

White Cloud Chamber of Commerce
Box 158
White Cloud MI 49349   (616) 689-6607

White Lake Area Chamber of Commerce
124 W. Hanson
Whitehall MI 49461-1027   (616) 893-4585

Whitmore Lake Chamber of Commerce
Box 454
Whitmore Lake MI 48189   (313) 449-8540

Williamston Area Chamber of Commerce
Box 53
Williamston MI 48895   (517) 655-1549

Wyoming Chamber of Commerce
395 54th St. SW
Wyoming MI 49548-5614   (616) 531-5990

Ypsilanti Convention & Visitors Bureau
125 N. Huron St.
Ypsilanti MI 48197   (313) 482-4920

Zeeland Chamber of Commerce
9 S. Church St.
Zeeland MI 49464   (616) 772-2494

Appendix B

Books & Resources

There are many books available on Michigan's water recreation and maritime history. Here is a sampling:

BOATING

Captain's Guide to the Great Lakes
  (Publisher Distribution Services)
    Pentwater to Mackinac Island
    White Lake to Milwaukee
    Point Washington to Manistee
    North Channel to Rattle Harbor
    Lower Lake Huron
Cruising Guide to the Great Lakes
Marjorie Cahn Brazer
  (Contemporary Books)
Cruising Northern Michigan's Inland Waterway
L. R. Meyer
  (RLM & Co.)
Mariner's Atlas Series
ChartCrafters Inc.
  (Gulf Publishing)
    Lake Michigan
    Lake Erie
Richardson's Chartbook & Cruising Guides
    Lake Huron Edition
    Lake Superior Edition
    Lake Michigan Edition
    Lake Erie Edition
Well-Favored Passage: Guide to Lake Huron's North Channel
Marjorie Cahn Brazer
  (Heron Books)

CANOEING

Canoeing Michigan Rivers
Jerry Dennis & Craig Date
  (Friede Publications)

DIVING

Diver's Guide to Michigan
Steve Harrington
 (Maritime Press)
Diving & Snorkeling Guide to the Great Lakes
Kathy Johnson & Greg Lashbrook
 (Pisces Books)

FISHING

Angler's Guide to Michigan's Great Lakes
Gregory L. Curtis, Anne T. Fisher & Daniel R. Talhelm
 (Michigan Natural Resources Magazine)
Angler's Guide to Ten Classic Trout Streams in Michigan
Gerth E. Hendrickson
 (University of Michigan Press)
Fish Michigan -- 100 Southern Michigan Lakes
Tom Huggler
 (Friede Publications)
Fish Michigan -- Great Lakes
Tom Huggler
 (Friede Publications)
Michigan's 50 Best Fishing Lakes
Kenneth S. Lowe
 (Michigan United Conservation Clubs)
Michigan Steelheading
Mike Modrzynski
 (Michigan United Conservation Clubs)
Trout Streams of Michigan
Janet D. Mehl
 (Michigan United Conservation Clubs)

LIGHTHOUSES

The Northern Lights: Lighthouses of The Upper Great Lakes
Charles K. Hyde
 (TwoPeninsula)

MARITIME HISTORY

Great Lakes Ships We Remember
Detroit Marine Historical Society
 (Freshwater Press)

Great Lakes Shipwrecks and Survivals
William Ratigan
 (William B. Eerdman Publishing)
Ladies of the Lakes
James Clary
 (Michigan Natural Resources Magazine)
Terrifying Steamboat Stories
James L. Donahue
 (A & M Publishing)

PARKS

Michigan State and National Parks
Tom Powers
 (Friede Publications)
Michigan State Parks
Jim DuFresne
 (Mountaineers)

MAPS & CHARTS

Hydrographic maps of about 2,500 inland maps are available from Michigan United Conservation Clubs.

Nautical charts of Michigan's Great Lakes are published by the National Oceanic and Atmospheric Administration.

For an index and price list, write to MUCC Map Center, Box 30235, Lansing MI 48909 or call 1-800-777-6720 (toll-free in Michigan) or 517-371-1041 (out of state).

ABOUT THE AUTHOR

Eric Freedman is an award-winning reporter for The Detroit News, assigned to the state Capitol Bureau in Lansing. He graduated from Cornell University and New York University Law School, worked as an aide to U.S. Rep. Charles B. Rangel, and began his journalism career with The (Albany, N.Y.) Knickerbocker News. He joined The Detroit News in 1984.

Freedman's freelance articles about travel, adventure and outdoor recreation have appeared in more than two dozen U.S. and Canadian newspapers and magazines including Soundings, Great Expeditions, Los Angeles Times, Boston Globe, Chicago Tribune, Milwaukee Sentinel, St. Petersburg Times, Chicago Sun-Times, Des Moines Register, Empire State Report, London (Ont.) Free Press, Pittsburgh Press and Toronto Globe & Mail.

He also is the author of *Pioneering Michigan*, a book about the people who lived and settled in Michigan before statehood.